PRINCIPAL ADMINISTRATIVE ASSOCIATE

(ADMINISTRATIVE ASSISTANT)

Edited by
Hy Hammer, Chief of
Examining Service Division
New York City Department
of Personnel (Ret.)

Prentice Hall
New York • London • Toronto • Sydney • Tokyo • Singapore

Eighth Edition

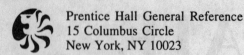

Prentice Hall General Reference
15 Columbus Circle
New York, NY 10023

Copyright © 1994, 1984, 1975 by Arco Publishing, a division
of Simon & Schuster, Inc.
All rights reserved
including the right of reproduction
in whole or in part in any form

An Arco Book

ARCO and PRENTICE HALL are registered trademarks
of Prentice-Hall, Inc.
Colophon is a trademark of Prentice-Hall, Inc.

Library of Congress Cataloging-in-Publication Data

Principal administrative associate (administrative assistant) / edited
      by Hy Hammer.—8th ed.
      p. cm.
      ISBN 0-671-84866-6
        1. Management—Examinations, questions, etc. 2. Supervision
of employees—Examinations, questions, etc. I. Hammer, Hy.
HD30.413.P74   1993   92-37104
658'.0076—dc20   CIP

Manufactured in the United States of America

1 2 3 4 5 6 7 8 9 10

CONTENTS

PART ONE
PRINCIPLES AND TECHNIQUES OF SUPERVISION

PART TWO
SAMPLE EXAMINATIONS FOR PRACTICE

WHAT THIS BOOK WILL DO FOR YOU

ARCO Publishing, Inc. has followed testing trends and methods ever since the firm was founded in 1937. We specialize in books that prepare people for tests. Based on this experience, we have prepared the best possible book to help *you* score high.

To write this book we carefully analyzed every detail surrounding the forthcoming examination . . .
- the job itself
- official and unofficial announcements concerning the examination
- all the previous examinations, many not available to the public
- related examinations
- technical literature that explains and forecasts the examination

CAN YOU PREPARE YOURSELF FOR YOUR TEST?

You want to pass this test. That's why you bought this book. Used correctly, your "self-tutor" will show you what to expect and will give you a speedy brush-up on the subjects tested in your exam. Some of these are subjects not taught in schools at all. Even if your study time is very limited, you should:
- Become familiar with the type of examination you will have.
- Improve your general examination-taking skill.
- Improve your skill in analyzing and answering questions involving reasoning, judgment, comparison, and evaluation.

- Improve your speed and skill in reading and understanding what you read—an important part of your ability to learn and an important part of most tests.

This book will tell you exactly what to study by presenting in full every type of question you will get on the actual test.

This book will help you find your weaknesses. Once you know what subjects you're weak in you can get right to work and concentrate on those areas. This kind of selective study yields maximum test results.

This book will give you the *feel* of the exam. Almost all our sample and practice questions are taken from actual previous exams. On the day of the exam you'll see how closely this book follows the format of the real test.

This book will give you confidence *now,* while you are preparing for the test. It will build your self-confidence as you proceed and will prevent the kind of test anxiety that causes low test scores.

This book stresses the multiple-choice type of question because that's the kind you'll have on your test. You must not be satisfied with merely knowing the correct answer for each question. You must find out why the other choices are incorrect. This will help you remember a lot you thought you had forgotten.

After testing yourself, you may find that you are weak in a particular area. You should concentrate on improving your skills by using the specific practice sections in this book that apply to you.

EXAMINATION ANNOUNCEMENT

PRINCIPAL ADMINISTRATIVE ASSOCIATE

THE GENERAL PROVISIONS OF THE NOTICE OF EXAMINATION AND THE GENERAL EXAMINATION REGULATIONS OF THE DEPARTMENT OF PERSONNEL APPLY TO THIS EXAMINATION AND ARE PART OF THIS NOTICE OF EXAMINATION. THEY ARE POSTED AND COPIES ARE AVAILABLE IN THE APPLICATION SECTION OF THE DEPARTMENT OF PERSONNEL AT 18 WASHINGTON STREET, NEW YORK, NEW YORK.

This examination is open to all eligible employees of all affected agencies of City government. A separate promotion eligible list will be established for each agency. This examination is also open to eligible employees of the New York City Health and Hospitals Corporation who meet the eligibility requirements listed below. The results of the examination will be made available to the New York City Health and Hospitals Corporation for the establishment of its own eligible list.

REQUIREMENTS

ELIGIBILITY: Open to each employee of all affected agencies of City government, or of the Health and Hospitals Corporation, who on the date of the written test (1) is permanently employed in the title of Office Associate; Office Machine Associate; Research Assistant; Research Assistant (Behavioral Sciences); Stenographic/Secretarial Associate; Stenographic Specialist; Senior Police Administrative Aide; Paralegal Aide; Information Assistant; Principal Shorthand Reporter; Public Relations Assistant; Editorial Assistant; Associate Reporter Stenographer (D.A.); Equipment Control Planner (Hospitals); Maintenance Control Scheduler; Manager, Print Shop; Supervising Police Communications Technician; Statistician; or Eligibility Specialist and (2) is not otherwise ineligible.

This examination is also open to former employees of the City of New York whose names are on preferred lists for Administrative Aide; Shop Clerk; Supervising Telephone Operator; Supervising Clerk; Supervising Clerk (Income Maintenance); Field Supervisor (VISTA); Legislative Clerk (Albany); Assistant Public Services Officer; Information Clerk (Department of Probation; Senior Toll Collector (Markets); Supervising Stenographer; Stenographer (Law); Shorthand Reporter; Supervising

Blueprinter; Supervising Blueprinter and Photostat Operator; Supervising Photostat Operator; Senior Police Administrative Aide; Paralegal Aide; Information Assistant; Public Relations Assistant; Editorial Assistant; Hearing Administrative Services Coordinator (Parking Violations Bureau); Research Assistant; Research Assistant (Behavioral Sciences); Principal Shorthand Reporter; Principal Telephone Operator; Grand Jury Stenographer; Hearing Reporter; Senior Hearing Reporter; Associate Reporter Stenographer (D.A.); Senior Legal Secretary; Equipment Control Planner (Hospitals); Maintenance Control Scheduler; or Manager, Print Shop; who were permanently employed in such title before their names were placed on the preferred lists, and who are not otherwise ineligible.

Also eligible is each employee of all affected agencies of City government, or of the New York City Health and Hospitals Corporation, who on the date of the written test: (1) is permanently employed in the title of Auditor of Accounts; Senior Auditor of Accounts; or Supervising Auditor of Accounts; (2) meets the minimum requirements specified below; and (3) is not otherwise ineligible.

The admission of employees in the title of Auditor of Accounts, Senior Auditor of Accounts, or Supervising Auditor of Accounts is on a collateral basis and applies to this examination only; it is not to be considered a precedent for future examinations.

MINIMUM REQUIREMENTS

1. A baccalaureate degree from an accredited college and two (2) years of satisfactory, responsible full-time paid experience in a governmental agency, business firm, civic organization or educational institution, conducting administrative or management studies, or assisting an executive in directing the administration of a large organizational segment, or directing or coordinating the administration of several small organizational segments, or performing any appropriate combination of these duties; or serving in a highly responsible secretarial capacity or as a supervisor of a large stenographic pool.

2. An associate degree from an accredited college or completion of two (2) years of study (60 credits) at an accredited college and four (4) years of satisfactory responsible full-time paid clerical or stenographic experience, at least two (2) years of which shall have been in an administrative capacity as described above; or

3. High school graduation or evidence of having passed an examination for a high school equivalency diploma and six (6) years of satisfactory, responsible full-time paid clerical or stenographic experience, at least two (2) years of which shall have been in an administrative capacity as described under subdivision 1; or

4. Education and/or experience which is equivalent to 1, 2, or 3. However, all candidates must possess the two (2) years of administrative experience as described under subdivision 1.

JOB DESCRIPTION

DUTIES AND RESPONSIBILITIES: This class of positions encompasses responsible office, supervisory or administrative work of varying degrees of difficulty and with varying degrees of latitude for independent initiative and judgment. There are several assignment levels within this class of positions. The following are typical assignments within this class of positions. All personnel perform related work.

Assignment Level I

Under general supervision, with some latitude for independent initiative and judgment, performs one of the following difficult and responsible supervisory or administrative functions:

Supervises a large office engaged in routine clerical activities or supervises a small office engaged in departmental, administrative or management activities; or performs difficult and responsible administrative or personnel management work. Supervises a group or section of subordinate personnel in the clerical and related activities performed in an income maintenance center. Performs difficult and responsible administrative work required for the conduct of hearings, control processing, and integrity of dispositions of parking violations; performs related work.

Under general supervision, with considerable latitude for the exercise of independent judgment, makes the necessary arrangements of service and activities in connection with public events, ceremonies, luncheons and City Hall receptions.

Under direction, performs difficult and responsible administrative work in the capacity of secretary or assistant to a high level executive.

Assignment Level II

Under direction, with considerable latitude for independent action or decision, performs difficult and responsible supervisory or administrative work in any one or more of the following:

Administers all matters pertaining to the general municipal telephone system. Supervises a very large office engaged in routine clerical or personnel management work.

Assignment Level III

Under general direction and with wide latitude for the exercise of independent initiative and judgment, performs the following:

Supervises an exceptionally large office engaged in routine activities,

or supervises a very large office engaged in departmental
administrative or management activities. Performs exceptionally
difficult and responsible independent, specialized administrative or
management work related to accounts and budgeting, methods and
organization, etc. Plans, directs and supervises a minimal personnel
management program covering a large number of employees, or a well-
developed personnel management program including several major
personnel activities, covering a moderate number of employees or
performs appropriate professional duties in a personnel program headed
by an employee of higher rank.

TEST INFORMATION

TESTS: Seniority, weight 15; written, weight 85, 70% required. The
written test will be of the multiple-choice type and may include
questions on reading comprehension and English usage; evaluation of
job problems and human relations; supervision and administration,
including planning and organizing work, and staff training; personnel
management; payroll administration; departmental budgeting;
arithmetic reasoning; and standards of employee conduct, including
provisions of Mayor's Executive Order No. 16 and related areas.

PART ONE

Principles and Techniques
of Supervision

SUPERVISING SKILLED WORKERS

Effective supervision involves the application of certain basic concepts. The questions that follow illustrate the principles of supervising skilled employees. Each question is followed by an explanation of the concept illustrated. In this way, you can see the practical applications of the supervisory principles you have been reading about, and you will be able to apply these concepts in other similar situations.

1. A supervisor, George Gordon, has received orders for a work assignment to be carried out by his unit. He has firmly decided on methods for carrying out this assignment which he believes will lead to its completion both properly and expeditiously. He has no intention whatsoever of changing his mind. After he has reached his decision he calls a staff conference to discuss various alternative methods of carrying out the assignments without making clear that he has already decided upon the method to be used. To hold a conference of this type would generally be a

   (A) good idea, because subordinates are likely to carry the assignment through better if they believe that they devised the methods used

   (B) good idea, because the staff will have the opportunity and be properly motivated to gain knowledge and experience in methodology without endangering staff performance

   (C) poor idea, because it would be a failure on the part of the supervisor to show the firm leadership which the unit has a right to expect

   (D) poor idea, because the discovery by the staff that they had not actually participated in deciding upon methods to be used would have an adverse effect upon their morale.

Answer: **(D)** It is an accepted concept that where employees are consulted as to methods of work performance before they are instituted, a higher level of morale will exist. Higher morale leads to increased and superior work production.

2. A supervisor is put in charge of a special unit. She is exceptionally well qualified for this assignment by her training and experience. One of her very close personal friends has been working for some time in this unit. Both the supervisor and her friend are certain that the rest of the people in the unit, many of whom have been in the bureau for a long time, know of this close relationship. Under these circumstances, the most advisable action for the supervisor to take is to

   (A) ask that either she be allowed to return to her old assignment, or, if that cannot be arranged, that her friend be transferred to another unit

   (B) avoid any overt sign of favoritism by acting impartially and with greater reserve when dealing with her friend than with the rest of the staff

   (C) discontinue any socializing with her friend either inside or outside the office so as to eliminate any gossip or dissatisfaction

   (D) talk the situation over with her friend and arrive at a mutually acceptable plan of proper office decorum.

Answer: (A) and (D) This question accepts an alternate answer to the original answer of (D). Actually the correct course of action for a supervisor to follow when a close personal friend is assigned to her unit is for the two of them to arrive at a decision as to just how they will conduct themselves during working hours on the job. This can be accomplished at a meeting called by the supervisor. Answer (A) provides an alternate solution as it actually eliminates the problem by reassignment or transfer. But that course of action may not be in the best interests of the agency if the services of the subordinate are required in that particular unit.

3. Experts in the field of personnel relations feel that it is generally a bad practice for subordinate employees to become aware of pending or contemplated changes in policy or organizational set-up via the ''grapevine'' chiefly because
   (A) evidence that one or more responsible officials have proved untrustworthy will undermine confidence in the agency
   (B) the information disseminated by this method is seldom entirely accurate and generally spreads needless unrest among the subordinate staff
   (C) the subordinate staff may conclude that the administration feels the staff cannot be trusted with the true information
   (D) the subordinate staff may conclude that the administration lacks the courage to make an unpopular announcement through official channels.

Answer: (B) Most rumors deal with bad news. As the rumor is spread from employee to employee, it is likely to be altered and exaggerated. When a supervisor learns about a rumor that is causing unrest among employees, steps should be taken immediately to inform employees of the true situation.

4. One factor which might be given consideration in deciding upon the optimum span of control of a supervisor over immediate subordinates is the position of the supervisor in the hierarchy of the organization. It is generally considered proper that the number of subordinates immediately supervised by a higher, upper echelon, supervisor

   (A) is unrelated to and tends to form no pattern with the number supervised by lower level supervisors
   (B) should be about the same as the number supervised by a lower level supervisor
   (C) should be larger than the number supervised by a lower level supervisor
   (D) should be smaller than the number supervised by a lower level supervisor.

Answer: (D) As the work of the subordinates becomes more complex, the supervisor's span of control decreases. The functions of workers increase in complexity as they ascend the ladder of hierarchy in an organization.

5. When an experienced subordinate who has the authority and information necessary to make a decision on a certain difficult matter brings the matter to the supervisor without having made the decision, it would generally be best for the supervisor to
   (A) agree to make the decision for the subordinate after the subordinate has explained why it is difficult to make the decision and after a recommendation has been made
   (B) make the decision for the subordinate, explaining the reasons for arriving at the decision
   (C) refuse to make the decision, but discuss the various alternatives with the subordinate in order to clarify the issues involved
   (D) refuse to make the decision, explaining that the subordinate is deemed to be fully qualified and competent to make the decision.

Answer: (C) The key words are *experienced* and *authority*. If an employee has been given the authority to make a decision and has the experience to make it, the most the supervisor should do is to point out the alternative courses of action as a means of guidance.

6. The *least* important of the following reasons why a particular activity should be assigned to a unit which performs activities dissimilar to it is that

(A) close coordination is needed between the particular activity and other activities performed by the unit

(B) it will enhance the reputation and prestige of the unit supervisor

(C) the unit makes frequent use of the results of this particular activity

(D) the unit supervisor has a sound knowledge and understanding of the particular activity.

Answer: **(B)** This question asks the *least* important reason for assigning a particular activity to a unit. Choices (A), (C) and (D) contain good reasons for the assignment of an activity to a unit. Very few things in personnel administration are done to enhance the reputation and prestige of an individual. The assignment of work is definitely not one of them.

7. In a psychological study of leadership, it was found that it is possible to predict the behavior of a new employee in a leadership position more accurately on the basis of the behavior of the predecessor in the post than on the behavior of that employee in his or her previous job. The best explanation of this observation is that there is a tendency

(A) to select similar types of personalities to fill the same type of position

(B) for a newly appointed employee to avoid instituting basic changes in operational procedures

(C) for a given organizational structure and set of duties to produce similar patterns of behavior

(D) for increased responsibility to impose more mature patterns of behavior on an incumbent.

Answer: **(C)** Most people will react similarly under set conditions. In other words, the idiosyncracies of a job tend to determine the behavior of the incumbent.

8. One of your workers has relatives who raise chickens. One day, you mention in casual conversation that you bought some eggs of poor quality at the grocery store. The following Monday the worker places a box of fresh eggs on your desk. You express thanks and offer payment, which is refused. On several occasions thereafter, the worker brings in additional eggs but still refuses to take payment, obviously proud of these products and seeming to take great pleasure in sharing them with you. However, you begin to hear rumors that the other workers believe that you and the worker are very friendly and that this individual is receiving special privileges from you. You should

(A) explain the situation to the worker, pointing out that the worker is being hurt by the conditions because of the feelings of others

(B) ignore the situation since the worker is merely being friendly and is actually receiving no favors in return

(C) supervise this worker more carefully than the others to insure that the worker will not take advantage of the situation

(D) refuse all gifts from the worker thereafter without further explanation.

Answer: **(A)** This choice presents the best of the four courses of action. There is nothing in the question which leads one to believe that the intent of the worker is anything but harmless. If these actions are creating a situation which could have repercussions, it would be best for the supervisor to have a talk with the worker where they could agree on another course of conduct.

9. Lax supervision has been blamed largely on the unwillingness of supervisors to supervise their rank-and-file. The chief reason for this unwillingness to supervise is based mainly on the supervisor's

(A) failure to accept modern concepts of proper supervision and its methods

(B) doubt his or her ability to keep pace with modern techniques and developments

(C) own inability to adhere to the same high standards of performance which are required of subordinates

(D) fear of complaints from subordinates and desire to avoid unpleasantness.

Answer: **(D)** Lax supervision is the result of supervisors deliberately avoiding the workers on the job. Such supervisors are aware that their subordinates have cause for complaint or are operating under adverse conditions. They know that if they encounter their workers on the job, they will be recipients of many complaints.

10. In making assignments, a supervisor attempts to fit the employees to the jobs. This procedure is
    (A) good; chiefly because it is a definite policy which lends itself to analysis and conclusions
    (B) poor; chiefly because a job should be fitted to the employee
    (C) good; chiefly because accomplishment of the mission is the primary goal
    (D) poor; chiefly because no consideration is paid to human values and relationships.

Answer: (C) This situation should first be evaluated as a good one. Choice (A) is nothing but gobbledygook. Choice (C) is correct; a worker should be fitted to a job, not a job to a worker. In other words, a job must exist before an individual is assigned to it.

11. The effectiveness of the work of a unit depends in a large measure on that unit's will to work. The best of the following methods for the unit supervisor to employ in order to increase the will of the members of the unit to work is for the unit supervisor to
    (A) allow each worker to proceed at his or her own pace
    (B) be constantly on guard for any laxity among the workers
    (C) provide comfortable working facilities for the workers
    (D) clearly discuss with the workers the functions and objectives of the agency.

Answer: (D) Of the four choices, this is the only one that would have a beneficial effect on employee morale and would therefore result in better work performance. When an employee is aware of the functions and objectives of the agency and can see the part that his or her work plays in attaining these objectives, the employee is likely to do a better job.

12. While supervising a crew performing inspectional duties you come across practices on an installation that are on the fringe of many law violations. For you to imply to the owner that your department will conduct frequent inspections of the premises until some of the questionable conditions on the property are eliminated is
    (A) proper mainly because the owner may be persuaded by it to maintain satisfactory conditions
    (B) improper mainly because the owner may feel that this is harassment
    (C) proper mainly because any means which result in the elimination of hazardous conditions are permissible
    (D) improper because threats which may not be carried out should not be made.

Answer: (A) This action may be evaluated as proper because it will most likely result in improvement of the conditions in question at the installation. Choice (C) is not true at all; the word *any* is much too positive.

13. A supervisor in charge during a hazardous operation made a great effort to give orders in a normal tone of voice and generally to act in a normal manner, as though the situation was routine and without danger. In this situation, the supervisor's behavior was
    (A) improper mainly because the workers are not alerted to their danger
    (B) proper mainly because danger is part of the job and should be faced without flinching
    (C) improper mainly because the supervisor is not behaving normally or honestly
    (D) proper mainly because the subordinates also will tend to act calmly.

Answer: (D) The supervisor's action should first be evaluated as proper. Choice (D) is correct and logical. Choice (B) is not true at all because even though the workers are aware of the danger connected with their job, it is perfectly normal to be afraid during dangerous situations. At any rate loss of composure is infectious. If the supervisor became excited, such conduct would surely be carried over to the workers.

14. The main reason for a supervisor to delegate authority to a subordinate is to
    (A) develop the leadership potential of the subordinate
    (B) make the authority equal to the responsibility of an assignment
    (C) free the supervisor for more important tasks
    (D) obtain new and better methods of performing the duties assigned.

Answer: (C) A supervisor who is bogged down with too much detail work will be unable to devote sufficient time to supervisory duties. Supervisors are paid to supervise, and if they do not have sufficient time to devote to this, they are derelict in the performance of their duties.

15. A chief of an inspectional division encounters a subordinate in the course of an inspection. The inspector is in the process of issuing violations for five infractions. The chief of the division considers four of the violations clear violations of the law, but the fifth the chief considers a borderline case which should not have been handled by issuing a violation order. In this situation, the best of the following courses for the chief to take is to
    (A) direct the inspector to cancel the violation order for the borderline situation
    (B) say nothing to the inspector at this time but later warn against unduly strict interpretation of the law
    (C) accept the inspector's findings without any comment at this time or later
    (D) question the inspector closely about various sections of the law to determine whether that individual has a proper understanding of its requirements.

Answer: (C) This situation involves a sensitive area. The inspection of violations sometimes is a matter of individual interpretation. The inspector has been delegated the authority to perform the inspection and should be permitted to perform it unimpeded, especially since the point in question is not definite one way or the other.

16. Although there is a normal distinction between the successive ranks of supervision in an agency, the greatest distinction and change in rank occurs when a worker becomes a supervisor. This is true chiefly because the supervisor
    (A) must be better informed than subordinates in all aspects of the work
    (B) must learn to assume new and more complex duties
    (C) becomes responsible for the first time for the job performance of members of the staff
    (D) has greater responsibility and authority than the subordinates being supervised.

Answer: (C) For the first time the worker will be responsible for the performance of others.

17. It has been said that the success or failure of the work of the unit rests on the unit supervisor. If the supervisor wants to stimulate growth among the workers, it would generally be best to
    (A) set an easy pace for the workers so that they will not become confused because of having to learn too much too rapidly
    (B) set the pace for the workers so that the job is never too easy, but is a constant challenge calling for more and better work
    (C) spot check the workers' case records at irregular intervals in order to determine whether they are performing their duties properly
    (D) see to it that the broad objectives and goals of the department are periodically communicated and interpreted to the workers.

Answer: (B) When work standards are set at a level where they may be attained with little effort they will tend to create boredom among the organization's employees. Work standards should be set so that a considerable effort must be made to attain them, although they should not be set so high that they are out of reach and discourage the workers.

18. For a supervisor to encourage workers to think about the reasons for a policy is
    (A) advisable, mainly because the workers are then more likely to apply the policy appropriately
    (B) inadvisable, mainly because the workers may then apply the policy too flexibly
    (C) advisable, mainly because the workers then feel that they have participated in policy making

(D) inadvisable, mainly because the workers may interpret the policy incorrectly if they misunderstand its meaning.

Answer: (A) If workers understand the reasons behind the setting of a policy and just why it has been put into effect, they will support that policy with much more enthusiasm than if they believe it to be an arbitrary decision on the part of management.

19. "A good supervisor should know when to refer a matter to a superior and when to handle it personally." Of the following, the situation which a supervisor would most appropriately refer to a superior is
    (A) poor cooperation by a subordinate
    (B) a complaint about poor service
    (C) a disagreement between two subordinates
    (D) a breakdown of recently purchased equipment.

Answer: (D) Supervisors should be able to handle most aspects of the job by themselves. The first three choices involve a complaint of poor work by subordinates or everyday personnel problems. These are within the province of the supervisor and should be handled by the supervisor alone. However, supervisors are usually not responsible for the purchase of equipment, and if equipment breaks down they should seek the aid of the individual responsible for its purchase or maintenance.

20. A supervisor who plans work properly and has no difficulty in meeting deadlines insists that new workers pattern their activities on the supervisor's model in every detail. This method is
    (A) undesirable, chiefly because such compliance can cause antagonism and hamper the workers' growth
    (B) undesirable, chiefly because this method cannot work as successfully for the new workers
    (C) desirable, chiefly because the supervisor's methods have proved successful and will eliminate waste
    (D) desirable, chiefly because the untrained worker needs guidelines to follow.

Answer: (A) In the first place, this supervisor is not allowing for individual differences. Secondly, the supervisor is stifling initiative by insisting that everyone perform as is best for the supervisor. No two people are exactly alike. What is good for one person may not be good for the next person.

21. For a supervisor, to encourage competitive feelings among the staff is
    (A) advisable, chiefly because the workers will perform more efficiently when they have proper motivation
    (B) inadvisable, chiefly because the workers will not perform well under the pressure of competition
    (C) advisable, chiefly because the workers will have a greater incentive to perform their job properly
    (D) inadvisable, chiefly because the workers may focus their attention on areas where they excel and neglect other essential aspects of the job.

Answer: (D) This situation should first be appraised as an inadvisable one. A supervisor should not encourage competitiveness among employees, but rather encourage harmony, coordination and team spirit. The reason given in choice (D) is much better than the one in choice (B) because the condition in choice (B) may not turn out to be true.

22. In selecting tasks to be assigned to a new worker, the supervisor should assign those tasks which
    (A) give the worker the greatest variety of experience
    (B) offer the worker the greatest opportunity to achieve concrete results
    (C) present the worker with the greatest stimulation because of their interesting nature
    (D) require the least amount of contact with outside agencies.

Answer: (B) Success is known to follow other successes. If new employees are assigned tasks they are reasonably sure to be successful in, it will give them the confidence to tackle the other tasks assigned.

23. An essential element of administrative control over the operations for which a superior is responsible is that the superior
    (A) should personally perform an important task instead of assigning a competent subordinate to perform it
    (B) should personally check every ordered action taken by subordinates to insure that they have been properly performed
    (C) who has issued an order to a subordinate should ascertain that it has been carried out properly
    (D) who has assigned an important task to subordinates should inform them that they, the subordinates, will be held fully accountable for its proper execution.

Answer: (C) It is the ultimate responsibility of a superior officer to see that the work assigned to subordinates is carried out in a proper manner.

24. Of the following, the factor which is *least* important in determining the number of subordinates a superior can effectively supervise is the
    (A) type of work being done
    (B) abilities of superior and subordinates
    (C) level of command in the organization
    (D) overall size of the department.

Answer: (D) The concept in question here deals with *span of control*. The type of work being performed, the abilities of the supervisor and subordinates, and the level of command in the organization all are pertinent to the number of subordinates the supervisor is able to supervise effectively. The overall size of the department is not a factor at all.

25. Of the following activities, generally the *least* proper function of a centralized procedure section is
    (A) issuing new and revised procedural instructions
    (B) coordinating forms revision and procedural changes
    (C) accepting or rejecting authorized procedural changes
    (D) controlling standard numbering systems for procedural releases.

Answer: (C) The other three choices depict proper functions of a centralized procedure section. This section, however, is a coordinating unit and it would not have the authority to rule on the validity of authorized procedural changes.

26. A proposal is made to allow a large measure of planning responsibility to each departmental division rather than to place sole responsibility in a central planning division. Adoption of such decentralized planning would lead to
    (A) more effective planning; plans will be conceived in terms of the existing situations and will be more likely to be carried out willingly
    (B) less effective planning; a central planning division will have a more objective overall view than any operating division can possibly achieve
    (C) more effective planning; operating divisions are usually better equipped technically than the central planning divisions and thus better able to make valid plans
    (D) less effective planning; personnel in an operating division do not have the time to plan efficiently and painstakingly.

Answer: (A) In many instances the function of planning will be carried out most effectively if the individual units are permitted to do it on their own. This is true because they are nearer the work and are in a better position to construct effective plans. In addition, they would be more willing to carry out plans which emanated from within their own unit than if the plans were formulated elsewhere.

27. In some jurisdictions work performance above the call of duty is rewarded by special assignments and consideration for promotion to higher ranks. A basic weakness of this system is that it
    (A) tends to inspire ambitious young employees deliberately to seek situations in which they can excel and which will enhance their standing in the eyes of their superiors
    (B) tends to weaken respect for the senior members of the agency since the system described favors younger employees

(C) overlooks the fact that the rapid growth of organizations tends to give all employees the opportunity to encounter situations which will win them attention

(D) tends to penalize to an unfair extent those employees who are most productive.

Answer: (D) In a setup such as described, promotion and special assignments would go to those who happen to be in situations which are likely to be rewarded. Those employees who simply performed their routine work well would not have the opportunity for promotion or special assignments.

28. For a supervisor to permit subordinates to participate in the decision-making process is generally desirable, when practicable, primarily because
(A) it leads to the elimination of grievances
(B) better solutions may be obtained
(C) individual development requires an ever-expanding view of operations
(D) the supervisor is forced to "keep on his toes" under the stimulation of interchange of ideas.

Answer: (B) This is strictly a case of many heads being better than one. Valid suggestions may come from the most unlikely sources.

29. A crew is faced with a troublesome problem. The supervisor calls all subordinates to a meeting, outlines the problem and asks them to give spontaneously any ideas that occur to them as possible ways of handling it. Each idea suggested is written down, and later discussed carefully. The chief advantage of the procedure employed by the supervisor is that
(A) time is not wasted on needless talk
(B) ideas are obtained which otherwise might not be developed
(C) there is less tendency for the meeting to stray from the subject under discussion
(D) subordinates receive training in analysis of problems and evaluation of solutions.

Answer: (B) This is an excellent manner of obtaining various outlooks which may then be developed until they satisfactorily meet a given situation. Choices (A) and (C) are fallacious statements.

Although the statement in choice (D) may be true to an extent, it is not the main purpose of the meeting at all. The meeting was called by the supervisor to get help from subordinates in solving a problem.

30. A new procedure is about to be instituted in your division. Before presenting it to your staff you try to think of what objections they may raise and how to deal with these objections. Of the following, the best reason for this practice is that the
(A) employees will respect your competence when you can handle their objections on the spot
(B) analysis involved will help you better to understand the new procedure
(C) objections can be channeled upwards and the procedure revised before it is implemented
(D) knowledge you have of your employees' ways of thinking and behaving will be increased.

Answer: (A) Supervisors will enhance the chances of a new procedure being accepted willingly by subordinates if they are prepared to answer any objections raised while presenting it to them. Any indecisiveness will be looked upon as a sign that the supervisor does not really understand the procedure and that the order for a change was arbitrary and not well thought out.

31. A recently assigned supervisor is greatly antagonized by one subordinate. Of the following, the most useful first step the supervisor could take with respect to this individual is to
(A) determine the chances of transferring the person
(B) tactfully ascertain from the staff their reactions to this individual as well as the individual's reputation as a worker
(C) recognize that this is the well-known "halo" effect and make a conscious effort to be fair to this employee
(D) explain the situation to a superior and ask for advice.

Answer: (B) Perhaps the supervisor's initial impression was faulty and an attempt should be made to ascertain whether others who had close contact with the person in question reacted in the same way.

32. A senior supervisor institutes a policy of minimizing the amount of information passed on to subordinates since this supervisor feels the workers are overburdened with details. This practice is
    (A) proper; it is part of the job to act as a buffer for the staff
    (B) improper; the senior supervisor is trying to assume too many responsibilities
    (C) proper; the supervisor's leadership strength is increased by the degree to which subordinates turn to their superior for guidance
    (D) improper; the subordinates lack information which may be necessary to proper performance of their duties.

Answer: (D) This procedure should definitely be evaluated as improper. Subordinates must be well informed if they are to function effectively. Although choice (B) is correct to some degree, choice (D) is much better.

33. When unexpected obstacles arise during the course of operations, the supervisor must find means of overcoming them. Of the following, the most important factor in this endeavor is the supervisor's
    (A) attitude
    (B) advance planning
    (C) training
    (D) knowledge of procedures.

Answer: (A) All formulated plans leave room for the unexpected to happen because it usually does. Supervisors must not allow themselves to be rattled by the unexpected. They must be able to modify their plans to take care of any new situation that may arise.

34. Of the following duties to be performed, a supervisor would be *least* justified in delegating to a member, rather than performing personally, the
    (A) inspection of committee work
    (B) preparation of a report of an investigation of a complaint
    (C) follow-up training of a recently transferred employee
    (D) making out of inspection cards.

Answer: (A) The functions in choices (B), (C) and (D) are all suitable for delegation to a qualified subordinate by a supervisor. Inspection of committee work is not, because the supervisor would be directly responsible for the results of the committee.

35. The outcome that is most likely to result from setting work standards slightly higher than subordinates can achieve with ease is that they will have
    (A) clearly defined and perceivable objectives
    (B) a desire to avoid potential failure
    (C) the opportunity to enjoy gratifying success
    (D) an area about which they can safely complain.

Answer: (C) The best work standards are those which are set just slightly above what the average employee can easily attain. Workers must be made to extend themselves just a bit if they are to feel a sense of accomplishment.

36. You have a group of employees working under you on a special assignment. One of them is not competent. This individual resents your criticism and claims to be discriminated against. Close supervision is necessary for this person to do the job and yet any such supervision is resented by the worker. The best solution to this problem is to
    (A) prepare a written reprimand that will be made part of the employee's records and will be an official warning that there must be an improvement in conduct
    (B) permit the group to correct the situation since group action is usually more effective than corrective action imposed by the supervisor
    (C) recommend a change in assignment in an attempt to remove the employee from a work situation that is having an adverse effect
    (D) identify the real cause of the behavior problem and determine how the employee can be helped to find greater personal satisfaction from the job.

Answer: (C) This individual is working on a special assignment and is not doing a good job at it. A recommendation for a change in assignment in this instance is not really considered a transfer. The employee is obviously not suited for this *special* work. It should be kept in mind, however, that under ordinary circumstances, a transfer of an incompetent worker is not considered good personnel practice, because actually what is being done is to shift one supervisor's problem to another.

37. When a supervisor gives a valid command to a subordinate, there is a tacit understanding that the subordinate has the legal power to perform it. This is based on the principle that
    (A) the person to whom authority is granted becomes as accountable for its use as the superior who delegated the authority
    (B) responsibility for proper performance of an order cannot be placed without the delegation of the authority needed to execute it
    (C) only through the establishment of effective controls can a supervisor insure the proper execution of orders
    (D) superiors who give orders are responsible for seeing to it later that the orders have been carried out as assigned.

Answer: (B) Sufficient authority must be delegated with the responsibility to carry out a function.

38. Much has been said in recent years about the advisability of instituting suggestion programs or of inviting subordinates to participate in attempting to find solutions to company problems. In general, the most likely result of instituting either or both of these ideas would be
    (A) an increased motivation of the subordinates to do a better job
    (B) an increased need for disciplinary action against subordinates as a result of their feeling more free to introduce new ideas
    (C) a loss of efficiency resulting from the introduction of new ideas
    (D) a stifling of initiative among the subordinates.

Answer: (A) A well-run suggestion program will not only produce good ideas from some of the most unexpected sources, but it will also tend to make all members of the organization feel that they belong. Their ideas are not only wanted; they are appreciated.

39. A supervisor must frequently delegate authority to subordinates, and the success of the delegation depends in a large degree upon the ability of the subordinate to accept the delegated authority. Of the following, the most important factor in encouraging positive and whole-hearted acceptance on the part of a subordinate is that
    (A) the delegation be on a permanent basis
    (B) the assignment does not require greater effort than customarily exerted by the subordinate
    (C) appropriate members of the organization be duly notified and instructed to accept the delegation
    (D) the delegation does not involve assumption of authority over co-workers.

Answer: (C) Due notice must be given to affected parties when authority is delegated by the supervisor to a subordinate. In the absence of this notification the subordinate assuming the authority will not command the respect and cooperation of the workers necessary to fulfill the function.

40. An important principle of the science of supervision is that the span of control should be narrow enough to permit effective control. Of the following, the principle which is most *contradictory* to this is that
    (A) organizational levels should be kept to a minimum
    (B) employees should be grouped according to geographic areas
    (C) the units composing an organization have a tendency to grow away from each other and become independent
    (D) control should be placed in persons in key positions.

Answer: (A) It is an accepted concept that the levels of an organization should be kept down to as few as possible. However, if this would result in too broad a span of control, the levels in the organization would have to be adjusted. The span of control and the organizational levels are inversely related.

41. A chief of an inspectional division charged with seeing that safety regulations are enforced encounters a subordinate making an inspection of a factory. The subordinate is not sure just which

safety regulations are being violated, and seeks the aid of the chief. The chief and the subordinate discuss the possible violations in the presence of the factory manager, and then the chief directs the subordinate to issue summonses for specific violations. Discussing the problem in the presence of the factory manager was

(A) proper, mainly because the factory manager probably would realize the chief and a subordinate were not acting arbitrarily or unreasonably

(B) improper, mainly because the factory manager might prefer one of the approaches which was suggested and rejected

(C) proper, mainly because the activities of the department should, whenever possible, be open to the public

(D) improper, mainly because inaccurate statements may have been made during the preliminary discussion.

Answer: (D) The factory manager would most likely lose respect for the chief and the subordinate if any indecision as to the correct course of action was exhibited by the two officials in their preliminary discussion.

42. A good leader encourages subordinates to use their initiative, but realizes that such a practice has a price. Of the following, the main drawback is that subordinates will occasionally

(A) overstep the bounds of their authority
(B) make errors in judgment
(C) duplicate work of others
(D) engage in fruitless experimentation.

Answer: (B) The main danger involved when subordinates are permitted and encouraged to make their own decisions is that they probably do not have as much experience as their supervisors. However, a practice of encouraging subordinates to use their *initiative* will result in their development.

43. Of the following results, the most likely consequence of decentralization of authority and responsibility in an organization is

(A) improved discipline
(B) increased specialization of functions
(C) greater diversity in procedures
(D) greater interchangeability of personnel.

Answer: (C) When authority is decentralized, more people will be making decisions concerning courses of action. Therefore, it is probable that the same type of work may be performed differently from unit to unit in the same organization. When authority is centralized, decisions emit from one source in an organization and work procedures of a like nature will be handled similarly.

44. A special unit of a department is rife with rumors concerning plans for its future and the possibility of its abolition. As a result, morale and production of members assigned to it have suffered. To handle this situation, the supervisor in command adopts a policy of promptly corroborating factual rumors and denying false ones. This method of dealing with the problem will achieve some good results, but its chief weakness is that

(A) it gives status to the rumors by the attention paid to them
(B) the supervisor may not have the necessary information at hand to dispose promptly of all rumors
(C) it "chases" the rumors rather than forestalling them by giving information concerning the unit's future
(D) the supervisor may have confidential information which should not be divulged.

Answer: (C) This action is doing nothing to prevent these many rumors. The supervisor is just disposing of them as fast as he can after they occur.

SUPERVISING UNSKILLED WORKERS

Whatever the nature of your job, if it entails the supervision of unskilled workers there are certain basic concepts of supervision that will apply. The questions that follow illustrate the range of supervisory problems you will face. The explanations provided for each question spotlight the supervisory reasoning involved in each situation.

1. One of the workers in your crew complains about having to do a hard job. The best thing for you to do is to
   (A) ignore the worker
   (B) explain that all employees must do their fair share of the hard jobs
   (C) tell the worker that the next job will be an easy one
   (D) take the worker off this job.

Answer: **(B)** It usually works out well to have the undesirable tasks rotated among all workers of equal rank. All tasks cannot be desirable, but all have to be performed.

2. Employees will respect their supervisor most if the supervisor
   (A) acts sternly with them
   (B) does not show favoritism
   (C) is quick to criticize their errors
   (D) does not enforce all the rules and regulations.

Answer: **(B)** A supervisor who is impartial toward subordinates is most likely to be respected. A strict supervisor will not always gain the respect of subordinates, and a lenient supervisor is even less likely to be respected. Criticism of a subordinate's errors should always be handled with the greatest discretion.

3. The best supervisor is usually the
   (A) best mechanic
   (B) fastest worker

   (C) employee in service the longest
   (D) ablest leader.

Answer: **(D)** The successful supervisor must be a good leader and must be able to gain the support of employees in fulfilling his or her functions. A good worker does not necessarily make a good supervisor. The same can be said of a fast worker. An employee who has worked at the job for a long time does not necessarily acquire leadership ability.

4. One of your workers offers a suggestion to improve the method of doing a job. The best thing to do is to tell the worker
   (A) that the job has always been done the same way and therefore it must be the best way
   (B) that you will check the suggestion to see if it really is a better way of doing the job
   (C) to make the suggestion to the chief engineer
   (D) to discuss it with the other employees, and if they agree, you will try the suggested method.

Answer: **(B)** Some of the most useful suggestions come from those closest to the actual work. All suggestions should be carefully evaluated by the supervisor. Even if the entire suggestion is not valid, it may have its good points. Besides, the supervisor will do much to maintain the morale of the group if suggestions are encouraged.

5. Of the following, the statement that is correct is that
   (A) every worker can do the same amount of work

(B) the employee with the most seniority will work the fastest
(C) the strongest worker will do the most work
(D) the amount of work a person does can be increased by improving morale.

Answer: **(D)** Production and employee morale are directly related. When morale is high, production will be high; when morale is low, production will be poor.

6. Of the following, the best way for a supervisor to get subordinates to follow orders and directives willingly is to
   (A) ask for volunteers
   (B) explain the reasons behind the orders and directives
   (C) issue them in the form of a request or in a mild tone of voice
   (D) take part in carrying them out.

Answer: **(B)** A worker will be more likely to perform well if aware of the reason for carrying out a particular task.

7. Inefficient scheduling of work should be suspected when one notes that there are several employees
   (A) absent from work
   (B) in the rest room
   (C) loading a truck
   (D) waiting to use equipment.

Answer: **(D)** The fact that equipment is not available when necessary is usually indicative of poor scheduling of work. Workers who must wait around for equipment are losing valuable time.

8. Whenever you give an assignment to one of your experienced employees, you are asked a great many questions about it although the employee has successfully performed similar assignments in the past. The time you spend in answering the many questions about minor details takes you away from more important work. Under these circumstances, you should probably *first*
   (A) answer the questions in such a way that the employee will be discouraged from asking further questions

(B) ask the employee to question a fellow employee
(C) express your confidence in the employee's ability to carry out the assignment properly and suggest that the employee proceed with the assignment
(D) tell the employee that if the assignment is too difficult, you will give it to someone who does not raise so many questions.

Answer: **(C)** This individual is needlessly wasting the time of the supervisor and apparently lacks self-confidence. The supervisor should attempt to instill self-confidence in this employee through encouragement and praise whenever justified.

9. A supervisor's self-image should be primarily that of
   (A) boss of the crew
   (B) part of the top management team
   (C) skilled maintenance and repair mechanic in various fields
   (D) mechanic first and boss second.

Answer: **(A)** Paid to supervise, a supervisor's aim should be to achieve maximum production from subordinates and to attain the unit's objectives.

10. If, after you have been a supervisor for several years, you find that your staff never complains to you about working conditions or assignments, this is most probably a sign that
    (A) there is poor communication between you and your employees
    (B) the employees are interested mainly in their rate of pay
    (C) the employees have nothing to complain about
    (D) you are a very good supervisor.

Answer: **(A)** It is perfectly normal for workers to have some complaints. If a supervisor never receives any, the reason probably is a manner which does not encourage them. The supervisor's attitude should be one that makes it easy for the workers to come to the supervisor with work problems.

11. "The number of subordinates reporting directly to a superior should not be greater than the

number which can be supervised competently."
This could be an acceptable definition of
(A) chain of command
(B) span of control
(C) specialized functions
(D) unity of command.

Answer: **(B)** The concept of span of control relates to the number of subordinates any supervisor can effectively handle. This number may increase or decrease, depending on the type of work being performed, how effectively the subordinates are trained, the conditions they perform the work under, etc.

12. A characteristic which a supervisor should consider most desirable in a worker is
(A) willingness to work as much overtime as possible
(B) keeping aloof from co-workers
(C) the ability to carry out assignments properly
(D) the readiness to report gang gossip back to the supervisor.

Answer: **(C)** The worker who is most valuable to the organization is the one who does the job with the greatest possible efficiency. What good is willingness to work overtime if the job is not well done? Personality traits such as aloofness and willingness to gossip are not important unless they tend to interfere with work performance.

13. If a crew continues to work effectively when their supervisor is out sick for a day or two, it would most probably indicate that
(A) the supervisor has their full cooperation
(B) the supervisor apparently serves no useful function with this crew
(C) the crew is trying to curry favor
(D) the job is not too difficult.

Answer: **(A)** When a crew functions equally well whether the supervisor is absent or present, it is an indication that a high degree of morale exists. The staff is well-trained, cooperative and fully behind their supervisor in attainment of unit objectives.

14. A supervisor would be personally to blame for inefficiency resulting from
(A) improper planning of work assignments

(B) unforeseen delays in delivery of material
(C) departmental policy of job rotation
(D) frequent labor turnover.

Answer: **(A)** Poor planning causes delays in work through idle labor, lack of needed supplies, and improper staffing.

15. Supervisors are most likely to be held in high regard by their employees if they make it a practice to
(A) exchange advice with employees on personal problems
(B) are outspoken when pointing out employees' faults
(C) expect all employees to carry out any job with equal proficiency
(D) observe the same rules of conduct that employees are expected to observe.

Answer: **(D)** Supervisors will be respected by their subordinates if they observe the same rules of conduct that the subordinates are expected to follow. The exchange of advice on personal problems is a practice fraught with danger. If the advice does not have good results, it is bound to cause friction. An effective supervisor will use discretion while criticizing subordinates. Criticism should do good, not harm.

16. A supervisory practice which is most likely to lead to confusion and inefficiency is for the supervisor to
(A) issue orders only in writing
(B) relay orders to the staff through co-workers
(C) follow up on the orders after issuing them
(D) give orders verbally directly to the individual assigned to the job.

Answer: **(B)** Aside from the chance that a verbal order will not be relayed accurately, there is also the risk that some workers will resent being given an order by a fellow worker.

17. Several workers in your crew start a discussion during working hours of rumored changes in working conditions. This discussion can best be stopped by telling the workers that
(A) existing conditions are satisfactory

(B) you will check on the rumor
(C) working conditions do not concern them
(D) they should wait and see if the working conditions are changed.

Answer: **(B)** Uncertainty based on rumors of change can be demoralizing. As supervisor, you should assure the workers that you will find out if the rumor is valid and report back to them.

18. It has been said that the success of a unit performing routine work rests on the unit supervisor. If the supervisor wants to prevent boredom and to stimulate the workers' interest in their duties, it would generally be best to
   (A) set an easy pace for subordinates so that they will not become bored because of having to learn too much too rapidly
   (B) set the pace for subordinates so that the task is never too easy but is a constant challenge calling for more and better work
   (C) inspect subordinates on the job at irregular intervals in order to determine whether they are performing their duties properly
   (D) see to it that the objectives and goals of the department are properly communicated and interpreted to subordinates.

Answer: **(B)** A good work standard is not easily attained. Workers must be made to extend themselves to some degree or they are prone to becoming easily bored.

19. Frequently, when you, as a supervisor, have given instructions to your crew on how to do a job, a certain crew member has made a suggestion to you concerning a better way in which to do the job. The next time this person does this, you should
   (A) listen to the suggestion, express your thanks and adopt the suggestion if it seems good
   (B) listen to the suggestion, thank the person but don't adopt the suggestion
   (C) ask whether the person is trying to embarrass you
   (D) tell the individual to put the suggestion in writing so that you and your superior can examine and discuss it fully.

Answer: **(A)** If the person really suggests a better method for performing the job, by all means take advantage of it. This is bound to benefit the unit.

20. You, as a supervisor, are given an engineer's sketch of a certain trench to be excavated and a small piece of curbing to be removed from your area. This work is to be done by you and your crew. You do not fully understand the sketch. You should
   (A) first ask whether any member of the crew understands it
   (B) first ask your supervisor for help
   (C) do the work the best you can without seeking advice
   (D) wait until an engineer visits the job site and then request an explanation of the sketch.

Answer: **(B)** This goes for everyone, workers and supervisors alike. When in doubt about working instructions, ask questions. It is better to ask questions before starting the job than after it is done wrong.

21. One of the members of your crew who is a good worker prefers to be alone and rarely mixes with other crew members. As a supervisor you should
   (A) respect as far as possible the apparent desire to be alone
   (B) team this person up whenever possible with the most sociable members of the crew
   (C) urge other crew members to find out why this individual seldom talks with others
   (D) try to discover if there is anything abnormal in the personal life of the individual.

Answer: **(A)** As long as the job is properly done, permit the individual to be alone if it does not interfere with unit objectives.

22. A subordinate assigned to your ten-person crew asks to be excused from lifting any heavy objects for a period of one week to permit a sore thumb and index finger to heal. It would be best for you to
   (A) grant this request
   (B) ask for a medical certificate before granting the request

(C) suggest that this worker arrange with another crew member to do any heavy lifting work

(D) advise that this worker cannot be excused, but that there is no assurance that heavy lifting will be necessary that week.

Answer: **(A)** There is nothing in the question to indicate that the crew member is a malingerer; therefore, why not grant the request?

23. Since subordinates must carry out every order issued, it is the responsibility of the supervisor to
    (A) issue orders that are justified and clearly understood
    (B) issue orders sparingly
    (C) issue very important orders in writing
    (D) justify to subordinates the need for an order when it is issued.

Answer: **(A)** It is important indeed that a supervisor give orders which are not only valid but which are workable. The supervisor must make sure that they are issued in a manner which makes them easily understood.

24. If you are assigned to be supervisor over a crew which includes several employees who have been unfriendly to you in the past, the best course of action for you to take is to
    (A) give some excuse to be relieved of this assignment
    (B) supervise these employees more closely than the others
    (C) tell these employees right at the start that you will not tolerate any nonsense from them
    (D) treat them the same as you do the others under your supervision.

Answer: **(D)** Initially this situation calls for no special action at all. All should be treated exactly alike. However, if these employees do pose a problem, your position should be made quite clear. You will not tolerate any attitude that will interfere with satisfactory work performance. It is more important for a supervisor to command the respect of subordinates than to be liked by them.

25. It is most important for a supervisor to
    (A) acknowledge good work on the part of subordinates
    (B) know when a situation requires a decision from higher authority
    (C) make discipline strict but not lacking in personal sympathy
    (D) rotate the unpleasant work assignments.

Answer: **(B)** All supervisors should be aware of where their authority begins and ends. Without this information it is impossible for them to fulfill their functions properly. When a situation arises that calls for a decision to be made by a higher authority, the supervisor involved should not hesitate to consult that authority.

26. Some management authorities propose that work assignments be made by assigning a varied set of tasks to a group of employees and then allowing the group to decide for itself how to organize the work to be done. This method of assigning work is called "job enlargement." The one of the following which is considered to be the chief advantage of job enlargement is that it
    (A) encourages employees to specialize in the work they are assigned to do
    (B) reduces the amount of control that employees have over their work
    (C) increases the employees' job satisfaction
    (D) reduces the number of skills that each employee is required to learn.

Answer: **(C)** This situation results in the absence of specific orders to perform work. Employees who are given the opportunity to have at least some say in the work to be done are bound to receive greater satisfaction from its performance.

27. When you ask an employee to do some work from a high ladder, the employee requests another assignment because of a problem working in high places. In this case, it would be best for you to
    (A) give the employee another assignment as requested
    (B) insist that the employee do the job originally assigned
    (C) ask the employee to try to exchange assignments with another individual

(D) tell the employee to return to the reporting quarters while you start disciplinary action.

Answer: (A) There is nothing in the question to make one believe the individual has any other reason for asking to be excused from the task aside from a fear of heights. If at all possible, the supervisor should assign this task to another employee.

28. Although there is a normal disparity between successive ranks of employees in an organization, the greatest disparity and change in rank occur when a worker becomes a first-line supervisor. This is true chiefly because the first-line supervisor
    (A) must be better informed than subordinates
    (B) becomes responsible for the first time for the job performance of others
    (C) must learn to assume new and more complex duties
    (D) has greater responsibility and authority than the subordinates.

Answer: (B) There is a great difference in being responsible for your own work and being responsible for the work of others. A first-line supervisor makes this transition when assuming the new job.

29. If one of your workers informs you of an obvious error in a written order issued by you, it would be best for you to
    (A) tell the worker it is of no consequence and the order still stands since its intent is evident
    (B) point out that all orders issued by supervision must be carried out without questioning their accuracy
    (C) request that worker to say nothing to the others in order to keep their respect
    (D) immediately change the order to correct the obvious error.

Answer: (D) A supervisor should not only have an open mind, but should be a "big person." If an obvious error is brought to the attention of a supervisor by any subordinate, remedial action should be taken immediately. This is bound to result in the fostering of good relations between the supervisor and the subordinates.

30. In setting up a work schedule for a special job, it is least important for you to know
    (A) the pay rate of the various individuals assigned to you
    (B) when the employees will be available
    (C) the approximate time required to complete the job
    (D) when the material for the job will be available.

Answer: (A) The pay rate is the least important of the choices. When scheduling a job, the availability of labor and material is most important. When the job is to be completed is also pertinent. Although you are a supervisor, you are not required to know the pay rates of the various workers who will perform the work. You are not determining the cost of the job.

31. In measuring the work of subordinates, the supervisor of a unit performing routine work began by observing them at work. If a subordinate seemed to be busy, then the supervisor concluded that the subordinate was producing a great deal of work. On the other hand, the supervisor concluded that a subordinate who did not seem to be busy was not producing much work. The supervisor's work measurement method was faulty chiefly because
    (A) it did not use a standard against which a subordinate's work could be measured
    (B) the type of work performed by the subordinates did not lend itself to accurate measurement
    (C) the subordinates might not have worked at their normal rates if they were aware that their work was being observed
    (D) the supervisor may not have observed a subordinate's work for a long enough period of time.

Answer: (A) Observation in itself is a poor method of measuring work performance. What is lacking in this situation is the absence of the finished product. A supervisor should inspect the finished product for accuracy and then measure the amount done against a predetermined standard. Quantity of work performed may be easily measured by assigning a specific amount to be done during a set amount of time.

32. You find that your superior has a tendency to issue written orders which lack sufficient detail and clarity. As supervisor it is best that you
    (A) request that your superior issue all orders verbally
    (B) complain to the superior about the condition
    (C) ask for clarification on receiving the orders
    (D) use your own judgment.

Answer: (C) It is imperative that when an order is received it be thoroughly understood. The recipient of a seemingly unclear order should ask for immediate clarification before undertaking to carry out the order.

33. In acquainting a new employee with job details, it would be improper for a supervisor to talk about the
    (A) shortcomings of the workers in his crew
    (B) proper method for making inspection reports
    (C) rules and regulations of the department
    (D) special safety precautions.

Answer: (A) Obviously this is the one thing a supervisor must not do. The information in the other choices would all be proper to orient a new worker.

34. "Supervisory authority implies the acceptance of responsibility." This means chiefly that supervisors should
    (A) be accountable for their own actions
    (B) not give authority to members of the crew
    (C) not give advice to subordinates
    (D) keep complete records of serious errors.

Answer: (A) Supervisors should realize that they hold positions of responsibility and that their actions will be scrutinized very carefully by subordinates and superiors alike.

35. You are a supervisor and you learn that a certain subordinate is soon to be transferred to your crew. You know that this person has a reputation for being hard to handle and inclined to be belligerent. The one of the following that would be the *least* desirable thing for you to do

as a supervisor would be to
    (A) make reference to this reputation as soon as the subordinate joins the crew and state that you will not tolerate the slightest misbehavior
    (B) ask the subordinate about the kind of work previously done
    (C) try to discover whether the bad reputation is deserved or not
    (D) welcome the subordinate into the crew as just another member.

Answer: (A) This employee must be given an equal chance in spite of the bad reputation. Perhaps this bad reputation was gained because of conditions which were beyond control of the employee.

36. If a supervisor has a subordinate in the crew who is constantly blaming co-workers when jobs that this subordinate works on turn out unsatisfactorily, then it would be best for the supervisor to try to
    (A) assign the individual to jobs which will fix responsibility on him or her alone
    (B) reassign this person to work with different individuals
    (C) refer this employee to your superior for appropriate action
    (D) say or do nothing but give the employee a less-than-satisfactory service rating.

Answer: (A) This subordinate must be assigned to jobs where he or she can be held strictly responsible for their proper performance. In fact, it may be necessary to assign the employee to tasks that would have to be performed entirely alone. Then the employee would not be able to blame anyone else if the jobs were not done properly.

37. A worker, Jones, complains to you that you are giving another worker, Smith, a larger share of good details than others and mentions half a dozen specific examples of this. As their supervisor, it would be best for you to tell Jones
    (A) when Jones is a supervisor, Jones can make the assignments
    (B) why you have been giving these details to Smith
    (C) you will give Smith fewer such details in the future
    (D) you will give Jones more such details in the future than you will give Smith.

Answer: **(B)** Employee Jones is specific in this grievance and does deserve an explanation beyond a general denial. There is probably a good explanation for your assigning these duties to Smith. If your reasons are good, an explanation will probably alleviate the situation. The other three choices contain courses of action which are either arbitrary or not in the best interest of the unit.

38. As a supervisor, you realize that a subordinate who is a good employee has failed to carry out an assignment properly because your instructions were not thoroughly understood. The employee is aware that the assignment was not carried out properly but has concealed this from you and has not come to talk it over. As a supervisor, it would be best for you to
    (A) ask a co-worker friend to speak to the employee and try to develop more confidence in you
    (B) give the employee a mild reprimand
    (C) overlook this in view of the employee's record
    (D) try to establish a better relationship with this employee.

Answer: **(D)** This situation indicates that the subordinate is reluctant to communicate with the supervisor. The reason is probably based on a poor relationship between the two. Action should be taken to alleviate this.

39. One of the duties of a supervisor is to see to it that quality standards of work are maintained. An example of a standard of quality would be
    (A) how well a task had been performed
    (B) how fast the task had been performed
    (C) how many units of work were performed in a specific time
    (D) how long it took to fill out the reports connected with the work.

Answer: **(A)** The measurement of the quality of work performance will show how well work was performed. The other three choices contain examples of quantity performance.

40. For a supervisor to question a worker about personal problems would be most justified when the supervisor feels that
    (A) such problems can be solved
    (B) the supervisor has experienced similar problems in the past
    (C) the job performance of the worker is affected by such problems
    (D) the worker has a negative attitude toward such problems.

Answer: **(C)** Modern supervisory practice dictates that a supervisor is not to become involved in personal problems of subordinates unless the problems are affecting work performance.

41. It may happen sometimes that a supervisor will doubt the wisdom of an order received from a superior. However, in issuing this order to subordinates for execution, should the supervisor's doubts be mentioned?
    (A) no, because the supervisor can never be sure whether the doubts are entirely correct
    (B) yes, because the supervisor owes it to the subordinates to be completely frank with them
    (C) no, because criticism of such orders by the supervisor will create indecision among the employees
    (D) yes, because the employees may have some valuable suggestions to offer.

Answer: **(C)** A supervisor should support superiors if the support of subordinates is expected. It is a very poor practice indeed for the supervisor to show any disrespect for superiors to subordinates.

42. A certain supervisor, when giving an order, frequently accompanies it with a warning that disciplinary action will follow if the order is not carried out as directed. This practice is
    (A) desirable because it makes for a tightly knit, well-disciplined force
    (B) undesirable because it is likely to antagonize the staff and result in loss of their cooperation
    (C) desirable because the workers expect this type of supervision
    (D) undesirable because the warning will lose its effect eventually.

Answer: **(B)** This is a classic example of negative discipline. This type of action is designed to make subordinates work lest they be punished. It is seldom used at the present time because it cannot possibly have worthwhile results.

43. Your crew consistently performs more work than the crew headed by another supervisor. The other supervisor tells you that the high performance of your crew makes the other crew look bad. Under these circumstances, it would be best for you to
    (A) ignore the matter and have your crew continue working as before
    (B) report the matter to your superior for disciplinary action
    (C) slow your crew down somewhat to show the other supervisor that you are willing to cooperate
    (D) slow your crew down to the level of the other crew.

Answer: **(A)** It would be a poor practice indeed for the supervisor to slow up his more efficient crew so that the less efficient crew can compare favorably with it. It should work the other way around. The supervisor of the less efficient crew should institute the necessary training to attempt to catch up with the more efficient one.

44. You have reason to believe that one of the workers in your crew gossips about you behind your back. Under these circumstances, it is usually best to
    (A) attempt to find out which of your employees believes the gossip
    (B) find out what this worker's weak points are and bring them to the attention of your crew
    (C) ignore the matter
    (D) speak to the worker about it and request that the gossip be stopped.

Answer: **(C)** The supervisor in this instance should ignore the matter until it becomes a problem.

45. One of your subordinates wants to submit a suggestion to the Suggestion Program regarding the operation of the unit, but wants your advice first. The most advisable course of action for you to take is to
    (A) advise the subordinate that any suggestions concerning the unit should be made directly to you
    (B) give the subordinate advice provided your name is included on the suggestion
    (C) give the subordinate the desired advice
    (D) tell the subordinate that it would not be fair if you were to give any help.

Answer: **(C)** A suggestion program operates on the basis that suggestors should be encouraged to contribute ideas for operational improvement. It is not wise for the supervisor to show any animosity towards a contributor. Let the suggestor receive any credit due and feel that you are flattered that your advice has been sought.

46. A task has to be performed. You issue instructions to your crew as to how this should be done. One of your workers strongly objects and says that your instructions are wrong. You listen to the reasons, but you still think that you are right. Under these circumstances, you should
    (A) ask for opinions from others in the crew as to how the job should be done
    (B) contact another worker for an opinion
    (C) refer the matter to your superior for a decision
    (D) tell the worker to perform the job in accordance with your instructions.

Answer: **(D)** It is the function of the supervisor to make decisions as to how work is to be performed. The supervisor in this question has acted correctly by listening to this worker who has another way to do the job. However, if after listening to this worker the supervisor is still of the opinion that the original way is best, his subordinates should be ordered to proceed immediately to do the work according to his instructions.

47. You tell an employee to separate and store supplies in a certain way. The employee then asks you, "Why do you want me to do it this way?" You should answer the question by
    (A) advising the employee to figure out the reason

(B) explaining why you want it done in that particular way
(C) repeating your instructions more slowly
(D) telling the employee to follow your instructions without asking any questions.

Answer: (B) A worker will function more effectively if he or she can understand the reason why a job is performed in a particular manner. If the validity of the reason is doubted, the worker may consider the order arbitrary and be less likely to function effectively.

48. Assume that an employee shows you that you have made an error in issuing certain instructions. You admit your error. Such action on your part is desirable primarily because
(A) the job may be done correctly
(B) your employees will be encouraged to make similar corrections in the future
(C) you will gain a reputation for fairness
(D) your employees will realize that you will not make errors of this type in the future.

Answer: (A) This question states that the supervisor has been in error while issuing instructions. Of primary importance is that these instructions be corrected so that the work can be performed accurately. It is the responsibility of the supervisor to see that the work of the unit is accomplished in the most effective way.

49. Suppose that you are the supervisor of a small unit in an agency. One of your subordinates expressed dissatisfaction with a work assignment and wishes to discuss the matter with you. The employee is obviously very angry and upset. Of the following, the course of action that you should take first in this situation is to
(A) postpone discussion of the employee's complaint, explaining to him that the matter can be settled more satisfactorily if it is discussed calmly
(B) have the employee describe the complaint, correcting any erroneous charge against you
(C) permit the employee to present the complaint in full, withholding your comments until the full description of the complaint has been given

(D) promise the employee that you will review all the work assignments in the unit to determine whether or not any changes should be made.

Answer: (C) Many employee grievances are disposed of by merely permitting the aggrieved to sound off and "get it off his chest." The dissatisfaction may or may not be justified. In any case, the supervisor, by giving the subordinate the opportunity to state the complaint in full, will then be able to determine its validity.

50. Assume that the operations of a certain unit enable the supervisor to allow each subordinate wide discretion in selecting the kind and amount of work the individual chooses to do. However, in evaluating the work of subordinates, the supervisor places more emphasis on some areas of their work than on others. Factors such as number of applications processed and number of letters written are given great weight in evaluation, while factors such as number of papers filed and number of forms checked are given little weight. Hence, a subordinate who processes a large number of applications would receive a high evaluation even if very few forms have been checked. The supervisor's method of evaluation would most likely result in
(A) an increase in the amount of time spent on processing each application
(B) a backlog of papers waiting to be filed
(C) an improvement in the quality of letters written
(D) a decline in output in all areas of work.

Answer: (B) This situation is a poor one indeed. Workers would tend to spend time on work that the supervisor evaluated highly and neglect the work for which the supervisor did not assign credit.

51. As the newly appointed supervisor of a unit in an agency, you are about to design a system for measuring the quantity of work produced by your subordinates. The one of the following which is the first step that you should take in designing this system is to
(A) establish the units of work measurement to be used in the system
(B) determine the actual advantages and disadvantages of the system

(C) determine the abilities of each of your subordinates

(D) ascertain the types of work done in the unit.

Answer: (D) The first step in a program designed to measure the quantity (amount) of work performed by your subordinates is a determination of the different types of work being performed which are measureable.

52. "It has been said that the best supervisor is the one who gives the fewest orders." The one of the following supervisory practices that would be most likely to increase the number of orders that a supervisor must give to get out the work is to

(A) set general goals for subordinates and give them the authority for reaching the goals

(B) train subordinates to make decisions for themselves

(C) establish routines for subordinates' jobs

(D) introduce frequent changes in the work methods subordinates are using.

Answer: (D) When the performance of a job is not changed frequently, standard operating procedures can be set up, thus cutting down the amount of orders which are given by the supervisor. If the workers are aware of just what has to be done and how it should be done, the necessity for orders is lessened. However, if the work procedures are changed frequently, it will require more orders by the supervisor and closer supervision.

53. The one of the following supervisory practices that would be most likely to give subordinates in a unit of a public agency a feeling of satisfaction in their work is to

(A) establish work goals that take a long time to achieve

(B) show the subordinates how their work goals are related to the goals of the agency

(C) set work goals higher than subordinates can achieve

(D) refrain from telling subordinates that they are failing to meet their work goals.

Answer: (B) A worker who performs only part of a function should be shown just how that part contributes to the major goals of the agency. Only in this way will the worker be able to feel a sense of accomplishment.

54. For supervisors to listen to the personal problems which subordinates bring them is generally

(A) desirable; it is likely that the supervisor has broader experience in solving personal problems than do subordinates

(B) undesirable; the supervisor may be unable to solve such problems

(C) desirable; the supervisor can better understand subordinates' behavior on the job

(D) undesirable; permitting a subordinate to talk about personal problems may only make them seem worse.

Answer: (C) A supervisor should take an interest in a subordinate's personal problems when they are affecting the work of the subordinate.

55. Suppose that you are the supervisor of a small unit. You have given one of your subordinates, Smith, an assignment which must be completed by the end of the day. Because he is unfamiliar with the assignment, Smith will be unable to complete it on time. Your other subordinates are too busy to help Smith, but you have the time to help him complete the assignment. For you to help Smith complete the assignment would be

(A) desirable, because a supervisor is expected to be familiar with the work of subordinates

(B) undesirable, because Smith will come to depend on you to help him do his work

(C) desirable, because Smith is likely to appreciate your help and give you his cooperation when you need it

(D) undesirable, because a supervisor should not perform the same type of work as subordinates.

Answer: (C) A supervisor is paid primarily to supervise subordinates. However, helping in the work of one of the employees is justified when it is necessary to accomplish an objective and when there is no other way of getting the job done.

56. Of the following, generally the basic reason for using standard procedures in an agency is to

(A) provide sequences of steps for handling recurring activities

(B) facilitate periodic review of standard practices

(C) train new employees in the agency's policies and objectives

(D) serve as a basis for formulating agency policies.

Answer: (A) The key word in this question is *recurring*. If a function is going to be performed again and again in the future, why not set up a standard procedure for its performance? This will eliminate a great deal of instructional time.

57. Green is assigned to type weekly reports to be submitted to the supervisor, Brown. Brown tells Green that the reports should be neat in appearance. The first two reports submitted are unsatisfactory to Brown because they contain a few erasures, and Brown tells Green that the reports are unsatisfactory. The next two reports submitted are also unsatisfactory because they contain many erasures; however, Brown accepts these reports without criticizing them. The fifth report submitted contains fewer erasures than the previous reports, but it too is unsatisfactory, and this time Brown criticizes the erasures in an attempt to prevent the submission of unsatisfactory reports in the future. Green is puzzled and upset by this criticism. Brown's handling of Green was faulty chiefly because

(A) Brown did not give Green sufficient opportunity to correct the work

(B) Green may not have been capable of doing neat work

(C) Brown was inconsistent in the criticism of Green's work

(D) Brown should have criticized the reports containing many erasures rather than the reports with only a few erasures.

Answer: (C) The acceptance of unsatisfactory work at one time and the rejection of it at another time will undermine the standards that should be set for an employee. Green will never know what is expected. Standards should be consistent.

58. Assume that you are the head of a unit in an agency. From time to time, your subordinates are assigned to other units to do reception work and other duties. You receive a note from Mr.

Jones, the head of one of these other units, stating that the work of Miss Smith, one of your subordinates, was unsatisfactory when she worked for him, and asking you not to assign her to him again. Although Miss Smith has worked in your unit for a long time, this is the first time that anyone has complained about her work. The one of the following actions that you should take first in this situation is to ask

(A) the heads of the other units for whom Miss Smith has worked whether or not her work has been satisfactory

(B) Mr. Jones in what way Miss Smith's work has been unsatisfactory

(C) Miss Smith to explain in what way her work for Mr. Jones was unsatisfactory

(D) Mr. Jones which of your subordinates he would prefer to have assigned to him.

Answer: (B) Avoid general complaints of unsatisfactory work. They should always be specific so that, if valid, corrective measures can be taken.

59. Assume that in an office, correspondence is filed, according to the date received, in 12 folders, one for each month of the year. On January 1 of each year, correspondence dated through December 31 of the preceding year is transferred from the active to the inactive files. New folders are then inserted in the active files to contain the correspondence to be filed in the next year. Of the following, the chief disadvantage of this method of transferring correspondence from active to inactive files is that

(A) the inactive files may lack the capacity to contain all the correspondence transferred to them

(B) the folders prepared each year must be labeled the same as the folders in preceding years

(C) some of the correspondence from the preceding year may not be in the active files on January 1

(D) some of the correspondence transferred to the inactive files may be referred to as frequently as some of the correspondence in the active files.

Answer: (D) In this instance, material only a month old—and probably still very much current—would be placed in the inactive files.

60. "There are disadvantages as well as advantages in using statistical controls to measure specific aspects of subordinates' jobs." Of the following, that which can *least* be considered to be an advantage of statistical controls to a supervisor is that such controls may
    (A) reduce the need for close, detailed supervision
    (B) give the supervisor information needed for making decisions
    (C) stimulate subordinates whose work is measured by statistical controls to improve their performance
    (D) encourage subordinates to emphasize aspects being measured rather than their jobs as a whole.

Answer: **(D)** The workers would tend to work well in areas which could be revealed by the statistics. They would be less likely to give full effort to tasks for which they would not receive statistical credit.

61. In setting the work standard for a certain task, a unit supervisor took the total output of all the employees in the unit and divided it by the number of employees, thus establishing the average output as the work standard for the task. The method that the supervisor used to establish the work standard is generally considered to be
    (A) proper, since the method takes into account the output of the outstanding, as well as of the less-productive employees
    (B) improper, since the average output may not be what could reasonably be expected of a competent, satisfactory employee
    (C) proper, since the standard is based on the actual output of the employees who are to be evaluated
    (D) improper, since all the employees in the unit may be successful in meeting the work standard.

Answer: **(B)** The average of anything is seldom good enough. It is determined by the worst as well as the best, and there may be more employees below a reasonable standard than above it.

62. Assume that a system of statistical reports designed to provide information about employee work performance is put into effect in a unit of an agency. There is some evidence that the employees of this unit are working below their capacities. The information obtained from the system is to be used by management to improve employee work performance. The employees whose work is to be recorded by the reports resent them. Nevertheless, the employees' work performance improves substantially after the reporting system is put into effect, and before management has put the information to use. The one of the following which is the most accurate conclusion to be drawn from this situation is that
    (A) a statistical reporting system may fail to provide the information it is designed to provide
    (B) low employee morale may have been the cause of the employees' former level of work performance
    (C) a statistical reporting system designed only to provide information about problems may also help to solve the problems
    (D) willing employee cooperation is essential to the success of a system of statistical reports.

Answer: **(C)** In this instance the workers knew they were producing below their normal capacities and that as soon as the reporting system went into effect the finger would be pointed at them. As a result, they improved their work performance.

DISCIPLINE AS A TRAINING DEVICE

As a first-line supervisor, you will be expected to establish and maintain discipline among the workers under you. The questions in this chapter pinpoint some of the problems you may face. The explanations following each question illustrate the supervisory concepts behind the solutions to discipline problems.

1. If, as a disciplinary measure, you wish to reprimand a worker for some improper act or neglect of duty, it would *not* be good practice to
   (A) allow yourself a cooling-off period of several days before you administer the reprimand
   (B) give the worker a chance to reply to your criticism
   (C) be very specific about the particular act or neglect of duty for which you are reprimanding the worker
   (D) reprimand the worker when you are alone with him or her.

Answer: (A) The longer the cooling-off period, the more the infraction will tend to be separated from the resultant discipline in the mind of the employee. A reprimand, or any other disciplinary measure, should take place as soon after the infraction as possible.

2. Before you recommend that charges be preferred against one of your workers for an alleged infraction of the rules and regulations, you should make absolutely sure that
   (A) the charges will be sustained at the hearing
   (B) your superior will approve your recommendation
   (C) the worker's fellow employees will give testimony favorable to your side of the case
   (D) you have all the pertinent information on the case.

Answer: (D) Disciplinary action is a very serious matter. You are instituting a procedure which may result in something being taken away from a person. The supervisor should precede disciplinary action with a thorough investigation and collection of pertinent facts. A missing fact can throw a different light on the situation.

3. The one of the following which would *not* be an acceptable practice for a supervisor to observe when criticizing a subordinate is to
   (A) focus attention on the act to be criticized instead of on the person
   (B) express the criticism in general rather than specific terms
   (C) refer to previous instances of poor performance
   (D) avoid humor or sarcasm when making the criticism.

Answer: (B) The purpose of criticism of work performance is to point out specifically where it may be improved. If the criticism were general and not specific, the worker would not know what corrective action to take.

4. You are informed by another supervisor that some of your workers who have been assigned to work by themselves are loafing on the job. You should handle this situation by
   (A) telling the supervisor not to interfere in a matter between you and your workers

(B) calling the workers together to your office and reprimanding them

(C) changing the workers' assignment so that they work under your direct supervision at all times

(D) arranging to visit the workers on the job at more frequent intervals.

Answer: **(D)** There is nothing in the question to suggest that the motives of the informant are anything but good. If you have reason to believe any workers are guilty of loafing, you have only one course of action, closer and more direct supervision.

5. If one of your crew comes to work obviously drunk, the best thing to do is to
   (A) give the person an easy job where there is no possibility of injury
   (B) let the person "sleep it off" in the morning and start to work when the effects have apparently worn off
   (C) send the person home
   (D) give the person a hard job so as to "sweat it out."

Answer: **(C)** The action that a supervisor should take when one of the crew members reports for work drunk is quite clear. Send the individual home because of the obvious inability to perform the job.

6. The best way for a supervisor to handle a chronic troublemaker is to
   (A) give the troublemaker closer supervision and, if this is not enough, take disciplinary action
   (B) let the troublemaker know that the supervisor is watching very closely so as to "get something" specific on him or her
   (C) rely on the others in the section to bring the troublemaker into line
   (D) assign the troublemaker to the most undesirable details.

Answer: **(A)** A chronic troublemaker is bad for any organization. If close supervision does not help, more positive disciplinary action should be taken.

7. A supervisor who finds that it is frequently necessary to take disciplinary action against workers should

(A) ask for a new assignment for the good of the organization and to avoid a further clash of personalities

(B) examine his or her supervisory practices to see whether they are at fault

(C) realize that the workers are a "tough bunch" to supervise, and not consider it unusual

(D) understand that this is sometimes necessary in order to keep a disciplined force.

Answer: **(B)** Faulty supervisory practices are among the most common causes for the necessity of frequent disciplinary action. The supervisor who finds disciplinary problems a frequent occurrence should examine the supervisory practices used to see if they are at fault. If they are not, the supervisor should look elsewhere for the answer to the problems.

8. Two of your employees frequently argue with each other so that the work of your crew is disrupted. You should *first*
   (A) attempt to find out why the employees argue with each other
   (B) speak to the two individuals privately regarding their possible transfer to another crew
   (C) submit a report to your superior setting forth the facts
   (D) tell both employees that unless they stop arguing, you will see that they are given below-standard service ratings.

Answer: **(A)** If the work of a crew is being disrupted by repeated arguments between two workers, it is the function of the supervisor first of all to discover the cause of the arguments and then to take immediate corrective measures.

9. Although you have frequently spoken to one of your workers regarding the proper way of lifting objects, he persists in ignoring your instructions. He says that he knows the proper way of lifting, that you do not, and that he does not intend to hurt himself by following your instructions. Of the following, the best course of action for you to take is to
   (A) assign the man to tasks which do not involve heavy lifting
   (B) ignore the matter as long as the man does not hurt himself

(C) put your instructions on how to lift in writing and give a copy of your instructions to each man in the crew

(D) report the matter to your superior.

Answer: **(D)** The subordinate in this question is taking an unreasonable attitude. The supervisor is the boss and his orders should be obeyed because he is responsible for the performance of the work and all of the ramifications that may result from it. Choice (A) depicts an escape from reality, as does choice (B). Choice (C) unnecessarily involves others who have been obeying the instructions of the supervisor. Choice (D) depicts the only logical course of action to be followed.

10. "It is only when an individual in the crew gets out of line that disciplinary action should be taken and then only to re-establish the proper working relationships of the whole crew." The use of disciplinary action as discussed in this sentence suggests that disciplinary action should have as its main goal

(A) forgiveness
(B) punishment
(C) correction
(D) sympathetic understanding.

Answer: **(C)** The primary basis of disciplinary action is to train workers to correct their job performance and deportment, not to punish those guilty of rule infractions.

11. One of the members of your crew sometimes overstays the lunch period, thus interfering with the work of the entire crew. Of the following, the most desirable action you should take *first* is to

(A) assign the worker to less desirable details whenever you get a chance
(B) warn the employee of the failure to observe time regulations
(C) report the lateness in returning from lunch for disciplinary action
(D) arrange for this person's lunch hour to be at a different time from that of the others.

Answer: **(B)** Your *first* action should be a warning. The employee is interfering with the output of the entire crew. If the warning does not work, more drastic and positive measures should be taken.

12. You have in your section a subordinate who is a good worker, but who very often complains about department policies. As a supervisor, you should

(A) arrange to transfer this employee to another section where a better adjustment could perhaps be made
(B) give this person department material explaining the reasons for such policies
(C) talk to this worker privately and try to change the attitude and to stop the complaints
(D) tell the other subordinates to ignore the complaints since the individual is such a good worker.

Answer: **(C)** A worker who constantly complains about departmental policies creates a bad situation. A private talk with this individual may help to change the outlook. The supervisor may be able to show convincingly that there are good reasons for departmental policies.

13. You have reason to believe that one of your employees is stealing merchandise from the storehouse. When you question the individual, you are told that the merchandise was borrowed and would be returned. Under these circumstances, you should probably

(A) disregard the matter until such time as you have evidence which will stand up in court
(B) offer to accompany the employee home to pick up the property in question
(C) report the matter to your superior
(D) ask that the property be returned as soon as the employee has finished using it.

Answer: **(C)** This person has removed merchandise from the premises without permission. This is a serious matter. If the intention was to borrow the merchandise, the employee should have asked for permission to do so. In view of the employee's admission, choices (A), (B), and (D) offer no acceptable course of action. Choice (C) would be the wisest to take on the basis of the evidence given.

14. Of the following, usually the *poorest* reason for transferring a worker is to

(A) grant a doctor's request that the employee work nearer his or her home

(B) discipline the worker
(C) relieve the monotony of work assignments
(D) take care of changes in workload.

Answer: **(B)** A transfer which takes place solely for disciplinary reasons is a poor practice indeed. Nothing is being done to solve the problem. What is actually being done is to transfer one supervisor's problem to another supervisor.

15. You have observed that a subordinate in your crew does good work only when under close supervision. Whenever not being carefully supervised, the subordinate tends to loaf on the job. The most important consequence of this observation for you as a supervisor should be to
(A) try to change the subordinate's attitude and warn of possible disciplinary action
(B) let the subordinate work alone without supervision and check in at unexpected intervals
(C) let the subordinate work with another employee and ask the latter periodically whether the subordinate does a good day's work
(D) order the subordinate to produce as much work as the others.

Answer: **(A)** A worker who performs well under close supervision only is not particularly valuable. The cost of supervising the employee closely may not be worthwhile. Therefore, it is up to the supervisor to change the worker's attitude in any way possible.

16. A member of your crew dislikes performing a particular task which is a part of the job. This employee hates to do such a task, saying that it is very unpleasant work. Your best reply as a supervisor would be
(A) "Can you suggest anyone else for the job?"
(B) "I am sorry but it is a part of the job and everyone must take a turn."
(C) "The job isn't so bad once you get used to it."
(D) "Why complain? The job only takes a couple of minutes!"

Answer: **(B)** Wherever possible, unpleasant tasks should be rotated among all of the workers. It makes these jobs less distasteful if everyone takes a turn doing them.

17. In hearings involving employees charged with violations of the department's code of discipline, one of the main breaches of discipline is failing to obey orders. The chief implication this should have for the supervisor is that he or she should
(A) issue orders in writing whenever this is practicable
(B) make assignments to teams of workers as often as possible so that the workers in a team can check each other
(C) make sure orders are understood and check on their implementation as soon as possible
(D) take disciplinary action promptly for failure to obey orders.

Answer: **(C)** Since failure to carry out the order is a breach of discipline, it would be wise for a supervisor to make sure that orders are thoroughly understood when they are issued, so if they are not carried out, it can be attributed to an unwillingness on the part of the subordinate and not to a misunderstanding.

18. Of the following, the *poorest* supervisory practice would be for a supervisor to
(A) assign responsibility for some routine tasks to an assistant
(B) praise a worker merely for the purpose of maintaining pleasant relations
(C) give more supervision to a new employee than to an older one
(D) personally instruct a new employee in his or her duties.

Answer: **(B)** Praise must be deserved to be of value; otherwise, it may become a harmful instrument. If praise is meted out without good reason, it will lose its meaning. Choices (A) and (D) contain examples of good supervisory practices.

19. When a supervisor issues orders to an employee and this employee regularly does not carry them out properly, who is to be blamed?
(A) An investigation should be made to find out if the supervisor or the employee is to be blamed
(B) Nobody is to be blamed; some workers just do poor work

(C) The supervisor cannot be blamed if it can be shown that the worker was given proper orders

(D) The supervisor must share some of the blame for such regularly poor performance.

Answer: **(D)** The supervisor is responsible to see that orders are carried out properly. If they are not, it is necessary to determine why they are not and to take appropriate corrective measures. Perhaps the employee needs disciplining or more training. Both of these are the responsibility of the supervisor.

20. One of your subordinates often slows down the work of the crew by playing practical jokes. The best way to handle this situation is to
    (A) assign this person to more unpleasant jobs
    (B) warn the subordinate that this practice must stop at once
    (C) ignore the situation because the subordinate will soon tire of it
    (D) ask your superior to transfer this individual to another crew.

Answer: **(B)** Practical jokers who interfere with production must be "sat on" at once. Immediate and perhaps very positive action should be taken without delay.

21. One of your workers comes to you and complains in an angry manner about having been chosen by you for some particular assignment. In your opinion, the subject of the complaint is trivial and unimportant, but it seems to be quite important to your worker. The best of the following actions for you to take in this situation is to
    (A) allow the worker to continue talking until calmed down and then explain the reasons why this individual was chosen for that particular assignment
    (B) warn the worker to "moderate your tone of voice at once because you are bordering on insubordination"
    (C) tell the worker in a friendly tone not to make a tremendous fuss over an extremely minor matter

(D) point out that you are the worker's immediate supervisor and that you are running the unit in accordance with official policy.

Answer: **(A)** An imagined grievance is real enough in the mind of the aggrieved. Many a grievance can be disposed of by merely permitting the aggrieved to talk and complain. After the employee has finished complaining, it would then be appropriate for the supervisor to point out the weaknesses of the complaint.

22. A supervisor hears a worker apparently giving the wrong information to a client and immediately issues a severe reprimand. For the supervisor to reprimand the worker at this point is poor chiefly because
    (A) instruction must precede correct performance
    (B) oral reprimands are less effective than written reprimands
    (C) the worker was given no opportunity to explain the reason for the action
    (D) more effective training can be obtained by discussing the errors with a group of workers.

Answer: **(C)** The supervisor acted much too hastily. It would have been better to permit the subordinate to offer an explanation. If a good explanation is forthcoming, the supervisor who has acted hastily in the reprimand will be embarrassed and the subordinate hurt.

23. You are the newly-appointed supervisor of a small unit in a company. One of your subordinates, Mr. Smith, a competent employee, has resented your appointment as his supervisor and has not been as cooperative toward you as you have wanted him to be. One day, Mr. Smith fails to observe an important rule of the company. You are required to reprimand any employee who fails to observe the rule. The one of the following courses of action you should take in this situation is to
    (A) attempt to overcome Mr. Smith's resentment by explaining to him that although you should reprimand him, you will not do so

(B) reprimand Mr. Smith after pointing out to him that he failed to observe the rule

(C) tell Mr. Smith that if he becomes more co-operative, you will overlook his failure to observe the rule

(D) tell Mr. Smith that although you did not originate the rule, nevertheless you are required to reprimand him.

Answer: (B) This is not the time to pacify Mr. Smith. He has failed to observe an important rule and he deserves an appropriate reprimand. You will never get his cooperation until you win his respect, and you are not likely to win his respect by pussy-footing.

24. One of your subordinates has violated an important rule of the agency. For such a violation, you are required to impose discipline in the form of a reprimand given in private. Of the following, the most important reason for disciplining the employee for violating the rule is to
(A) obtain compliance with the rule
(B) punish the employee for the violation in an impartial manner
(C) establish your authority to administer discipline
(D) impress upon all the employees in the unit the need for observing the rule.

Answer: (A) Discipline is essentially a training process. In this case, it is most useful as a means to impress upon employees the importance of observing rules.

25. Rumors have arisen to the effect that one of the workers under your supervision, who is supposed to be making field visits during afternoon hours, has instead been attending classes at a local university. The best of the following ways for you to approach this problem is to
(A) disregard the rumors since, like most rumors, they probably have no actual foundation in fact
(B) have a discreet investigation made in order to determine the actual facts prior to taking any other action
(C) inform the worker that you know what has been going on, and that such behavior is overt dereliction of duty and is punishable by dismissal

(D) review the work record and spot check the cases of the worker. Take no further action unless the quality of work is below average for the unit.

Answer: (B) The rumors may or may not be true. A discreet investigation should reveal the facts without injuring the party in question if innocent.

26. A supervisor, who was promoted to a position a year ago, has supervised a certain assistant supervisor for this one year. The work of the assistant supervisor has been very poor because this person has done a minimum of work, refused to take sufficient responsibility, been difficult to handle, and required very close supervision. Apparently due to the increasing insistence of the supervisor that the caliber of work be improved, the assistant supervisor resigns, stating that the demands of the job are too much. The opinion of the previous supervisor, who had supervised this assistant supervisor for two years, agrees substantially with that of the new supervisor. Under such circumstances, the best of the following actions the supervisor can take in general is to
(A) recommend that the resignation be accepted and that the individual be rehired should he or she later apply to do the job
(B) recommend that the resignation be accepted and that the individual not be rehired should he or she later apply
(C) refuse to accept the resignation but try to persuade the assistant supervisor to accept psychiatric help
(D) refuse to accept the resignation, promising the assistant supervisor that supervision will be lessened in the future since the assistant supervisor is now so experienced.

Answer: (B) This question is replete with information which indicates that the assistant supervisor is an unsatisfactory employee. There is not one word or reason listed to mitigate the unsatisfactory work. If this person resigns, the only course of action is to accept the resignation.

27. Two employees under your supervision who are required to work together are not able to get along with each other. You have attempted to

remedy this situation, but without any success. One is an older person who has been in the section for many years, and the other is recently appointed and younger. Both individuals are capable employees. Of the following, the most advisable course of action for you to take is to recommend that the
(A) older employee be transferred
(B) two individuals be given below-average service ratings
(C) younger person be discharged at the end of a probationary period
(D) younger person be transferred.

Answer: (D) Although an employee transfer is usually not looked upon as a solution to a problem, this instance is an exception. Both are capable employees, but they cannot get along, even though they must work together. Their capabilities preclude discharging the younger person or giving a below-standard rating for either. It would be more equitable to transfer the younger employee rather than the older one.

28. The key to effective discipline is in the hands of the supervisor at all levels. The most important link in the disciplinary chain is, however, the
(A) first-level supervisor, who works closely with the employees and must constantly evaluate their competency and integrity
(B) second-level supervisor, who must consider whether positive or negative discipline is appropriate in the case at hand
(C) administrator, who is responsible ultimately for the competency and integrity of every supervisor
(D) company head, since discipline does not emanate from the bottom of an organization—it is only from the top that good discipline flows.

Answer: (A) The first-level supervisor comes in closest contact with those on the job. Good supervisory practices will go a long way toward limiting disciplinary action in an organization.

29. A proposal has been made that a table of standard penalties be established for infractions of the rules whereby there would be a set penalty for each type of infraction and this penalty

would be applied automatically. To institute such a system would be
(A) undesirable; it would be almost impossible to work out a fair and equitable table of penalties
(B) desirable; it would assure that no worker would be subjected to a more drastic penalty than any other
(C) undesirable; it prevents the exercise of judgment in fitting the penalty to the individual and the background of the situation
(D) desirable; it creates an understanding among workers as to what they may expect, thereby causing them to be less likely to question the application of a proper penalty.

Answer: (C) This proposal must be evaluated as undesirable. It leaves no room at all for individual differences and extenuating circumstances which might have led to a rule infraction. Choice (C) is better than choice (A) because it gives a more valid reason for finding the procedure undesirable.

30. "All infractions should be met with equally fair, but firm, treatment, even if the infraction is of a minor nature." For a supervisor to follow this rule would, generally, be
(A) advisable; alertness on the part of the superior is normal and expected
(B) inadvisable; the severity of any disciplinary action should not exceed the seriousness of the offense
(C) advisable; overlooking minor infractions may lead to serious trouble
(D) inadvisable; the supervisor's time could be occupied more profitably by spending it on serious company affairs instead of on trivial matters.

Answer: (C) This statement of procedure should first be evaluated as an advisable one. When subordinates notice that they can get away with committing minor infractions they are likely to get away with committing more serious infractions. Choice (A) is an irrelevant answer.

31. A supervisor notices a subordinate doing the wrong thing and issues a reprimand in the fol-

lowing terms: "What is the matter with you? Can't you follow simple instructions? Your errors are just carelessness and have got to stop." For the supervisor to reprimand a subordinate in this manner is poor chiefly because

(A) instruction must precede correct performance

(B) oral reprimands are less effective than written reprimands

(C) the subordinate was given no opportunity to explain

(D) more effective training can be obtained by discussing the errors with a group of subordinates.

Answer: (C) This type of reprimand accomplishes little good because it is one-sided. The subordinate should at least be given the opportunity to offer an explanation for what was done.

32. When dealing with newly assigned subordinates, a supervisor has been following the practice of promptly bringing to their attention their first violation of the rules and regulations. This practice is generally

(A) advisable, chiefly because the subordinate must be taught as promptly as possible just who is in charge

(B) inadvisable, chiefly because the subordinate is relatively new at this point and should be treated with greater leniency

(C) advisable, chiefly because at this point mild disciplinary measures may be very effective

(D) inadvisable, chiefly because the subordinate may come to feel that the superior is setting too high a standard of expected performance.

Answer: (C) This course of action should definitely be evaluated as an advisable one. Overlooking minor infractions will tend to lead to major violations of rules and regulations. As for choice (A), this would be a rather extreme and childish way to show a newcomer who was in authority.

33. A supervisor who gives a subordinate a tongue lashing or bawling out uses a dubious technique of leadership even if done in private. Of the following, the main objection to this practice is that generally the

(A) subordinate does not have an adequate opportunity to reply in defense

(B) point at issue tends to be obscured and the matter becomes a personal clash between individuals

(C) past records of the subordinate and all the surrounding circumstances of the incident are not adequately considered

(D) incident becomes widely known and undermines the authority of the supervisor.

Answer: (B) A tongue lashing usually results in ill will between the supervisor and the subordinate who is receiving it. It seldom does any good and should be saved for rare occasions when no other course of action is found acceptable. It is difficult for an adult to accept a bawling out from another adult.

SUPERVISORY RESPONSIBILITIES

Every supervisor has many varied responsibilities. However, they are all directed at getting the work out in the most efficient manner possible. The following questions, culled from previous tests for supervisory positions, indicate the scope of the supervisor's responsibilities. An answer key is provided at the end of the test.

1. In addition to general supervisory ability, one of the desirable qualifications of a supervising officer is the ability to
   (A) be publicized effectively as an outstanding leader
   (B) deal with staff in such a manner that disagreements will be eliminated
   (C) refrain from taking any action which would incite criticism
   (D) inspire others and to remain openminded in discriminating between relative values.

2. An important responsibility that you have as a supervisor is to make certain that all required work is completed on time. Of the following, the procedure which is most likely to lead to accomplishing this aim is for you to
   (A) require every subordinate to submit a daily work report
   (B) schedule the work and keep track of its progress
   (C) impress your subordinates with the importance of getting work done on time
   (D) hold each employee responsible for the work assigned.

3. Listed below are several supervisory duties and a method of accomplishing each duty. While the duties are all correct, only one method of performing the duty is correct. It is
   (A) to see that discipline is maintained by adhering to a set of rules without deviation of any kind in any case

   (B) to see that there is unity of command by making every employee directly responsible and answerable to the chief
   (C) to see that there is competent and vigorous management of the department by means of clear lines of authority and distinct statements of duties
   (D) to see that everything is subject to proper control by having all decisions, both general and detailed, come from the supervisor.

4. Under the best administrative conditions, "authority" becomes a problem of
   (A) responsibility and leadership
   (B) the scientific issuance of orders
   (C) the determination of the relative worth of existing rules and regulations
   (D) constructive criticism.

5. Of the following, the *least* desirable procedure for a supervisor to follow is to
   (A) be flexible in planning and carrying out assignments
   (B) insist that agency reports conform strictly to the regulations
   (C) avoid schedules or routines when busy
   (D) organize his or her own work before taking responsibility for helping others in theirs.

6. "Subordinates must obey orders without delay or question, but at the same time the supervisor

takes on a definite responsibility." Of the following, the most acceptable statement concerning such responsibility is that the supervisor should

(A) issue orders in a positive and decisive manner
(B) explain to subordinates the reason for each command issued
(C) issue only those orders which can be justified
(D) avoid issuing orders except as a last resort.

7. A sound organization structure may be said to exist when
(A) there is a division in lines of authority
(B) executive authority and responsibility are co-equal
(C) lines of authority are left undefined to encourage initiative
(D) many subordinates are reporting directly to the supervisor.

8. When one exceeds the "span of control" in a department, it is almost inevitable to have
(A) over-disciplined work
(B) delineation of responsibility
(C) over-specialization
(D) undisciplined work.

9. The major function of a supervisor with regard to the departmental policies is to
(A) review them critically to uncover obsolete or unworkable items
(B) transmit all statements of policy to subordinates without comment
(C) interpret policy to subordinates
(D) make the decision as to policy whenever subordinates point out conflicting provisions.

10. In supervising a new employee, the one of the following which is not generally accepted as a good basic principle is to
(A) allow the employee to take some responsibility at once
(B) prevent any temporary dependence on the supervisor

(C) allow the employee to make mistakes, without any advance instructions and to learn by experience
(D) hold the employee to the perfect execution of every rule of the department until all policies are learned.

11. Although it is not necessary to list and define every supervisory responsibility, it is essential for an individual placed in a supervisory position first to
(A) clarify lines of authority both to oneself and to subordinates
(B) learn to adjust to the particular managerial group
(C) assume responsibility for the errors of subordinates
(D) delegate work to others to conserve time for handling complicated cases.

12. The most basic of the following duties of a supervisor is that of
(A) seeing that the departmental rules are enforced
(B) properly delegating authority to qualified individuals
(C) seeing that each employee adequately performs the work assigned
(D) getting along well with the employees.

13. On being promoted to a supervisory position, an individual should recognize that the position is primarily one of
(A) security
(B) power
(C) responsibility
(D) authority.

14. The supervisor has a reputation for being "conscientious." The best example of this statement is that the supervisor is one who
(A) feels obligated to do what he or she believes is right
(B) frequently makes suggestions for improvement in procedure
(C) has good personal relationships with superiors and subordinates
(D) is accustomed to hard work.

15. If a supervisor is indefinite in assigning subordinates responsibilities for various phases of work, this action is most likely to result in
    (A) valuable training through use of their own initiative
    (B) the assuming of authority by those who are most willing to do so
    (C) friction, misunderstanding, and ineffective work
    (D) the work being done by those most capable of doing it.

16. The principal cause of a good supervisor's failure to be successful as a manager is most likely due to
    (A) unwillingness to assume administrative and supervisory responsibilities of the new position
    (B) a sense of inferiority or frustration
    (C) reluctance to give up routine responsibilities with which the supervisor is familiar
    (D) a lack of appreciation of the new responsibilities involved.

17. "A supervisor should be a leader whose subordinates will follow with enthusiasm." A competent supervisor should realize that this type of leadership is most effectively based upon
    (A) close observance of precisely formulated rules and regulations
    (B) diligent study by both employees and administrators
    (C) respect and confidence of the employees
    (D) strict and invariable discipline.

18. "Every supervisor who has had occasion to teach subordinates how to operate a new piece of equipment has seen trial-and-error learning, in which the worker fumbles about until he strikes upon the proper procedure by accident." Of the following, the most accurate statement concerning trial-and-error learning in training is that
    (A) trial-and-error learning should be reduced by the supervisor through proper guidance
    (B) the supervisor will find it most effective to allow trial-and-error learning to precede specific training

    (C) trial-and-error learning is more permanent than any other type of learning
    (D) trial-and-error learning is more efficient per unit time than any other type of learning.

19. If a supervisor uses authority to obtain acceptance of ideas, the cause most probably is that
    (A) subordinates have little respect for their supervisor if he or she fails to use authority
    (B) discipline depends upon subordinates' recognition of the supervisor's absolute authority
    (C) the introduction of new ideas is solely the responsibility of the subordinate
    (D) the ideas do not warrant consideration on their own merit.

20. The recommendation has been made that interviews with dissatisfied employees be discontinued and that grievances be accepted in writing only. This recommendation is
    (A) desirable primarily because personal interviews tend to be emotionally upsetting to employees and frequently to administrators as well
    (B) undesirable primarily because there is no point in encouraging needless correspondence when a short interview may settle the matter
    (C) undesirable primarily because it will tend to dehumanize a procedure in which human values may be receiving insufficient consideration
    (D) desirable primarily because the amount of time that administrators spend on grievances will be decreased.

21. Impartiality is considered to be one of the most important qualifications of a supervisor. This is so mainly because
    (A) the supervisor should rotate responsibility among the members of the staff
    (B) a supervisor should be able to train subordinates to be impartial
    (C) impartiality and intellectual honesty are closely related
    (D) staff cooperation tends to deteriorate when a supervisor shows favoritism.

22. "A common difference among supervisors is that some are not content unless they are out in front in everything that concerns their unit, while others prefer to run things by pulling strings, by putting others out in front and by stepping into the breach only when necessary." Generally speaking, an advantage this latter method of operation has over the former is that it
    (A) results in a higher level of morale over a sustained period of time
    (B) gets results by exhortation and direct stimulus
    (C) makes it unnecessary to calculate integrated moves
    (D) makes the personality of the supervisor felt down the line.

23. The head of a unit is responsible for the quality and accuracy of the work performed by the staff. In handling errors made by members of the staff, the unit head should be concerned chiefly with
    (A) determining how best to reprimand the persons responsible for the errors
    (B) finding out who is ultimately responsible for the errors
    (C) recording each error made by a staff member in that staff member's personal record
    (D) preventing such errors from being made again.

24. The supervisor of a large central typing bureau is responsible for the accuracy of the work performed by subordinates. Of the following procedures which might be adopted to insure the accurate copying of long reports from rough draft originals, the most effective one is to
    (A) examine the rough draft for errors in grammar, punctuation, and spelling before assigning it to a typist to copy
    (B) glance through each typed report before it leaves her bureau to detect any obvious errors made by the typist
    (C) have another employee read the rough draft original to the typist who typed the report, and have the typist make whatever corrections are necessary
    (D) rotate assignments involving the typing of long reports equally among all the typists in the unit.

25. "The successful supervisor wins victories through preventive rather than through curative action." Of the following, the most accurate statement on the basis of this quotation is that
    (A) success in supervision may be measured more accurately in terms of errors corrected than in terms of errors prevented
    (B) anticipating problems makes for better supervision than waiting until these problems arise
    (C) difficulties that cannot be prevented by the supervisor cannot be overcome
    (D) the solution of problems in supervision is best achieved by scientific methods.

Questions 26 to 29 are to be answered solely on the basis of the information contained in the following paragraph:

"Good personnel relations in an organization depend upon mutual confidence, trust, and good will. The basis of confidence is understanding. Most troubles start with people who do not understand each other. When the organization's intentions or motives are misunderstood, or when reasons for actions, practices, or policies are misconstrued, complete cooperation from individuals is not forthcoming. If management expects full cooperation from employees, it has a responsibility of sharing with them the information which is the foundation of proper understanding, confidence, and trust. Personnel management has long since outgrown the days when it was the vogue to 'treat them rough and tell them nothing.' Up-to-date personnel management provides all possible information about the activities, aims, and purposes of the organization. It seems altogether creditable that a desire should exist among employees for such information which the best-intentioned executive might think would not interest them and which the worst-intentioned would think was none of their business."

26. The paragraph implies that one of the causes of the difficulty which an organization might have with its personnel relations is that its employees
    (A) have not expressed interest in the activities, aims, and purposes of the organization
    (B) do not believe in the good faith of the organization

(C) have been able to give full cooperation to the organization

(D) do not recommend improvements in the practices and policies of the organization.

27. According to the paragraph, in order for an organization to have good personnel relations, it is *not* essential that
    (A) employees have confidence in the organization
    (B) the purposes of the organization be understood by the employees
    (C) employees have a desire for information about the organization
    (D) information about the organization be communicated to employees.

28. According to the paragraph, an organization which provides full information about itself to its employees
    (A) understands the intentions of its employees
    (B) satisfies a praiseworthy desire among its employees
    (C) is managed by executives who have the best intentions toward its employees
    (D) is confident that its employees understand its motives.

29. Of the following, the most suitable title for the paragraph is
    (A) The Foundations of Personnel Relations
    (B) The Consequences of Employee Misunderstanding
    (C) The Development of Personnel Management Practices
    (D) The Acceptance of Organizational Objectives.

30. "A line supervisor can play an important role in helping subordinates to make healthy mental, emotional, and social adjustments." The one of the following which would *not* be considered to be a part of the supervisor's role in helping subordinates to make these adjustments is to
    (A) ascertain which subordinates are likely to develop maladjustments

(B) recognize indications of these types of maladjustments

(C) refer subordinates displaying signs of maladjustments to specialists for assistance

(D) create a work environment that will tend to minimize subordinates' preoccupations with personal problems.

31. You are a supervisor in charge of a unit of clerical employees. One of your subordinates, Mr. Smith, has not seemed to be his usual self in the past several weeks, but, rather, has seemed to be disturbed. In addition, he has not been producing his usual quantity of work and has been provoking arguments with his colleagues. He approaches you and asks if he may discuss with you a problem which he believes has been affecting his work. As Mr. Smith begins to discuss the problem, you immediately realize that, although it may be disturbing to him, it is really a trivial matter. Of the following, the *first* step that you should take in this situation is to
    (A) permit Mr. Smith to continue to describe his problem, interrupting him only when clarification of a point is needed
    (B) tell Mr. Smith that his becoming unduly upset about the problem will not help to solve it
    (C) point out that you and your subordinates have faced more serious problems and that this one is a relatively minor matter
    (D) suggest that the problem should be solved before it develops into a serious matter.

32. Assume that a supervisor praises subordinates for satisfactory aspects of their work only when about to criticize them for unsatisfactory aspects of their work. Such a practice is undesirable primarily because
    (A) the subordinates may expect to be praised for their work even if it is unsatisfactory
    (B) praising subordinates for some aspects of their work while criticizing other aspects will weaken the effects of the criticisms
    (C) subordinates would be more receptive to criticism if it were followed by praise
    (D) subordinates may come to disregard praise and wait for criticism to be given.

33. Since a recent promotion, an employee has become very irritable and frequently loses his temper. Of the following, the most advisable action for the employee's supervisor to take *first* is to
    (A) have the employee take a supervisor training course
    (B) suggest that the employee get counseling or similar help
    (C) try to determine the reason for the employee's irritability
    (D) warn the employee that he may be demoted to his former position.

34. "Interest is essentially an attitude of continuing attentiveness, found where activity is satisfactorily self-expressive. Whenever work is so circumscribed that the chance for self-expression or development is denied, monotony is present." On the basis of this quotation, it is most accurate to state that
    (A) tasks which are repetitive in nature do not permit self-expression and therefore create monotony
    (B) interest in one's work is increased by financial and non-financial incentives
    (C) jobs which are monotonous can be made self-expressive by substituting satisfactory working conditions
    (D) workers whose tasks afford them no opportunity for self-expression find such tasks to be monotonous.

35. "The improvement in skill and the development of proper attitudes are essential factors in the building of correct work habits." Of the following, the most valid implication of this quotation for a supervisor is that
    (A) the more skillful an employee is, the better the attitude toward the job
    (B) developing proper attitudes in subordinates toward their work is more time-consuming for the supervisor than improving their skill
    (C) the improvement of a worker's skill is only part of a supervisor's job
    (D) correct work habits are established in order to either improve the skill of workers or develop in them a proper attitude toward their work.

36. Of the following, the greatest work incentive that a supervisor should recognize is that
    (A) everyone has a desire for approval or recognition
    (B) fear may drive persons to do better work
    (C) rivalry is a spur to effort
    (D) constant watching will produce better work.

37. If an intelligent employee assigned to a routine job is inclined to be restless, a supervisor could most probably correct this situation by
    (A) transferring or recommending the transfer of the employee to a more responsible job, if possible
    (B) praising the employee's work before the other workers
    (C) explaining to the employee that not everyone in the job can be freed from routine duties
    (D) offering constructive criticism and urging the employee to take more interest in the job.

38. In order to maintain the best morale in the staff, a supervisor preferably should
    (A) tell the inefficient worker to "get busy"
    (B) praise the good worker in the presence of the staff
    (C) maintain fairness and impartiality consistently
    (D) give sarcastic criticism to the slow worker whenever the occasion demands.

39. If an employee is emotionally upset when coming to a supervisor with a problem, the supervisor should, in most instances
    (A) inquire into the employee's personal problems for the cause of the emotional disturbance
    (B) postpone the conference until the employee has regained his self-control
    (C) give an immediate decision satisfactory to the employee
    (D) help the employee to become calmer before discussing a solution.

40. Of the following responsibilities of a supervisor, the most important is
    (A) becoming acquainted with the personal problems of each subordinate

(B) assigning and evaluating work

(C) keeping a daily record of work completed by each subordinate

(D) smoothing out personal frictions and jealousies among the subordinates.

41. The chief task of a supervisor of a trained clerical staff with the normal work load to perform is to

(A) give continual direction to each employee

(B) keep up potential or intensity of group effort

(C) revise rules and regulations in order to impress the staff with the autocratic rights of the supervisor

(D) criticize the work of each employee regularly in order to show superior knowledge.

42. The immediate task of a supervisor of a clerical staff, augmented by an increase in temporary employees to put out an increased volume of work in accordance with a well-established routine, is to

(A) assign and train the new subordinates

(B) develop written instructions covering every detail of the procedure and outlining the responsibility

(C) develop and maintain high morale

(D) keep exact records of the work production (quantity and quality) of each employee.

43. If a subordinate makes a work suggestion that would give better service but would result in gain by some persons and in loss by others, the supervisor should

(A) agree to put over the employee's wishes at once

(B) discuss the suggestion fully with the employee and state that it will receive due consideration

(C) praise the employee for the suggestion, saying that you will discuss it at a later date

(D) tell the employee that the suggestion will be filed for reference.

44. Often a staff wastes time doing a particular routine or in traveling about while working. The first possibility a supervisor should investigate

as the cause of this situation is

(A) lack of interest in the work

(B) poor working conditions

(C) improper work habits caused by inadequate supervision

(D) poor planning and organization caused by a lack of supervision.

45. Of the following ways in which a supervisor may expect to obtain conformance among the employees to the rules and regulations of office conduct in an organization, ordinarily the most effective would be to

(A) post the rules and regulations in a conspicuous place

(B) discuss instances of nonconformity in staff meetings

(C) delegate to the employees the responsibility for seeing that rules and regulations are observed

(D) personally observe the rules and regulations.

46. A supervisor can best develop an employee's understanding of a job and skill in performing it by

(A) insisting on high standards

(B) thorough, patient teaching

(C) encouraging trial and error on the part of the learner

(D) constantly "driving" the learner.

47. If it becomes necessary for a supervisor to hold a corrective interview with a worker, good practice dictates that the reprimand should be given

(A) in private, in an authoritative manner

(B) informally, in the presence of other workers

(C) by publicly centering attention on the person rather than on the work

(D) in private, in a firm, decisive manner.

48. In teaching a procedure to any member of the staff, which method is the most desirable for a supervisor to follow? To teach the procedure by

(A) giving the worker the written procedure and having him or her learn by doing the work

(B) "absorption," through the constant observation of another worker until the procedure is mastered

(C) telling the worker "how" to do the task, and then criticizing every time an error is made

(D) assigning the worker to work with an experienced employee until the techniques used by the experienced employee are learned.

49. When arguments arise between employees over the advantage of seating arrangements to give the best light, of the following, the best procedure for a supervisor to follow to deal with the situation efficiently and fairly is to

(A) issue a memorandum explaining the correct way such matters should be handled

(B) reprimand the offenders before the entire staff and explain to all the way such matters should be handled

(C) arbitrarily change the seating arrangement

(D) arrange the seating so that the light is good for the greatest number according to the type of work requiring the best lighting.

50. In attempting to improve the work habits of the staff, the chief concern of a supervisor should be to

(A) assume that correct work habits will develop from employees observing the good habits of others in the group

(B) make scientific time studies of the workmanship of all employees before attempting to correct any work habits

(C) permit each employee to use individuality in performing the assigned tasks so as not to stifle initiative

(D) teach and re-teach the employees to use properly and consistently the methods and tools at hand.

51. If you were to design a form for office use, of the following, which consideration should come first?

(A) the limit to the number of items to be included

(B) the purpose the form is to fulfill

(C) the expense involved

(D) the necessity for the form.

52. What principle of proper supervisory relationship to subordinates is suggested to the supervisor by the old saying:

"Twice I did well, and I heard never
Once I did ill, and that I heard ever!"

(A) to make a continuous fuss over a fault or error

(B) to give credit when due

(C) to make an example of the inefficient worker

(D) to use the inefficient as instruments to spur the efficient to greater effort.

53. When an unusual emergency arises and you, as the supervisor, are unable to get an interview with your superior about the handling of the situation, the best procedure for you to follow is to

(A) handle the case according to your own judgment without bringing the case to the attention of your superior

(B) break into your superior's office with your problem

(C) take a particular action and prepare a memorandum to your superior on the case, stating what action has been taken and that you have tried unsuccessfully to get an interview

(D) delay action until your superior can give the matter attention.

54. If, as a supervisor, you find yourself in a position where your authority is not clear and well-defined, the best procedure for you to follow is to

(A) take hold hard and supervise the work and workers strictly

(B) take it easy, regardless of output, in order to be on good terms with the other employees

(C) make an outline of your responsibilities and submit it to your superior for approval

(D) "keep an eye on the work" until indefiniteness in assigning and announcing your responsibilities is cleared up by your superior.

55. Competent supervisors are "leaders, not order- ing but serving their subordinates." The most important proof that a supervisor is carrying out leadership functions in dealing with subor- dinates is that he or she
(A) maintains complete production records of all subordinates
(B) reminds subordinates of the supervisor's authoritative powers
(C) considers every employee an important in- dividual and helps employees to develop in the job
(D) compares the successes and failures of the subordinate with other fellow workers.

Answer Key

1. D	12. C	23. D	34. D	45. D
2. B	13. C	24. C	35. C	46. B
3. C	14. A	25. B	36. A	47. D
4. A	15. C	26. B	37. A	48. A
5. C	16. A	27. C	38. C	49. D
6. C	17. C	28. B	39. D	50. D
7. B	18. A	29. A	40. B	51. B
8. D	19. D	30. A	41. B	52. B
9. C	20. D	31. A	42. A	53. C
10. A	21. D	32. D	43. B	54. C
11. A	22. A	33. C	44. D	55. C

SUPERVISORY PROBLEMS

Supervisors encounter problems constantly. Deciding how and when to deal with each situation is an essential aspect of the supervisor's job. The questions that follow present some of the problems you are likely to face as a supervisor. The correct solutions are provided at the end of the test.

1. Suppose that an employee newly assigned under your supervision appears to lack confidence in the performance of duties. Of the following, the best action for you to take is to
   (A) warn employee that he or she is being observed constantly and that the poor quality of his or her work is being given special consideration
   (B) give employee an assignment which you believe he or she will be able to perform well
   (C) assign employee to exceptionally difficult tasks which you believe will constitute a definite challenge
   (D) assign employee to tasks on which he or she will be required to work alone.

2. Assume that you are a supervisor and that an employee with a long and excellent record in your company has recently begun to exhibit laziness and lack of interest in the work. Of the following, the best course of action for you as the superior to follow is to
   (A) call the attention of the other employees specifically to this case to demonstrate that good work requires constant, diligent application
   (B) start disciplinary action immediately against this employee as you would against any other employee
   (C) overlook the matter until the employee again demonstrates the usual high quality of work
   (D) interview the employee and attempt to determine the reason for this unusual behavior.

3. If a supervisor has an employee who is willing and tries hard but has consistently proved to be incompetent, the best of the following things to do is to
   (A) pay no attention to the case
   (B) report the case to superiors
   (C) encourage the employee by assigning light duties
   (D) continue to give the employee regular work, with reprimands if the work is not up to standard.

4. An employee of long and otherwise good standing exhibits laziness for a period of time. The best course for the supervisor to follow is to
   (A) ignore the matter until the employee can straighten it out
   (B) reprimand the employee before fellow workers
   (C) reprimand the employee in a private interview and threaten disciplinary action
   (D) interview the employee and attempt to straighten the matter out in an amicable manner.

5. Suppose you have just been promoted to supervisor. The best way to attain your aims and gain the good-will of those working under you would be by
   (A) trying to instill in each employee an idea of true efficiency
   (B) confidentially asking each employee's advice as to necessary changes
   (C) continuing the policies of your predecessor, gradually introducing needed changes

(D) immediately revamping the entire department along the proper lines.

6. Suppose that a newly appointed supervisor is finding it difficult to organize work. Of the following, the most appropriate suggestion that could be made in this situation is that the supervisor should
(A) review the workload in order to simplify and condense it
(B) immediately allocate some of the supervisory tasks to employees
(C) break the total job into its component parts and plan the time needed for each part
(D) make a list of all the tasks that have to be attended to and check them off as they are completed.

7. Suppose that you have the task of formulating a plan for the purpose of making the operation of a particular activity more efficient. In general, you should pay *least* regard to the
(A) length of time consumed in the activity
(B) degree of prestige accrued to you resulting from the activity
(C) value of the end product of the activity
(D) number of persons involved in the activity.

8. If a situation arises in line of duty which to you is not clearly covered by rules and regulations, you should
(A) use your best judgment in the matter
(B) refer the matter to a superior officer
(C) do as the majority of the staff thinks best
(D) consult with your supervisor.

9. For five years a supervisor has been successful in performing the job. A new employee in the company makes a suggestion concerning a change in procedure. The supervisor should
(A) tell the employee that, in view of the present smooth operations, no changes are necessary
(B) tell the employee that the change suggested is contrary to policy
(C) give careful consideration to the proposed change
(D) make the change, but hold the employee responsible if it works out badly.

10. As a result of an examination, you receive an appointment as a supervisor and are transferred to another office. The first thing that you should do is to
(A) realize that skill in dealing with people will come with experience
(B) analyze your new position
(C) read recognized texts on supervision
(D) carefully observe the techniques of experienced supervisory personnel.

11. It comes to the bureau chief's attention that a particular employee has gone to his supervisor to discuss a seemingly trivial personal matter. Later, the supervisor, thinking the situation humorous, told others in the department about it. In this situation, the bureau chief should
(A) do nothing, since most of the staff enjoyed the joke
(B) do nothing, since this is the supervisor's business and he is in charge of the group
(C) do nothing, because the employee should use discretion about the type of thing with which he bothers the supervisor
(D) call this situation to the supervisor's attention as violation of supervision in breaking any confidence, no matter how small, which was placed in the supervisor by a subordinate.

12. Occasional outbursts of temper
(A) should be excused in a supervisor
(B) are inexcusable in a supervisor
(C) are to be expected from all employees
(D) are an effective supervisory technique.

13. If you are asked a technical question by one of your employees and do not know the answer, you should
(A) attempt to answer it the best you can
(B) tell the employee that you do not know the answer but that you will get the information
(C) tell the employee that you are too busy to explain at the moment
(D) suggest that the employee not bother you with things which can be found out directly.

14. One of the factors making it difficult for supervisors to introduce new methods which will alter procedures that have been in existence for some time is
    (A) the tendency of people to dislike something old because it is old
    (B) the feeling of distrust which people have for the ideas of "experts"
    (C) the nearly universal tendency of all people to dislike change
    (D) the tendency of people to change rapidly in their likes and dislikes.

15. When presenting a completely new idea to a group of employees, the most important principle of learning to be observed is
    (A) to relate the new idea to some familiar idea or activity previously learned
    (B) to point out how difficult the new idea is to learn
    (C) to give the employee printed material to read on the new idea
    (D) to break down the new principle into constituent parts before presenting the whole.

16. A new division head, after studying an inspection procedure which has been in use for a long time, decided that it was unsatisfactory. Thereupon, a recommendation was made to the supervisor of the department that the procedure be discontinued and that a new inspection procedure be instituted which made no use of present personnel and ignored the existing procedure. This recommendation is, in general
    (A) satisfactory; procedures which have been used for a long time tend to lose their value
    (B) unsatisfactory; procedures which have been used for a long time have obviously stood the test of time
    (C) satisfactory; when new procedures are instituted it is best to leave no stone unturned
    (D) unsatisfactory; plans should make as much use as possible of existing procedures and personnel before requesting new resources.

17. A very busy supervisor is requested by subordinates to take care of some detail which seems quite unimportant in comparison with other things demanding attention. The supervisor should
    (A) explain the busy schedule of the moment and ask subordinates to bring the matter up at a later date at which time the supervisor will be glad to look into it
    (B) make note of the request in a conspicuous place, explaining that other things must be done first, but that this matter will be taken care of by a certain time, and see that it is done by that time, regardless of how many important things are waiting
    (C) make the subordinates happy by telling them that the matter will be taken care of at once, even though the supervisor knows it will not be attended to for some time
    (D) tell the subordinates in a nice way that the supervisor is too busy to bother with such matters.

18. A supervisor made a practice of distributing agenda to all participants before a staff meeting was to be held. In general, this practice is
    (A) good; participants can give thought to the problems prior to discussion
    (B) bad; participants are less spontaneous and candid in their discussions
    (C) good; protracted discussion of one topic and neglect of others is prevented
    (D) bad; the problem of keeping the discussions confidential is made more difficult.

19. Assume that you have been appointed a supervisor. Of the following, the best justification for learning from the bureau chief as much as possible about those whom you are to supervise is that
    (A) personality problems usually disappear with knowledge of individual differences
    (B) knowledge of individual employee characteristics often aids in the effective handling of those employees
    (C) no supervisor can be effective on the job without a cooperative relationship with his or her superior
    (D) treating subordinates impartially leads to more effective leadership.

20. If an employee's performance is poor, the supervisor should first

(A) tell the entire department about it

(B) record all errors, and recommend dismissal

(C) call attention privately to errors and offer suggestions for improvement

(D) give the employee only menial tasks involving no responsibility.

21. In order to make it easier for a new employee to remember how a specific piece of work is to be done, the supervisor should

(A) watch the newcomer until there is no possibility of an error

(B) ask the new employee if there are any questions concerning the work

(C) explain the reasons for doing the work in the manner specified

(D) refer the employee to selected books on the general subject of the work being done.

22. To settle a dispute or conflict between two employees, which one of the following actions should you take?

(A) have both present their points of view and arguments in a written memorandum and on this basis make your decision

(B) require that the two individuals settle the case between themselves

(C) call each separately, and after hearing their cases presented, decide the issue

(D) bring both in for a conference at the same time and make the decision in their presence.

23. If a supervisor learns that some member of the staff has been given orders by supervisors of other branches of the department, the best of the following procedures to take would be to

(A) preserve department morale by disregarding the occurrence

(B) discuss the matter with his or her superior

(C) tell the member of the staff to disregard the orders

(D) tell the supervisors who issued the orders to confine their authority to those under their jurisdiction.

24. When a new employee under your supervision makes an error on the job, it is best to correct the employee

(A) a few days later

(B) immediately

(C) after the same error has been made several times

(D) at the next general meeting of your subordinates, without mentioning names.

25. In order to be sure that the day-to-day job is adequately accomplished by subordinates, a supervisor should

(A) make a planned effort to develop the capabilities of each individual so that each can take on the full responsibility inherent to the position

(B) perform that work for an employee which the employee has not yet learned to do, if it is apparent that the individual will be able to learn quickly

(C) make a personal day-to-day review of all the work done by the staff in order that an adequate evaluation may be made of each subordinate

(D) issue detailed written instructions to each person in preference to arranging scheduled conferences, since written instructions are more definite.

26. You are in charge of an office in which each member of the staff has a different set of duties, although each has the same title. No member of the staff can perform the duties of any other member of the staff without first receiving extensive training. Assume that it is necessary for one member of the staff to take on, in addition to the regular work, an assignment which any member of the staff is capable of carrying out. The one of the following considerations which would have the most weight in determining which staff member is to be given the additional assignment is the

(A) quality of the work performed by the individual members of the staff

(B) time consumed by individual members of the staff in performing their work

(C) level of difficulty of the duties being performed by individual members of the staff

(D) relative importance of the duties being performed by individual members of the staff.

27. Assume that you are the supervisor of a large number of clerks in a unit in a city agency. Your unit has just been given an important assignment which must be completed a week from now. You know that, henceforth, your unit will be given this assignment every six months. You or any one of your subordinates who has been properly instructed can complete this assignment in one day. This assignment is of a routine type which is ordinarily handled by clerks. There is enough time for you to train one of your subordinates to handle the assignment and then have the subordinate do it. However, it would take twice as much time for you to take this course of action as it would for you to do the assignment yourself. The one of the following courses of action which you should take in this situation is to

(A) do the assignment yourself as soon as possible without discussing it with any of your subordinates at this time
(B) do the assignment yourself and then train one of your subordinates to handle it in the future
(C) give the assignment to one of your subordinates after training the individual to handle it
(D) train each of your subordinates to do the assignment on a rotating basis after you have done it yourself the first time.

28. In making job assignments to subordinates, a supervisor should follow the principle that each individual is generally capable of

(A) performing one type of work well and less capable of performing other types well
(B) learning to perform a wide variety of different types of work
(C) performing best the type of work in which the individual has had experience
(D) learning to perform any type of work in which training has been given.

29. Investigation of the high employee turnover in an office reveals that a principal cause of this turnover is the arrogant attitude of the supervisor. The supervisor is otherwise very competent and his office always does a superior job. Of the following, the most advisable course of action for the department to take is to

(A) assign somebody to assist the supervisor
(B) have the supervisor brought up on charges
(C) transfer the supervisor to another office
(D) try to change the supervisor's attitude.

30. One section has not been able to keep up with the rest of the agency in getting its work out. It is discovered that an employee in that section does very little work. The other employees resent this since it means they have an increased workload. The section head sits in a private office and is not aware of what is going on. Of the following, the most advisable action for the agency to take is to

(A) arrange for the employees to get more supervision
(B) discharge the employee who is at fault
(C) reorganize the entire agency
(D) transfer the supervisor.

31. A department employee makes an error in totaling the figures in a budget request. Of the following, the most advisable course of action for the supervisor to take is to

(A) bring the attention of the entire office to the employee's mistake and emphasize the need for accuracy
(B) stress the need for accuracy and ask the employee to total the figures again
(C) relieve the employee of any duties involving computational skills
(D) reprimand the employee and issue a warning that more drastic action will be taken if a similar error is made.

Answer Key

1. B	12. B	22. D
2. D	13. B	23. B
3. B	14. C	24. B
4. D	15. A	25. A
5. C	16. D	26. B
6. C	17. A	27. C
7. B	18. A	28. B
8. A	19. B	29. D
9. C	20. C	30. A
10. B	21. C	31. B
11. D		

PART TWO

Sample Examinations
for Practice

ANSWER SHEET FOR SAMPLE PRACTICE EXAMINATION I

1 Ⓐ Ⓑ Ⓒ Ⓓ	24 Ⓐ Ⓑ Ⓒ Ⓓ	47 Ⓐ Ⓑ Ⓒ Ⓓ	70 Ⓐ Ⓑ Ⓒ Ⓓ
2 Ⓐ Ⓑ Ⓒ Ⓓ	25 Ⓐ Ⓑ Ⓒ Ⓓ	48 Ⓐ Ⓑ Ⓒ Ⓓ	71 Ⓐ Ⓑ Ⓒ Ⓓ
3 Ⓐ Ⓑ Ⓒ Ⓓ	26 Ⓐ Ⓑ Ⓒ Ⓓ	49 Ⓐ Ⓑ Ⓒ Ⓓ	72 Ⓐ Ⓑ Ⓒ Ⓓ
4 Ⓐ Ⓑ Ⓒ Ⓓ	27 Ⓐ Ⓑ Ⓒ Ⓓ	50 Ⓐ Ⓑ Ⓒ Ⓓ	73 Ⓐ Ⓑ Ⓒ Ⓓ
5 Ⓐ Ⓑ Ⓒ Ⓓ	28 Ⓐ Ⓑ Ⓒ Ⓓ	51 Ⓐ Ⓑ Ⓒ Ⓓ	74 Ⓐ Ⓑ Ⓒ Ⓓ
6 Ⓐ Ⓑ Ⓒ Ⓓ	29 Ⓐ Ⓑ Ⓒ Ⓓ	52 Ⓐ Ⓑ Ⓒ Ⓓ	75 Ⓐ Ⓑ Ⓒ Ⓓ
7 Ⓐ Ⓑ Ⓒ Ⓓ	30 Ⓐ Ⓑ Ⓒ Ⓓ	53 Ⓐ Ⓑ Ⓒ Ⓓ	76 Ⓐ Ⓑ Ⓒ Ⓓ
8 Ⓐ Ⓑ Ⓒ Ⓓ	31 Ⓐ Ⓑ Ⓒ Ⓓ	54 Ⓐ Ⓑ Ⓒ Ⓓ	77 Ⓐ Ⓑ Ⓒ Ⓓ
9 Ⓐ Ⓑ Ⓒ Ⓓ	32 Ⓐ Ⓑ Ⓒ Ⓓ	55 Ⓐ Ⓑ Ⓒ Ⓓ	78 Ⓐ Ⓑ Ⓒ Ⓓ
10 Ⓐ Ⓑ Ⓒ Ⓓ	33 Ⓐ Ⓑ Ⓒ Ⓓ	56 Ⓐ Ⓑ Ⓒ Ⓓ	79 Ⓐ Ⓑ Ⓒ Ⓓ
11 Ⓐ Ⓑ Ⓒ Ⓓ	34 Ⓐ Ⓑ Ⓒ Ⓓ	57 Ⓐ Ⓑ Ⓒ Ⓓ	80 Ⓐ Ⓑ Ⓒ Ⓓ
12 Ⓐ Ⓑ Ⓒ Ⓓ	35 Ⓐ Ⓑ Ⓒ Ⓓ	58 Ⓐ Ⓑ Ⓒ Ⓓ	81 Ⓐ Ⓑ Ⓒ Ⓓ
13 Ⓐ Ⓑ Ⓒ Ⓓ	36 Ⓐ Ⓑ Ⓒ Ⓓ	59 Ⓐ Ⓑ Ⓒ Ⓓ	82 Ⓐ Ⓑ Ⓒ Ⓓ
14 Ⓐ Ⓑ Ⓒ Ⓓ	37 Ⓐ Ⓑ Ⓒ Ⓓ	60 Ⓐ Ⓑ Ⓒ Ⓓ	83 Ⓐ Ⓑ Ⓒ Ⓓ
15 Ⓐ Ⓑ Ⓒ Ⓓ	38 Ⓐ Ⓑ Ⓒ Ⓓ	61 Ⓐ Ⓑ Ⓒ Ⓓ	84 Ⓐ Ⓑ Ⓒ Ⓓ
16 Ⓐ Ⓑ Ⓒ Ⓓ	39 Ⓐ Ⓑ Ⓒ Ⓓ	62 Ⓐ Ⓑ Ⓒ Ⓓ	85 Ⓐ Ⓑ Ⓒ Ⓓ
17 Ⓐ Ⓑ Ⓒ Ⓓ	40 Ⓐ Ⓑ Ⓒ Ⓓ	63 Ⓐ Ⓑ Ⓒ Ⓓ	86 Ⓐ Ⓑ Ⓒ Ⓓ
18 Ⓐ Ⓑ Ⓒ Ⓓ	41 Ⓐ Ⓑ Ⓒ Ⓓ	64 Ⓐ Ⓑ Ⓒ Ⓓ	87 Ⓐ Ⓑ Ⓒ Ⓓ
19 Ⓐ Ⓑ Ⓒ Ⓓ	42 Ⓐ Ⓑ Ⓒ Ⓓ	65 Ⓐ Ⓑ Ⓒ Ⓓ	88 Ⓐ Ⓑ Ⓒ Ⓓ
20 Ⓐ Ⓑ Ⓒ Ⓓ	43 Ⓐ Ⓑ Ⓒ Ⓓ	66 Ⓐ Ⓑ Ⓒ Ⓓ	89 Ⓐ Ⓑ Ⓒ Ⓓ
21 Ⓐ Ⓑ Ⓒ Ⓓ	44 Ⓐ Ⓑ Ⓒ Ⓓ	67 Ⓐ Ⓑ Ⓒ Ⓓ	90 Ⓐ Ⓑ Ⓒ Ⓓ
22 Ⓐ Ⓑ Ⓒ Ⓓ	45 Ⓐ Ⓑ Ⓒ Ⓓ	68 Ⓐ Ⓑ Ⓒ Ⓓ	
23 Ⓐ Ⓑ Ⓒ Ⓓ	46 Ⓐ Ⓑ Ⓒ Ⓓ	69 Ⓐ Ⓑ Ⓒ Ⓓ	

SAMPLE PRACTICE EXAMINATION I

DIRECTIONS FOR ANSWERING QUESTIONS

Each question has four suggested answers, lettered
A, B, C, and D. Decide which one is the best answer
and on the sample answer sheet find the question
number which corresponds to the answer that you have
selected and darken the area with a soft pencil.

The time allowed for the entire examination is
4½ hours.

Part 1

Weight 80, 70% Required

1. As a Principal Administrative Associate in a bureau of a city agency, you have been asked by the head of the bureau to recommend whether or not the work of the bureau requires an increase in the permanent staff of the bureau. Of the following questions, the one whose answer would most likely assist you in making your recommendation is:

    (A) Are some permanent employees working irregular hours because they occasionally work overtime?
    (B) Are the present permanent employees satisfied with their work assignments?
    (C) Are temporary employees hired to handle seasonal fluctuations in work load?
    (D) Are the present permanent employees keeping the work of the bureau current?

2. In making job assignments to subordinates, a supervisor should follow the principle that each individual generally is capable of

    (A) performing one type of work well and less capable of performing other types well
    (B) learning to perform a wide variety of different types of work

(C) performing best the type of work in which experience has been had

(D) learning to perform any type of work in which training is given.

3. Assume that, as Principal Administrative Associate, you are the supervisor of a large number of clerks in a unit in a city agency. Your unit has just been given an important assignment which must be completed a week from now. You know that, henceforth, your unit will be given this assignment every six months. You or any one of your subordinates who has been properly instructed can complete this assignment in one day. This assignment is of a routine type which is ordinarily handled by office aides. There is enough time for you to train one of your subordinates to handle the assignment and then have him or her do it. However, it would take twice as much time for you to take this course of action as it would for you to do the assignment yourself. The one of the following courses of action which you should take in this situation is to

(A) do the assignment yourself as soon as possible without discussing it with any of your subordinates at this time

(B) do the assignment yourself and then train one of your subordinates to handle it in the future

(C) give the assignment to one of your subordinates after training him or her to handle it

(D) train each of your subordinates to do the assignment on a rotating basis after you have done it yourself the first time.

4. You are in charge of an office in which each member of the staff has a different set of duties, although each has the same title. No member of the staff can perform the duties of any other member of the staff without first receiving extensive training. Assume that it is necessary for one member of the staff to take on, in addition to regular work, an assignment which any member of the staff is capable of carrying out. The one of the following considerations which would have the most weight in determining which staff member is to be given the additional assignment is the

(A) quality of the work performed by the individual members of the staff

(B) time consumed by individual members of the staff in performing their work

(C) level of difficulty of the duties being performed by individual members of the staff

(D) relative importance of the duties being performed by individual members of the staff.

5. The one of the following causes of clerical error which is usually considered to be <u>least</u> attributable to faulty supervision or inefficient management is

(A) inability to carry out instruction

(B) too much work to do

(C) an inappropriate record-keeping system
(D) continual interruptions.

6. Suppose you are the Principal Administrative Associate in charge of a large unit in which all of the clerical staff perform similar tasks. In evaluating the relative accuracy of the office aides, the office aide who should be considered to be the <u>least</u> accurate is the one

(A) whose errors result in the greatest financial loss
(B) whose errors cost the most to locate
(C) who makes the greatest percentage of errors in the work
(D) who makes the greatest number of errors in the unit.

7. Assume that under a proposed procedure for handling employee grievances in a public agency, the first step to be taken is for the aggrieved employee to submit the grievance as soon as it arises to a grievance board set up to hear all employee grievances in the agency. The board, which is to consist of representatives of management and of rank and file employees, is to consider the grievance, obtain all necessary pertinent information, and then render a decision on the matter. Thus, the first line supervisor would not be involved in the settlement of any of the subordinates' grievances except when asked by the board to submit information. This proposed procedure would be generally undesirable

chiefly because

(A) the board may become a bottleneck to delay the prompt disposition of grievances
(B) the aggrieved employees and their supervisors have not been first given the opportunity to resolve the grievances themselves
(C) employees would be likely to submit imaginary, as well as real, grievances to the board
(D) the board will lack first-hand, personal knowledge of the factors involved in grievances.

8. "Sometimes jobs in private organizations and public agencies are broken down so as to permit a high degree of job specialization." Of the following, an important effect of a high degree of job specialization in a public agency is that employees performing

(A) highly specialized jobs may not be readily transferable to other jobs in the agency
(B) similar duties may require closer supervision than employees performing unrelated functions
(C) specialized duties can be held responsible for their work to a greater extent than can employees performing a wide variety of functions
(D) specialized duties will tend to cooperate readily with employees performing other types of specialized duties.

9. Assume that you are the supervisor of a clerical unit. One of your subordinates

violates a rule, a violation which requires that the employee be suspended from work for one day. The violated rule is one that you have found to be unduly strict and you have recommended to the management that the rule be changed or abolished. The management has been considering your recommendation but has not yet reached a decision on the matter. In these circumstances, you should

(A) not initiate disciplinary action, but, instead, explain to the employee that the rule may be changed shortly
(B) delay disciplinary action on the violation until the management has reached a decision on changing the rule
(C) modify the disciplinary action by reprimanding the employee and explaining that further action may be taken when the management has reached a decision on changing the rule
(D) initiate the prescribed disciplinary action without commenting on the strictness of the rule or on your recommendation.

10. Assume that a supervisor praises his subordinates for satisfactory aspects of their work only when he is about to criticize them for unsatisfactory aspects of their work. Such a practice is undesirable primarily because

(A) his subordinates may expect to be praised for their work even if it is unsatisfactory
(B) praising his subordinates for some aspects of their work while criticizing other aspects will weaken the effects of the criticisms
(C) his subordinates would be more receptive to criticism if it were followed by praise
(D) his subordinates may come to disregard praise and wait for criticism to be given.

11. The one of the following which would be the best reason for an organization to eliminate a procedure for obtaining and recording certain information is that

(A) it is no longer legally required to obtain the information
(B) there is no advantage in obtaining the information
(C) the information could be compiled on the basis of other information available
(D) the information obtained is sometimes incorrect.

12. In determining the type and number of records to be kept in an organization, it is important to recognize that records are of value primarily as

(A) raw material to be used in statistical analysis
(B) sources of information about the organization's activities
(C) by-products of the activities carried on by the organization
(D) data for evaluating the effectiveness of the organization.

13. Aside from requirements imposed by authority, the

frequency with which reports are submitted or the length of the interval which they cover should depend principally on the

(A) availability of the data to be included in the reports
(B) amount of time required to prepare the reports
(C) extent of the variations in the data with the passage of time
(D) degree of comprehensiveness required in the reports.

14. Organizations that occupy large, general, open-area offices sometimes consider it desirable to build private offices for the supervisors of large bureaus. The one of the following which is generally not considered to be a justification of the use of private offices is that they

(A) lend prestige to the person occupying the office
(B) provide facilities for private conferences
(C) achieve the maximum use of office space
(D) provide facilities for performing work requiring a high degree of concentration.

15. The least important factor to be considered in planning the layout of an office is the

(A) relative importance of the different types of work to be done
(B) convenience with which communication can be achieved
(C) functional relationships of the activities of the office

(D) necessity for screening confidential activities from unauthorized persons.

16. The one of the following which is generally considered to be the chief advantage of using data processing equipment in modern offices is to

(A) facilitate the use of a wide variety of sources of information
(B) supply management with current information quickly
(C) provide uniformity in the processing and reporting of information
(D) broaden the area in which management decisions can be made.

17. In the box design of office forms, the spaces in which information is to be entered are arranged in boxes containing captions. Of the following, the one which is generally not considered to be an acceptable rule in employing box design is that

(A) space should be allowed for the lengthiest anticipated entry in a box
(B) the caption should be located in the upper left corner of the box
(C) the boxes on a form should be of the same size and shape
(D) boxes should be aligned vertically whenever possible.

18. As a management tool, the work count would generally be of least assistance to a unit supervisor in

(A) scheduling the work of the unit

(B) locating bottlenecks in the work of the unit

(C) ascertaining the number of subordinates needed

(D) tracing the flow of work in the unit.

19. Of the following, the <u>first</u> step that should be taken in a forms simplification program is to make a

(A) detailed analysis of the items found on current forms

(B) study of the amount of use made of existing forms

(C) survey of the amount of each kind of form on hand

(D) survey of the characteristics of the more effective forms in use.

20. The work distribution chart is a valuable tool for an office supervisor to use in conducting work simplification programs. Of the following questions, the one which a work distribution chart would generally be <u>least</u> useful in answering is:

(A) What activities take the most time?

(B) Are the employees doing many unrelated tasks?

(C) Is work being distributed evenly among the employees?

(D) Are activities being performed in proper sequence?

21. Assume that as Principal Administrative Associate, you conduct, from time to time, work performance studies in various sections of your organization. The units of measurement used in any study depend on the particular study and may be number of letters typed,

number of papers filed, or other suitable units. It is most important that the units of measurement to be used in a study conform to the units used in similar past studies when the

(A) units of measurement to be used in the study cannot be defined sharply

(B) units of measurement used in past studies were satisfactory

(C) results of the study are to be compared with those of past studies

(D) results of the study are to be used for the same purpose as were those of past studies.

22. As it is used in auditing, an internal check is a

(A) procedure which is designed to guard against fraud

(B) periodic audit by a public accounting firm to verify the accuracy of the internal transactions of an organization

(C) document transferring funds from one section to another within an organization

(D) practice of checking documents twice before they are transmitted outside an organization.

23. Of the following, the one which can <u>least</u> be considered to be a proper function of an accounting system is to

(A) indicate the need to curtail expenditures

(B) provide information for future fiscal programs

(C) record the expenditure of funds from special appropriations

(D) suggest methods to

expedite the
collection of revenues.

24. Assume that a new unit is to
be established. The unit is
to compile and tabulate data
so that it will be of the
greatest usefulness to the
high-level administrators in
the company in making
administrative decisions.
In planning the organization
of this unit, the question
that should be answered
first is:

(A) What interpretations
are likely to be made of
the data by the
high-level administrators
in making decisions?
(B) At what point in the
decision-making process
will it be most useful
to inject the data?
(C) What types of data will
be required by
high-level administrators
in making decisions?
(D) What criteria will the
high-level administrators
use to evaluate the
decisions they make?

25. The one of the following
which is the chief
limitation of the
organization chart as it
is generally used in
business and government is
that the chart

(A) engenders within
incumbents feelings of
rights to positions
they occupy
(B) reveals only formal
authority relationships,
omitting the informal
ones
(C) shows varying degrees of
authority even though
authority is not subject
to such differentiation
(D) presents organizational
structure as it is rather

than what it is supposed
to be.

26. The degree of
decentralization that is
effective and economical in
an organization tends to
vary inversely with the

(A) size of the organization
(B) availability of adequate
numbers of competent
personnel
(C) physical dispersion of
the organization's
activities
(D) adequacy of the
organization's
communications system.

27. The one of the following
which usually can least be
considered to be an
advantage of committees as
they are generally used in
government and business is
that they

(A) provide opportunities
for reconciling varying
points of view
(B) promote coordination by
the interchange of
information among the
members of the committee
(C) act promptly in
situations requiring
immediate action
(D) use group judgment to
resolve questions
requiring a wide range
of experience.

28. Managerial decentralization
is defined as the
decentralization of
decision-making authority.
The degree of managerial
decentralization in an
organization varies
inversely with the

(A) number of decisions made
lower down the
management hierarchy
(B) importance of the

decisions made lower down the management hierarchy

(C) number of major organizational functions affected by decisions made at lower management levels

(D) amount of review to which decisions made at lower management levels are subjected.

29. Some policy-making commissions are composed of members who are appointed to overlapping terms. Of the following, the chief advantage of appointing members to overlapping terms in such commissions is that

(A) continuity of policy is promoted

(B) the likelihood of compromise policy decisions is reduced

(C) responsibility for policy decisions can be fixed upon individual members

(D) the likelihood of unanimity of opinion is increased.

30. If a certain public agency with a fixed number of employees has a line organizational structure, then the width of the span of supervision is

(A) inversely proportional to the length of the chain of command in the organization

(B) directly proportional to the complexity of tasks performed in the organization

(C) inversely proportional to the competence of the personnel in the organization

(D) directly proportional to the number of levels of supervision existing in the organization.

31. Mr. Brown is a Principal Administrative Associate in charge of a section of clerical employees. The section consists of four units, each headed by a unit supervisor. From time to time, he makes tours of his section for the purpose of maintaining contact with the rank and file employees. During these tours, he discusses with these employees their work production, work methods, work problems, and other related topics. The information he obtains in this manner is often incomplete or inaccurate. At meetings with the unit supervisors, he questions them on the information acquired during his tours. The supervisors are often unable to answer the questions immediately because they are based on incomplete or inaccurate information. When the supervisors ask that they be permitted to accompany Mr. Brown on his tours and thus answer his questions on the spot, Mr. Brown refuses, explaining that a rank and file employee might be reluctant to speak freely in the presence of his supervisor. This situation may best be described as a violation of the principle of organization called

(A) span of control

(B) delegation of authority

(C) specialization of work

(D) unity of command.

Each of questions 32 to 36 consists of a quotation which contains one word that is incorrectly used because it is not in keeping with the meaning that the quotation is evidently intended to convey. For each of these questions, you are to select the incorrectly used word and substitute for it one of the words lettered A, B, C, or D, which helps best to convey the meaning of the quotation. Darken the space on your answer sheet accordingly.

32. "There has developed in recent years an increasing awareness of the need to measure the quality of management in all enterprises and to seek the principles that can serve as a basis for this improvement."

    (A) growth
    (B) raise
    (C) efficiency
    (D) define.

33. "It is hardly an exaggeration to deny that the permanence, productivity, and humanity of any industrial system depend upon its ability to utilize the positive and constructive impulses of all who work and upon its ability to arouse and continue interest in the necessary activities."

    (A) develop
    (B) efficiency
    (C) state
    (D) inspiration.

34. "The selection of managers on the basis of technical knowledge alone seems to recognize that the essential characteristic of management is getting things done through others, thereby demanding skills that are essential in coordinating the activities of subordinates."

    (A) training
    (B) fails
    (C) organization
    (D) improving.

35. "Only when it is deliberate and when it is clearly understood what impressions the ease of communication will probably create in the minds of employees and subordinate management, should top management refrain from commenting on a subject that is of general concern."

    (A) obvious
    (B) benefit
    (C) doubt
    (D) absence.

36. "Scientific planning of work requires careful analysis of facts and a precise plan of action for the whims and fancies of executives that often provide only a vague indication of the work to be done."

    (A) substitutes
    (B) development
    (C) preliminary
    (D) comprehensive.

37. Within any single level of government, the administrative authority may be concentrated or dispersed. Of the following plans of government, the one in which administrative authority would be dispersed the most is the

    (A) mayor plan
    (B) mayor-council plan
    (C) commission plan
    (D) city manager plan.

38. In general, the courts may review a decision of an administrative agency with rule-making powers. However, the courts will usually

refuse to review a decision of such an agency if the only question raised concerning the decision is whether or not the

(A) decision contravenes public policy
(B) agency has abused the powers conferred upon it
(C) decision deals with an issue which is within the jurisdiction of the agency
(D) agency has applied the same rules of evidence as are used in the courts.

39. A legislature sometimes delegates rule-making powers to the administrators of a public agency. Of the following, the chief advantage of such delegation is that

(A) the frequency with which the legality of the agency's rules is contested in court will be reduced
(B) the agency will have the flexibility to adjust to changing conditions and problems
(C) mistakes made by the administrators or the legislature in defining the scope of the agency's program may be easily corrected
(D) the legislature will not be required to approve the rules formulated by the agency.

40. "Some municipalities have delegated the functions of budget preparation and personnel selection to central agencies, thus removing these functions from operating departments." Of the following, the most important reason why

municipalities have delegated these functions to central agencies is that

(A) the performance of these functions presents problems that vary from one operating department to another
(B) operating departments often lack sufficient funds to perform these functions adequately
(C) the performance of these functions by a central agency produces more uniform policies than if these functions are performed by the operating departments
(D) central agencies are not controlled as closely as are operating departments and so have greater freedom in formulating new policies and procedures to deal with difficult budget and personnel problems.

41. Of the following, the most fundamental reason for the use of budgets in governmental administration is that budgets

(A) minimize seasonal variations in work loads and expenditures of public agencies
(B) facilitate decentralization of functions performed by public agencies
(C) provide advance control on the expenditure of funds
(D) establish valid bases for comparing present governmental activities with corresponding activities in previous periods.

42. In some governmental jurisdictions, the chief

executive prepares the budget for a fiscal period and presents it to the legislative branch of government for adoption. In other jurisdictions, the legislative branch prepares and adopts the budget. Preparation of the budget by the chief executive rather than by the legislative branch is

(A) desirable primarily because the chief executive is held largely accountable by the public for the results of fiscal operations and should therefore be the one to prepare the budget

(B) undesirable primarily because such a separation of the legislative and executive branches leads to the enactment of a budget that does not consider the overall needs of the government

(C) desirable primarily because the preparation of the budget by the chief executive limits legislative review and evaluation of operating programs

(D) undesirable primarily because responsibility for budget preparation should be placed in the branch that must eventually adopt the budget and appropriate the funds for it.

43. The one of the following which is generally the <u>first</u> step in the budget-making process of a municipality that has a central budget agency is

(A) determination of available sources of revenue within the municipality

(B) establishment of tax rates at levels sufficient to achieve a balanced budget in the following fiscal period

(C) evaluation, by the central budget agency, of the adequacy of the municipality's previous budgets

(D) assembling, by the central budget agency, of the proposed expenditures of each agency in the municipality for the following fiscal period.

44. It is advantageous for a municipality to issue serial bonds rather than sinking fund bonds chiefly because

(A) an issue of serial bonds usually includes a wider range of maturity dates than does an issue of sinking fund bonds

(B) appropriations set aside periodically to retire serial bonds as they fall due are more readily invested in long term securities at favorable rates of interest than are appropriations earmarked for redemption of sinking fund bonds

(C) serial bonds are sold at regular intervals while sinking fund bonds are issued as the need for funds arises

(D) a greater variety of interest rates is usually offered in an issue of sinking fund bonds.

45. "The principle of filling all higher grade jobs in an organization by promotion implies a necessary corollary." Of the following,

the most accurate statement of the corollary referred to in the quotation is that

(A) concrete salary incentives should be provided from the lowest to the highest position in the public service

(B) entrance into the public service should be restricted to persons with minimum educational requirements

(C) a minimum of at least one year of service in the appropriate lower grade should be required before promotion

(D) entrance tests for the public service should measure general capacity rather than skill in highly specialized fields.

46. The chief assumption underlying the provisions for a salary range with a miniumum, a maximum, and intervening steps for each class in the compensation plans of most organizations is that

(A) the granting of periodic increments to employees encourages staff stability at the lowest possible cost

(B) job offers made at a step higher than the minimum of a salary range are a positive aid to recruitment

(C) automatic salary increments provide an incentive to employees to improve their job performances from year to year

(D) an employee's value to the employer tends to increase with the

passage of time.

47. Selection of candidates for employment on the basis of aptitude test results is made on the assumption that the candidates making the highest test scores

(A) possess the most knowledge about the job for which they were tested

(B) will need a minimum amount of training on the job for which they were tested

(C) will be the most satisfactory employees after they have received training

(D) are those who will have the highest interest in succeeding on the job for which they were tested.

48. In position classification, the one of the following factors which is of least importance in classifying a clerical position is the

(A) degree of supervision under which the work of the position is performed

(B) amount of supervision exercised over other positions

(C) training and experience of the incumbent of the position

(D) extent to which independent judgment must be exercised in performing the duties of the position.

49. The position classifying bureau of the central personnel agency in a public jurisdiction is normally not responsible for

(A) allocating individual positions to classes

(B) assigning titles to classes of positions
(C) establishing minimum qualifications for positions
(D) determining which positions are necessary.

50. The one of the following which is generally considered to be an essential element in the process of classifying a position is the

   (A) comparison of the position with similar and related positions
   (B) evaluation of the skill with which the duties of the position are being performed
   (C) number of positions similar to the position being classified
   (D) determination of the salary being paid for the position.

51. Of the following, the least important objective of a modern performance evaluation system is to

   (A) validate selection procedures
   (B) improve the quality of supervision
   (C) furnish a basis for the construction of a position classification plan
   (D) foster the development of good employee performance.

52. Some organizations conduct exit interviews with employees who quit their jobs. The one of the following which is generally considered to be the chief value to an organization of such an interview is in

   (A) ascertaining from the

employee the reasons for leaving the job
   (B) obtaining reliable information on the employee's work history with the agency
   (C) persuading the employee to reconsider the decision to quit
   (D) giving the employee a final evaluation of work performance.

53. The rate of labor turnover in an organization may be arrived at by dividing the total number of separations from the organization in a given period by the average number of workers employed in the same period. In arriving at the rate it is assumed that those separated are replaced. If the rate of turnover is excessively low in comparison with other similar organizations, it usually indicates that

   (A) the organization is stagnant
   (B) promotions within the organization are made frequently
   (C) the organization's recruitment policies have been ineffective
   (D) suitable workers are in short supply.

54. In a training program for supervisory personnel, the aspect for which it is usually most difficult to develop adequate information is the

   (A) determination of the training needs of the supervisory personnel in the agency
   (B) establishment of the objectives of the program
   (C) selection of suitable training methods for the

program
(D) evaluation of the
effectiveness of the
training program.

55. You are conducting a
training conference for new
supervisors on supervisory
techniques and problems.
when one of the participants
in the conference proposes
what you consider to be an
unsatisfactory solution for
the problem under
discussion, none of the
other participants questions
the solution or offers an
alternate solution. For
you to tell the group why
the solution is
unsatisfactory would be

(A) desirable chiefly
because satisfactory
rather than
unsatisfactory solutions
to the problems should
be stressed in the
conference
(B) undesirable chiefly
because the participants
themselves should be
stimulated to present
reasons why the proposed
solution is
unsatisfactory
(C) desirable chiefly
because you, as the
conference leader, should
guide the participants
in solving conference
problems
(D) undesirable chiefly
because the proposed
unsatisfactory solution
may be useful in
illustrating the
advantages of a
satisfactory solution.

56. It is generally best that
the greater part of
in-service training for the
operating employees of an
agency in a public
jurisdiction be given by

(A) a team of trainers from
the central personnel
agency of the
jurisdiction
(B) training specialists on
the staff of the
personnel unit of the
agency
(C) a team of teachers from
the public school system
of the jurisdiction
(D) members of the regular
supervisory force of the
agency.

57. You are responsible for
training a number of your
subordinates to handle
some complicated procedures
which your unit will adopt
after the training has been
completed. If approximately
30 hours of training are
required, and you can arrange
the training sessions during
working hours as you see
fit, learning would
ordinarily be best effected
if you scheduled the
trainees to devote

(A) a half day each week to
the training until it is
completed
(B) one full day each week to
the training until it is
completed
(C) a half day every day to
the training until it is
completed
(D) full time to the training
until it is completed.

58. Assume that you are giving a
lecture for the purpose of
explaining a new procedure.
You find that the employees
attending the lecture are
asking many questions on the
material as you present it.
Consequently, you realize
that you will be unable to
cover all of the material you
had intended to cover, and
that a second lecture will be
necessary. In this situation,

the most advisable course of
action for you to take would
be to

(A) answer the questions on
the new procedure as
they arise
(B) answer the questions
that can be answered
quickly and ask the
employees to reserve
questions requiring
lengthier answers for
the second lecture
(C) suggest that further
questions be withheld
until the second lecture
so that you can cover as
much of the remaining
material as possible
(D) refer the questions back
to the employees asking
them.

59. As a Principal Administrative
Associate, you are conducting
a training conference
dealing with administrative
principles and practices.
One of the members of the
conference, Mr. Smith,
makes a factual statement
which you know to be
incorrect, and which may
hinder the development of
the discussion. None of the
other members attempts to
correct Mr. Smith or to
question him on what he has
said, although until this
point, the members have
participated actively in the
discussions. In this
situation, the most advisable
course of action for you to
take would be to

(A) proceed with the
discussion without
commenting on Mr. Smith's
statement
(B) correct the statement
that Mr. Smith has made
(C) emphasize that the
material discussed at
the conference is to

serve only as a guide
for handling actual work
situations
(D) urge the members to
decide for themsleves
whether or not to accept
factual statements made
at the conference.

60. With the wholehearted
support of top management,
the training bureau of an
organization schedules a
series of training
conferences for all the
supervisory and
administrative employees in
order to alter their
approaches to the problems
arising from the interaction
of supervisors and
subordinates. During the
conferences, the
participants discuss
solutions to typical
problems of this type and
become conscious of the
principles underlying the
these solutions. After the
series of conferences is
concluded, it is found that
the first-line supervisors
are not applying the
principles to the problems
they are encountering on the
job. Of the following, the
most likely reason why these
supervisors are not putting
the principles into practice
is that

(A) the training conferences
have not changed the
attitudes of these
supervisors
(B) these supervisors are
reluctant to put into
practice methods with
which their subordinates
are unfamiliar
(C) the conference method is
not suitable for human
relations training
(D) the principles which
were covered in the
conferences are not

suitable for solving
actual work problems.

61. Assume that you are the
leader of a training
conference dealing with
supervisory techniques and
problems. One of the
problems being discussed is
one with which you have had
no experience, but two of
the participants have had
considerable experience
with it. These two
participants carry on an
extended discussion of the
problem in the light of
their experiences and it is
obvious from their
discussion that they
understand the problem
thoroughly. It is also
obvious that the other
participants in the
conference are very much
interested in the discussion
and are taking notes on the
material presented. For you
to permit the two
participants to continue
until the amount of time
allowed for discussion of
the problem has been
exhausted would be

(A) desirable chiefly
because their
discussion, which is
based on actual work
experience, may be more
meaningful to the other
participants than would
a discussion which is
not based on work
experience
(B) undesirable chiefly
because they are
discussing the material
only in the light of
their own experiences
rather than in general
terms
(C) desirable chiefly
because the introduction
of the material by two
of the participants

themselves may put the
other participants at
ease
(D) undesirable chiefly
because the other
participants are not
joining in the
discussion of the
problem.

62. You are a Principal
Administrative Associate in
charge of a unit of clerical
employees. One of your
subordinates, Mr. Smith,
has not seemed to be his
usual self in the past
several weeks, but, rather,
has seemed to be disturbed.
In addition, he has not been
producing his usual quantity
of work and has been
provoking arguments with
his colleagues. He
approaches you and asks if he
may discuss with you a
problem which he believes has
been affecting his work.
As Mr. Smith begins to
discuss the problem, you
immediately realize that,
although it may be
disturbing to him, it is
really a trivial matter. Of
the following, the first
step that you should take in
this situation is to

(A) permit Mr. Smith to
continue to describe his
problem, interrupting
him only when
clarification of a point
is needed
(B) tell Mr. Smith that his
becoming unduly upset
about the problem will
not help solve it
(C) point out that you and
your subordinates have
faced more serious
problems and that this
one is a relatively
minor matter
(D) suggest that the problem
should be solved before

it develops into a
serious matter.

63. "A line supervisor can play
an important role in
helping subordinates to make
healthy mental, emotional,
and social adjustments."
The one of the following
which would not be
considered to be a part of
the supervisor's role in
helping subordinates to make
these adjustments is to

(A) ascertain which
subordinates are likely
to develop
maladjustments
(B) recognize indications of
these types of
maladjustments
(C) refer subordinates
displaying signs of
maladjustments that he
or she cannot handle to
specialists for
assistance
(D) create a work
environment that will
tend to minimize
subordinates'
preoccupations with
personal problems.

64. "One of the principal
duties of management is to
secure the most effective
utilization of personnel."
The one of the following
which would contribute least
to effective utilization and
development of personnel is

(A) the use of training
programs designed to
prepare employees for
future tasks
(B) a comprehensive list of
skills and abilities
needed to perform the
work effectively
(C) a systematic effort to
discover employees of
high potential and to
develop them for future

responsibilities
(D) the assignment of
employees to duties
which require the
maximum use of their
abilities.

65. During a training session
for new employees, an
employee becomes upset
because he is unable to
solve a problem presented to
him by the instructor. Of
the following actions which
the instructor could take,
the one which would be most
likely to dispel the
employee's emotional state
is to

(A) give him a different
type of problem which he
may be able to solve
(B) minimize the importance
of finding a solution to
the problem and proceed
to the next topic
(C) encourage the other
participants to
contribute to the
solution
(D) provide him with hints
which would enable him
to solve the problem.

66. Studies in human behavior
have shown that an employee
in a work group who is
capable of producing
substantially more work than
is being produced by the
average of the group
generally

(A) will tend to produce
substantially more work
than is produced by the
average member of the
group
(B) will attempt to become
the informal leader of
the group
(C) will tend to produce less
work than he is capable
of producing
(D) will attempt to

influence the other members of the group to increase their production.

67. Studies of organizations show that formal employee participation in the formulation of work policies before they are put into effect is most likely to result in

   (A) a reduction in the length of time required to formulate the policies
   (B) an increase in the number of employees affected by the policies
   (C) a reduction in the length of time required to implement the policies
   (D) an increase in the number of policies formulated within the organization.

68. "No matter how elaborate a formal system of communication is in an organization, the system will always be supplemented by informal channels of communication, such as the 'grapevine.' Although such informal channels of communication are usually not highly regarded, they sometimes are of value to an organization." Of the following, the chief value of informal channels of communication is that they serve to

   (A) transmit information that management has neglected to send through the formal system of communication
   (B) confirm information that has already been received through the formal system of communication
   (C) hinder the formation of employee cliques in the organization
   (D) revise information sent through the formal system of communication.

69. The one of the following which is generally considered to be the most important advantage of the written questionnaire method of obtaining information is that this method

   (A) assures accuracy of response greater than that obtained from other methods
   (B) gives the persons to whom the questionnaire is sent the opportunity to express their opinions and feelings
   (C) makes it possible to obtain the responses of many persons at small cost
   (D) permits errors in the information obtained to be corrected easily when they are discovered.

70. In collecting objective data for the evaluation of procedures which are used in the unit, an administrator should, in every case, be careful

   (A) to take an equal number of measurements from each source of information
   (B) not to allow beliefs about the values of the procedures to influence the choice of data
   (C) to apply statistical methods continuously to the data as they are gathered to assure maximum accuracy
   (D) not to accept data which

are inconsistent with the general trend established by verified data.

71. Assume that the law enforcement division in a public jurisdiction employs only males who are 5 feet 8 inches or taller. To expect the heights of these employees to be normally distributed is unjustified primarily because

    (A) the distribution of a random sample is not usually the same as the distribution of the population from which the sample was drawn
    (B) no maximum height requirement has been established
    (C) height is a characteristic which is not normally distributed in the general population of males
    (D) the employees are not a representative sample of the general population of males.

Questions 72 to 75 are to be answered solely on the basis of the information contained in the following paragraph:

"A standard comprises characteristics attached to an aspect of a process or product by which it can be evaluated. Standardization is the development and adoption of standards. When they are formulated, standards are not usually the product of a single person, but represent the thoughts and ideas of a group, leavened with the knowledge and information which are currently available. Standards which do not meet certain basic requirements become a hindrance rather than an aid to progress. Standards must not only be correct, accurate, and precise in requiring no more and no less than what is needed for satisfactory results, but they must also be workable in the sense that their usefulness is not nullified by external conditions. Standards should also be acceptable to the people who use them. If they are not acceptable, they cannot be considered to be satisfactory, although they may possess all the other essential characteristics."

72. According to the preceding paragraph, a processing standard that requires the use of materials that cannot be procured, is most likely to be

    (A) incomplete
    (B) inaccurate
    (C) unworkable
    (D) unacceptable.

73. According to the preceding paragraph, the construction of standards to which the performance of job duties should conform is most often

    (A) the work of the people responsible for seeing that the duties are properly performed
    (B) accomplished by the person who is best informed about the functions involved
    (C) the responsibility of the people who are to apply them
    (D) attributable to the efforts of various informed persons.

74. According to the preceding paragraph, when standards

call for finer tolerances than those essential to the conduct of successful production operations, the effect of the standards on the improvement of production operations is

(A) negative
(B) nullified
(C) negligible
(D) beneficial.

75. The one of the following which is the most suitable title for the preceding paragraph is

(A) The Evaluation of Formulated Standards
(B) The Attributes of Satisfactory Standards
(C) The Adoption of Acceptable Standards
(D) The Use of Process or Product Standards.

Questions 76 to 79 are to be answered solely on the basis of the information contained in the following paragraph:

"Good personnel relations in an organization depend upon mutual confidence, trust, and good will. The basis of confidence is understanding. Most troubles start with people who do not understand each other. When the organization's intentions or motives are misunderstood, or when reasons for actions, practices, or policies are misconstrued, complete cooperation from individuals is not forthcoming. If management expects full cooperation from employees, it has a responsibility of sharing with them the information which is the foundation of proper understanding, confidence, and trust. Personnel

management has long since outgrown the days when it was the vogue to 'treat them rough and tell them nothing.' Up-to-date personnel management provides all possible information about the activities, aims, and purposes of the organization. It seems altogether creditable that a desire should exist among employees for such information which the best-intentioned executive might think would not interest them and which the worst-intentioned would think was none of their business."

76. The preceding paragraph implies that one of the causes of the difficulty which an organization might have with its personnel relations is that its employees

(A) have not expressed interest in the activities, aims, and purposes of the organization
(B) do not believe in the good faith of the organization
(C) have not been able to give full cooperation to the organization
(D) do not recommend improvements in the practices and policies of the organization.

77. According to the preceding paragraph, in order for an organization to have good personnel relations, it is not essential that

(A) employees have confidence in the organization
(B) the purposes of the organization be

understood by the
employees
(C) employees have a desire
for information about
the organization
(D) information about the
organization be
communicated to
employees.

78. According to the paragraph,
an organization which
provides full information
about itself to its
employees

(A) understands the
intentions of its
employees
(B) satisfies a
praiseworthy desire
among its employees
(C) is managed by executives
who have the best
intentions toward its
employees
(D) is confident that its
employees understand its
motives.

79. The one of the following
which is the most suitable
title for the paragraph is

(A) The Foundations of
Personnel Relations
(B) The Consequences of
Employee Misunderstanding
(C) The Development of
Personnel Management
Practices
(D) The Acceptance of
Organizational
Objectives.

Questions 80 to 83 are to be
answered solely on the basis of
the information contained in the
following paragraph:

"Management, which is the
function of executive
leadership, has as its
principal phases the
planning, organizing, and

controlling of the
activities of subordinate
groups in the accomplishment
of organizational objectives.
Planning specifies the kind
and extent of the factors,
forces, and effects, and the
relationships among them,
that will be required for
satisfactory accomplishment.
The nature of the objectives
and their requirements must
be known before
determinations can be made as
to what must be done, how it
must be done and why, where
actions should take place,
who should be responsible,
and similar problems
pertaining to the
formulation of a plan.
Organizing, which creates the
conditions that must be
present before the execution
of the plan can be undertaken
successfully, cannot be done
intelligently without
knowledge of the
organizational objectives.
Control, which has to do
with the constraint and
regulation of activities
entering into the execution
of the plan, must be
exercised in accordance with
the characteristics and
requirements of the
activities demanded by the
plan."

80. The one of the following
which is the most suitable
title for the paragraph is

(A) The Nature of Successful
Organization
(B) The Planning of
Management Functions
(C) The Importance of
Organizational Objectives
(D) The Principal Aspects of
Management.

81. It can be inferred from the
paragraph that the one of the
following functions whose

existence is essential to the existence of the other three is the

(A) regulation of the work needed to carry out a plan
(B) understanding of what the organization intends to accomplish
(C) securing of information on the factors necessary for accomplishment of objectives
(D) establishment of the conditions required for successful action.

82. The one of the following which would not be included within any of the principal phases of the function of executive leadership as defined in the paragraph is

(A) determination of manpower requirements
(B) procurement of required material
(C) establishment of organizational objectives
(D) scheduling of production.

83. The conclusion which can most reasonably be drawn from the paragraph is that the control phase of managing is most directly concerned with the

(A) influencing of policy determinations
(B) administering of suggestion systems
(C) acquisition of staff for the organization
(D) implementation of performance standards.

84. A study reveals that Miss Brown files N cards in M hours, and Miss Smith files the same number of cards in T hours. If the two employees work together, the number of hours it will take them to file N cards is

(A) $\dfrac{N}{\dfrac{N}{M} + \dfrac{N}{T}}$

(B) $\dfrac{N}{T} + M + \dfrac{2N}{MT}$

(C) $N\left(\dfrac{M}{N} + \dfrac{N}{T}\right)$

(D) $\dfrac{N}{NT + MN}$

Questions 85 to 90 are to be answered solely on the basis of the information contained in the five charts below which relate to Bureau X in a City Department. The Bureau has an office in each of the five boroughs.

NUMBER OF UNITS OF WORK PRODUCED IN THE BUREAU PER YEAR

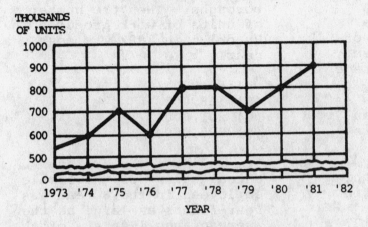

INCREASE IN THE NUMBER OF UNITS OF WORK PRODUCED IN 1982 OVER THE NUMBER PRODUCED IN 1973, BY BOROUGH

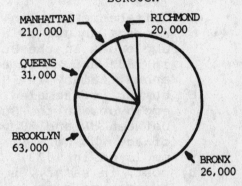

MANHATTAN 210,000
RICHMOND 20,000
QUEENS 31,000
BROOKLYN 63,000
BRONX 26,000

NUMBER OF MALE AND FEMALE EMPLOYEES PRODUCING THE UNITS OF WORK IN THE BUREAU PER YEAR

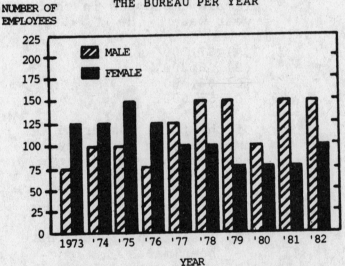

DISTRIBUTION OF THE AGES, BY PERCENT, OF EMPLOYEES ASSIGNED TO PRODUCE THE UNITS OF WORK IN THE YEARS 1973 and 1982

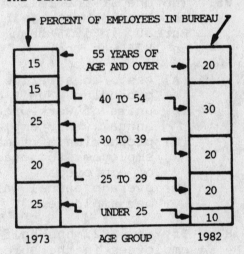

TOTAL SALARIES PAID PER YEAR TO EMPLOYEES ASSIGNED TO PRODUCE THE UNITS OF WORK IN THE BUREAU

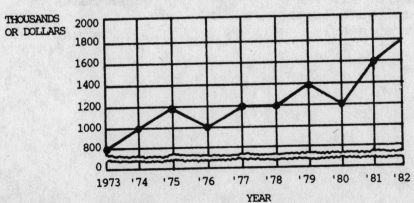

85. The information contained in the charts is sufficient to determine the

    (A) amount of money paid in salaries to employees working in Richmond in 1982
    (B) difference between the average annual salary of employees in the Bureau in 1982 and their average annual salary in 1981
    (C) number of female employees in the Bureau between 30 and 39 years of age who were employed in 1973
    (D) cost, in salary, for the average male employee in the Bureau to produce 100 units of work in 1978.

86. The one of the following which was greater, in the Bureau, in 1978 than it was in 1976 was the

    (A) cost, in salaries, of producing a unit of work
    (B) units of work produced annually per employee
    (C) proportion of female employees to total number of employees
    (D) average annual salary per employee.

87. If, in 1982, one-half of the employees in the Bureau 55 years of age and over each earned an annual salary of $8,400, then the average annual salary of all the remaining employees in the Bureau was most nearly

    (A) $6,350
    (B) $6,900
    (C) $7,060
    (D) $7,160.

88. Assume that, in 1973, the offices in Richmond and the Bronx each produced the same number of units of work. Also assume that, in 1973, the offices in Brooklyn, Manhattan and Queens each produced twice as many units of work as were produced in either of the other two boroughs. Then the number of units of work produced in Brooklyn in 1982 was most nearly

    (A) 69,000
    (B) 138,000
    (C) 201,000
    (D) 225,000.

89. If, in 1980, the average annual salary of the female employees in the Bureau was four-fifths as large as the average annual salary of the male employees, then the average annual salary of the female employees in that year was

    (A) $7,500
    (B) $6,200
    (C) $6,100
    (D) $6,000.

90. Of the total number of employees in the Bureau who were 30 years of age and over in 1973

    (A) at least 35 must have been females
    (B) less than 75 must have been males
    (C) no more than 100 must have been females
    (D) more than 15 must have been males.

PART 2

Weight 20

The head of your unit has assigned you to submit a report setting forth
your recommendations for a training program to be given to employees in
your unit who have been newly promoted to positions as first line
supervisors. The report should outline the subject matter areas to be
covered in the program, the training methods which would be most
effective in each of the areas outlined, and the criteria to be used
in evaluating the effectiveness of the program.

Prepare the report. It is to be addressed to the head of your unit and
you are to sign it "J. Doe." Your report will be rated on content,
organization of material, and English usage.

Write on one side of the essay answer paper only. Write legibly. No
credit will be given for material which cannot be read easily. Use
blue or black ink only.

Answer Key

1. D	16. B	31. D	46. D	61. A or D	76. B
2. B	17. C	32. B	47. C	62. A	77. C
3. C	18. D	33. C	48. C	63. A	78. B
4. B	19. B	34. B	49. D	64. B	79. A
5. A	20. D	35. D	50. A	65. D	80. D
6. C	21. C	36. A	51. C	66. C	81. B
7. B	22. A	37. C	52. A	67. C	82. C
8. A	23. D	38. D	53. A or B	68. A	83. D
9. D	24. C	39. B	54. D	69. C	84. A
10. D	25. B	40. C	55. B	70. B	85. B
11. B	26. D	41. C	56. D	71. D	86. B
12. B	27. C	42. A	57. C	72. C	87. C
13. C	28. D	43. D	58. A	73. D	88. C
14. C	29. A	44. A	59. B	74. A	89. D
15. A	30. A	45. D	60. A	75. B	90. A

EXPLANATIONS OF KEY POINTS BEHIND THESE ANSWERS
WILL BE FOUND IMMEDIATELY FOLLOWING

EXPLANATORY ANSWERS

Elucidation, clarification, explication, and a little help with the fundamental facts covered in Sample Practice Examination I. These are the points and principles likely to crop up in the form of questions on future tests.

1. (D) The key to this answer is the word _permanent_. The decision to the question of whether or not more staff is needed in an organization should be based solely on the ability of the staff to perform the work during normal times. If it cannot, more staff is needed. During busy periods, temporary help may be employed, but the permanent staff should be geared to normal times.

2. (B) Generally, most people are capable of performing many different types of work after undergoing the necessary training. It does not follow that an individual will perform _best_ a task because prior experience has been had. The individual's abilities may be much more suited towards the performance of tasks which he or she has not had the opportunity to work at previously.

3. (C) This question is replete with clues to indicate that you, as a supervisor, should train a subordinate to perform the assignment in question. _This assignment is to be repeated, proper instruction will permit_ _anyone to complete it in one day, it is of a routine nature, etc._

4. (B) All other considerations seem to be equal; it would therefore be up to the supervisor to select the subordinate who has the time to perform the function.

5. (A) There is not much a supervisor can do with a subordinate whose ability is limited. He or she can be developed and trained only so much. On the other hand, the supervisor can do much to eliminate the conditions mentioned in the other choices through proper planning and other supervisory maneuvering.

6. (C) The employee who is considered least accurate is the one who commits the highest percentage of errors while performing the work. In other words, if one employee performs 100 units of work and commits ten errors, that employee would be considered less accurate than the one who commits twelve errors while completing 150 units of work.

7. (B) The supervisor should

always be given first opportunity to dispose of a subordinate's grievance. A grievance that is permitted to go beyond this stage poses a problem.

8. (A) A job may be so highly specialized that it does not have another place in any other part of the organization. An individual who is performing that job would have to be retrained if the job were eliminated or if he or she is to be moved to any other part of the organization.

9. (D) Management formulates policy; the supervisor's function is to implement it.

10. (D) The supervisor limits his praise to occasions when he is about to criticize. His subordinates will expect criticism whenever praise is extended to them. The supervisor, by his actions, is indicating that criticism is more important to him than praise. This is indeed a poor practice.

11. (B) A function must be of value to an organization if it is to be continued. If it serves no purpose, it should be discontinued. If information may be compiled on the basis of other information available, it would be wasteful to duplicate the gathering of this information through an independent process.

12. (B) Records are not an end in themselves -- only a means to an end. They go beyond evaluating the effectiveness of an organization.

13. (C) The chief factor which governs the length of the interval between the submission of reports is the subjectivity to change of the information in the reports. If the information is likely to change on a daily basis, reports should be

submitted daily, etc.

14. (C) Private offices do not achieve maximum use of office space. The other three choices contain reasons to justify the use of private offices.

15. (A) The importance of the work to be done is given least consideration while planning an office layout. Functional relationships, communication and security deserve much more consideration.

16. (B) Data processing equipment can supply management with pertinent information much more quickly than workers keeping records manually are able to do.

17. (C) The size and the shape of the boxes on the form should be determined by the use they will be put to. There is no necessity for uniformity.

18. (D) A work count cannot trace the flow of work in a unit. This can be accomplished by a flow chart. The work count, a measurement of the work output of all the workers, can accomplish all of the objectives in the other three choices.

19. (B) If sufficient use is not being made of a form, why revise and simplify it? It would be better to eliminate it or to combine it with another form.

20. (D) The work distribution chart is an administrative tool which is used to indicate the functions each of the workers is performing and the time devoted to each. It does not show if the activities are being performed in proper sequence.

21. (C) If the units of measurement in a study are not similar to those used in past studies, it would be difficult to

compare the results of the study recently completed with those completed in the past.

22. (A) An internal check is a procedure instituted which is designed to guard against fraudulent acts. It is made use of when a suspicion exists in the minds of management that fraudulent acts may be taking place.

23. (D) An accounting system may be expected to carry out all of the functions in choices (A), (B) and, (C). The suggestion of methods to expedite the collection of revenues is an administrative function.

24. (C) The organization of a unit should be based upon the functions it is expected to perform. Therefore, the first step in the organization of a new unit would be the determination of just what that unit is expected to do.

25. (B) An organization chart depicts formal relationships in an organization only. Most organizations function effectively if informal relationships exist in addition to the formal relationships. An informal relationship is one where a function is performed without utilizing the formal lines of authority in an organization. For example: A clerk in one unit brings a letter down directly to the mail unit for mailing. The mailclerk and the clerk know it should be mailed. The mailclerk posts and mails the letter. If formal lines of authority were followed, the clerk would have to transmit the letter to his supervisor to bring to the supervisor of the mail unit so that he could assign the mailclerk to post and mail the letter.

26. (D) As an organization's communications system gains effectiveness and increases its activity, the necessity of decentralizing its operations decreases. Problems can be transmitted to management quickly and resultant solutions can then be transmitted back to the various units expeditiously.

27. (C) As a rule, committees do not act promptly. A meeting of several minds must be accomplished before a committee can act.

28. (D) As managerial decentralization in an organization increases, there will be a lesser review of decisions made at lower levels.

29. (A) Overlapping of the terms of members who serve on a commission precludes the possibility that the members of that commission will all be replaced at the same time. This will do away with the possibility that radical changes may take place with the formation of an entirely new commission.

30. (A) The number of employees remains constant. Therefore the span of control of each level will increase when the chain of command or the number of organizational levels decrease in number.

31. (D) Mr. Brown is in clear violation of the principle of unity of command which states that each individual in an organization should be responsible to but one superior.

32. (B) The word raise should be substituted for the word measure.

33. (C) The word <u>state</u> should be substituted for the word <u>deny</u>.

34. (B) The word <u>fails</u> should be substituted for the word <u>seems</u>.

35. (D) The word <u>absence</u> should be substituted for the word <u>ease</u>.

36. (A) The word <u>substitutes</u> should be used in place of the word <u>requires</u>.

37. (C) A commission is made up of several members. If a city is run by a commission, the authority to run it would be in the hands of its members. The mayor, mayor-council, and city manager plan of government all vest authority in but one individual for the main part.

38. (D) It is usually not necessary for an administrative agency to abide by the rules of evidence which predominate the administration of a court of law. The courts will most probably intervene when conditions exist as mentioned in the other choices.

39. (B) An agency which is given the authority to formulate rules concerning its operations will be able to pass appropriate measures to meet current requirements.

40. (C) Budgeting is performed most effectively if its function is vested in one agency.

41. (C) A budget is actually a plan in dollars and cents. It provides for a control on money which is to be spent during a budgetary period.

42. (A) Since the chief executive will be held responsible for the operation of the jurisdiction, he or she should be afforded sufficient budgetary power to provide for services which he or she deems necessary.

43. (D) The budget-making process begins with an assemblage of the alleged requirements of each of the agencies by the unit which is to prepare the budget.

44. (A) Self-explanatory.

45. (D) A worker who possesses a sizable capacity to learn can be trained to perform many jobs efficiently.

46. (D) Workers become more valuable to their employers merely on the basis of the amount of time they spend on a job. Skills in job performance are bound to improve with work experience until eventually a worker will reach top potential.

47. (C) An aptitude test is designed to indicate the amount a worker will benefit from the training given. An individual with a high rating on an aptitude test is likely to become an efficient worker after undergoing the necessary training to perform the job.

48. (C) The training and experience of the incumbent is not taken into consideration during the process of position classification. The education and experience of the incumbent may be far in excess of what is actually necessary for proper performance of the job.

49. (D) A classifying bureau is not responsible for determining the necessity of a job.

50. (A) A comparison of the position to be classified with other similar and related positions will aid in placing it in its proper category.

51. (C) A performance evaluation system does not form the basis for the construction of a position classification plan.

It does have as its objective all of the other points brought out in choices (A), (B), and (D).

52. (A) An organization should strive to retain its employees. A worker tends to increase in value with time and the training of new employees is costly. If the reason for a worker leaving the job is some fault in the operation of the agency, perhaps remedial action is called for.

53. (A and B) An organization which is stagnant will have a low turnover rate of personnel. Its workers are likely to become complacent and they will stay on the job. An organization with a policy of promotions from within will also tend to retain its employees because the promotion opportunities will act as an inducement for workers to remain with the organization.

54. (D) The most difficult part of any training program is the evaluation of its effectiveness.

55. (B) It is the function of the conference leader to stimulate the participants to produce the solutions to the problems brought before it.

56. (D) The supervisor of the workers to be trained is in the best position to extend the training to them. The supervisor is aware of their needs and can best evaluate the effectiveness of the training after its completion.

57. (C) The training period, since it is only to last thirty hours, should not be extended over too long a period. It should not be permitted to interfere excessively with the regular performance of work either.

58.   (A) This lecture covers a new procedure. Whenever new material is to be taught, each point must be thoroughly cleared up before the instructor may go on to the next part of the program.

59.   (B) It is true that the function of the conference leader is to stimulate the participants to contribute during the conference. However, if the correction of an obvious mistake is not forthcoming, it would be the duty of the conference leader to supply the correction in order to continue the conference's objectivity.

60.   (A) If a trainee is not convinced of the value of the material learned during a training program, he or she will not put it into practice.

61.   (A and D) This course of action has both undesirable and desirable aspects. The participants in the training conference are bound to learn from the experiences of the two active participants. However, this is a conference and a conference calls for the participation of all its members. Other points of view brought forward may be valuable and the conference leader should induce the other members to contribute whatever they are able to.

62.   (A) What may seem trivial in the mind of the Principal Administrative Associate evidently is not trivial in the mind of Mr. Smith.

63.   (A) It is definitely not the function of a supervisor to be concerned with which subordinate is likely to develop maladjustments sometime in the future. The supervisor should be concerned mainly with the problems which are in existence at the present time.

64. (B) A list of the skills and abilities needed to perform the work of the agency will, in itself, be of least value toward accomplishment of the effective utilization and development of personnel. The other choices contain information which is much more objective.

65. (D) This is the time the trainee needs to be encouraged. A discouraged trainee is not receptive to training.

66. (C) Generally, a worker will produce only what is expected, even if capable of producing more.

67. (C) When workers are permitted to participate in the formation of policies that affect their work, they are likely to cooperate in their implementation. From a management viewpoint, much can be learned from those closest to the actual work.

68. (A) Grapevines in an organization can and do serve a useful purpose. Note that this choice does not mention that the information has been deliberately withheld by management.

69. (C) One of the main advantages of the questionnaire method of obtaining information is that it is economical. Many people can be reached at a slight cost, as opposed to the personal interview method, which is both costly and time-consuming.

70. (B) An evaluation of a procedure must be kept objective. Actually, an administrator in the process of taking a survey to determine the effectiveness of a procedure can obtain the results he desires by limiting his selection of data to that which will serve to support his feelings concerning the matter.

71. (D) The heights of these males could not be normally distributed; they were taken from a select group. A normal distribution of any factor will result only if the sampling is representative of the whole item.

72. (C) Refer to the eighth line, but they must also be workable in the sense ....

73. (D) Refer to the third sentence in the paragraph.

74. (A) The result of the condition described in the question is definitely of no value.

75. (B) This paragraph speaks of the attributes of satisfactory performance standards -- not of their evaluation or adoption. The title in choice (D) is far off base and does not relate to the subject matter in the paragraph at all.

76. (B) This thought is made quite clear in the fifth sentence, which begins, If management expects full cooperation from employees ....

77. (C) The principal thought brought out in this paragraph is that good personnel relations are based on employee trust of the intentions of management. Although the information explaining why management acts as it does will lead to good personnel relations, there is nothing in the paragraph which implies that a desire for this information on the part of the workers must exist before good personnel relations in an organization can be accomplished.

78. (B) This thought is brought out in the final sentence of the paragraph.

79. (A) Of the titles contained in the four choices, this title is by far the best. The paragraph is essentially about the basis or foundation of good personnel relations in an organization.

80. (D) This paragraph covers all of the aspects of management. It goes beyond the planning phase and does not limit itself to the so-called successful organization. It is not principally devoted to the organizational objectives alone either.

81. (B) This is brought out in the third sentence, which begins, <u>The nature of the objectives</u> ....

82. (C) This paragraph states that the establishment of organizational objectives must be an accomplished fact before executive leadership can take over and do its part of the overall job. This thought is brought out in the third sentence of the paragraph.

83. (D) This thought is brought out in the final sentence of the paragraph which states that the control factor in an organization consists of seeing to it that the predetermined performance standards are being met up and down the line.

84. (A) One can best visualize the formula presented in this answer by assigning number values for each of the letters given.

85. (B) The total salaries paid for each year and the number of employees are indicated on the charts. The average salary for 1981 and 1982 can be obtained by dividing the number of employees into the total salaries paid for each of the two years. The difference can then be obtained by subtracting one result from the other.

The information in the other choices cannot be obtained from the facts presented in the charts.

86. (B) 1978

Units of work produced - 800,000.
Number of employees - 250 (100 female, 150 male).
Divide 250 into 800,000.
Result - 3,200 units of work produced by each employee during the year 1978.

1976

Units of work produced - 600,000.
Number of employees - 200 (75 male, 125 female).
Divide 200 into 600,000.
Result - 3,000 units of work produced by each employee during the year 1976.

87. (C)

Total of 250 employees in the year 1982 (100 male, 150 female). 20% of total (50) were over 55. ½ of this total of 50 (25) averaged $8,400 in salary during that year.
Total amount paid to these employees (25) was $8,400 multiplied by 25.
Result - $210,000.
Total salaries paid to all employees during 1982 - $1,800,000 (from chart).
Subtract $210,000 from $1,800,000.
Result - $1,590,000.
Subtract 25 employees (accounted for previously) from total of 250.
Result - 225.
For average of remaining employees' salaries, divide 225 into $1,590,000.
Result - $7,066.67. Nearest to answer (C), $7,060.

88. (C) During the year 1973, 550,000 units of work were produced in all of the five boroughs. The offices in Richmond and the Bronx each produced 1/8 of that total while the offices in the other three boroughs produced twice that amount of 1/4 of the total each. (Refer to information in the question.)

  1973 offices in Brooklyn produced 1/4 of the 550,000 units of work - 137,500 units of work.

From the pie chart, we can then determine that the borough of Brooklyn increased its output of work by 63,500 units in 1982 over the year 1973.

Add 63,500 to 137,500. Result - 201,000 units of work produced in the offices of Brooklyn in the year 1982.

89. (D) Total salaries paid during the year 1980 - $1,200,000. Total employees - 175 (100 males, 75 females).

This question can be answered most easily by utilizing the answers given in the choices. One begins at choice (A) using the salary of the males because it is easier to multiply by 100. (Move the decimal point two places to the right). Multiply $7,500 by 100. Result - $750,000. If this was the total deduction paid to male employees for that year, we can then deduct that amount from $1,200,000 and we would have the total paid to the female employees - $450,000. This figure can be divided by the total of 75 female employees, giving us an answer of $6,000 as the average salary paid to female employees during the year 1980. This figure proves to be 80% of the $7,500 paid to each male employee. From these figures an answer can be selected, (D) - which can be proven to be correct on the basis of the information given in the question.

90. (A) Total number of employees for the year 1973 - 200 (75 male, 125 female). 55% of that total were over 30 years of age - 110.

Therefore a minimum of 35 of the employees over 30 years of age must have been females because if all of the males were over 30 years of age, we would still have only a total of 75.

Now use the information supplied to you above which was selected from the chart showing the distribution by ages by percent and the bar chart indicating the number of female and male employees in the bureau. Try working out the information supplied in the other choices and you will determine that none of the information in the other choices can be substantiated.

Part 2

MODEL ANSWER-ESSAY QUESTION

To: Head of City Department   Subject: Training Course for Newly
                                              Appointed Supervisors
From: John Doe   Date: March 12, 1982

I.

1. Review of Basis of Existence of Agency
2. Rules and Regulations of Department Applicable to
   Supervisors and their Subordinates

For this part of the course, lectures would be appropriate for the
dispensing of new material while conferences could be used for the
balance.

II.

1. Human Relations in Supervision

    (A) Handling of Grievances   (E) Public Relations
    (B) Extending Recognition to   (F) Discipline
        the Subordinates   (G) Employee Suggestion
    (C) Training   Program
    (D) Employee Rating   (H) Safety at Work
                                      (I) Behavior on the Job

This part of the course can be taught by utilizing the lecture and
conference methods as well as using audio and visual aids whenever
possible. Role-playing would also be suitable to demonstrate correct
public relations and the safe way to work.

III.

1. Administration

    (A) Planning   (D) Staffing
    (B) Organizing   (E) Report Writing
    (C) Budgeting   (F) Coordinating the Work of
                                          the Unit

The lecture and conference methods would be suitable for the
dispensing of this part of the training.

The effectiveness of this training program may be evaluated in the
following manner:

1. Observation of trainees on the job after completion of
   training.
2. Service ratings of trainees and their subordinates.

3. Production records.
4. A comparison of the results of an examination given to the trainees before and after completion of the course.
5. Determination of the amount of the material taught in the training course which is subsequently put into practice by the trainees.
6. Determination of the level of morale of the units which trainees are assigned to supervise.
7. A questionnaire which the trainee is required to complete after the training course to determine his or her reaction to it.

JOHN DOE

ANSWER SHEET FOR SAMPLE PRACTICE EXAMINATION II

1 Ⓐ Ⓑ Ⓒ Ⓓ   26 Ⓐ Ⓑ Ⓒ Ⓓ   51 Ⓐ Ⓑ Ⓒ Ⓓ   76 Ⓐ Ⓑ Ⓒ Ⓓ

2 Ⓐ Ⓑ Ⓒ Ⓓ   27 Ⓐ Ⓑ Ⓒ Ⓓ   52 Ⓐ Ⓑ Ⓒ Ⓓ   77 Ⓐ Ⓑ Ⓒ Ⓓ

3 Ⓐ Ⓑ Ⓒ Ⓓ   28 Ⓐ Ⓑ Ⓒ Ⓓ   53 Ⓐ Ⓑ Ⓒ Ⓓ   78 Ⓐ Ⓑ Ⓒ Ⓓ

4 Ⓐ Ⓑ Ⓒ Ⓓ   29 Ⓐ Ⓑ Ⓒ Ⓓ   54 Ⓐ Ⓑ Ⓒ Ⓓ   79 Ⓐ Ⓑ Ⓒ Ⓓ

5 Ⓐ Ⓑ Ⓒ Ⓓ   30 Ⓐ Ⓑ Ⓒ Ⓓ   55 Ⓐ Ⓑ Ⓒ Ⓓ   80 Ⓐ Ⓑ Ⓒ Ⓓ

6 Ⓐ Ⓑ Ⓒ Ⓓ   31 Ⓐ Ⓑ Ⓒ Ⓓ   56 Ⓐ Ⓑ Ⓒ Ⓓ   81 Ⓐ Ⓑ Ⓒ Ⓓ

7 Ⓐ Ⓑ Ⓒ Ⓓ   32 Ⓐ Ⓑ Ⓒ Ⓓ   57 Ⓐ Ⓑ Ⓒ Ⓓ   82 Ⓐ Ⓑ Ⓒ Ⓓ

8 Ⓐ Ⓑ Ⓒ Ⓓ   33 Ⓐ Ⓑ Ⓒ Ⓓ   58 Ⓐ Ⓑ Ⓒ Ⓓ   83 Ⓐ Ⓑ Ⓒ Ⓓ

9 Ⓐ Ⓑ Ⓒ Ⓓ   34 Ⓐ Ⓑ Ⓒ Ⓓ   59 Ⓐ Ⓑ Ⓒ Ⓓ   84 Ⓐ Ⓑ Ⓒ Ⓓ

10 Ⓐ Ⓑ Ⓒ Ⓓ   35 Ⓐ Ⓑ Ⓒ Ⓓ   60 Ⓐ Ⓑ Ⓒ Ⓓ   85 Ⓐ Ⓑ Ⓒ Ⓓ

11 Ⓐ Ⓑ Ⓒ Ⓓ   36 Ⓐ Ⓑ Ⓒ Ⓓ   61 Ⓐ Ⓑ Ⓒ Ⓓ   86 Ⓐ Ⓑ Ⓒ Ⓓ

12 Ⓐ Ⓑ Ⓒ Ⓓ   37 Ⓐ Ⓑ Ⓒ Ⓓ   62 Ⓐ Ⓑ Ⓒ Ⓓ   87 Ⓐ Ⓑ Ⓒ Ⓓ

13 Ⓐ Ⓑ Ⓒ Ⓓ   38 Ⓐ Ⓑ Ⓒ Ⓓ   63 Ⓐ Ⓑ Ⓒ Ⓓ   88 Ⓐ Ⓑ Ⓒ Ⓓ

14 Ⓐ Ⓑ Ⓒ Ⓓ   39 Ⓐ Ⓑ Ⓒ Ⓓ   64 Ⓐ Ⓑ Ⓒ Ⓓ   89 Ⓐ Ⓑ Ⓒ Ⓓ

15 Ⓐ Ⓑ Ⓒ Ⓓ   40 Ⓐ Ⓑ Ⓒ Ⓓ   65 Ⓐ Ⓑ Ⓒ Ⓓ   90 Ⓐ Ⓑ Ⓒ Ⓓ

16 Ⓐ Ⓑ Ⓒ Ⓓ   41 Ⓐ Ⓑ Ⓒ Ⓓ   66 Ⓐ Ⓑ Ⓒ Ⓓ   91 Ⓐ Ⓑ Ⓒ Ⓓ

17 Ⓐ Ⓑ Ⓒ Ⓓ   42 Ⓐ Ⓑ Ⓒ Ⓓ   67 Ⓐ Ⓑ Ⓒ Ⓓ   92 Ⓐ Ⓑ Ⓒ Ⓓ

18 Ⓐ Ⓑ Ⓒ Ⓓ   43 Ⓐ Ⓑ Ⓒ Ⓓ   68 Ⓐ Ⓑ Ⓒ Ⓓ   93 Ⓐ Ⓑ Ⓒ Ⓓ

19 Ⓐ Ⓑ Ⓒ Ⓓ   44 Ⓐ Ⓑ Ⓒ Ⓓ   69 Ⓐ Ⓑ Ⓒ Ⓓ   94 Ⓐ Ⓑ Ⓒ Ⓓ

20 Ⓐ Ⓑ Ⓒ Ⓓ   45 Ⓐ Ⓑ Ⓒ Ⓓ   70 Ⓐ Ⓑ Ⓒ Ⓓ   95 Ⓐ Ⓑ Ⓒ Ⓓ

21 Ⓐ Ⓑ Ⓒ Ⓓ   46 Ⓐ Ⓑ Ⓒ Ⓓ   71 Ⓐ Ⓑ Ⓒ Ⓓ   96 Ⓐ Ⓑ Ⓒ Ⓓ

22 Ⓐ Ⓑ Ⓒ Ⓓ   47 Ⓐ Ⓑ Ⓒ Ⓓ   72 Ⓐ Ⓑ Ⓒ Ⓓ   97 Ⓐ Ⓑ Ⓒ Ⓓ

23 Ⓐ Ⓑ Ⓒ Ⓓ   48 Ⓐ Ⓑ Ⓒ Ⓓ   73 Ⓐ Ⓑ Ⓒ Ⓓ   98 Ⓐ Ⓑ Ⓒ Ⓓ

24 Ⓐ Ⓑ Ⓒ Ⓓ   49 Ⓐ Ⓑ Ⓒ Ⓓ   74 Ⓐ Ⓑ Ⓒ Ⓓ   99 Ⓐ Ⓑ Ⓒ Ⓓ

25 Ⓐ Ⓑ Ⓒ Ⓓ   50 Ⓐ Ⓑ Ⓒ Ⓓ   75 Ⓐ Ⓑ Ⓒ Ⓓ   100 Ⓐ Ⓑ Ⓒ Ⓓ

SAMPLE PRACTICE EXAMINATION II

DIRECTIONS FOR ANSWERING QUESTIONS

Each question has four suggested answers, lettered A, B,
C, and D. Decide which one is the best answer and on the
sample answer sheet find the question number and darken
the area with a soft pencil which corresponds to the
answer that you have selected.

Time allowed for the entire Examination: 4 Hours

1. The one of the following which best characterizes an agency in
    which delegation of authority is practiced on an organization-wide
    level is that the agency is

    (A) autocratic   (C) centralized
    (B) authoritarian   (D) decentralized.

2. The concept of the "chain of command" is most similar to which
    one of the following concepts?

    (A) span of control
    (B) matrix of task-force organization
    (C) scalar principle
    (D) functional departmentation.

3. The one of the following techniques which is <u>not</u> conducive to
    the establishment of an effective working relationship between
    employees and supervisors is

    (A) periodic discussion of job performance with employees
    (B) listening to employees when they discuss their job
        difficulties
    (C) observation of employees on the job, in both individual and
        group situations, in order to help them with job performance
    (D) treating all employees the same with respect to job
        performance and individual behavior.

4. Which of the following is a valid, commonly-raised objection to the establishment of work standards for office clerical workers?

(A) Routine clerical work is not subject to accurate measurement.
(B) Clerical work standards can only lower employee morale by creating undue pressure to produce work rapidly.
(C) Work standards are not effective tools for planning, scheduling, and routing clerical work.
(D) Some phases of many clerical jobs, such as telephone answering or information gathering, cannot be readily or accurately measured.

5. Of the following, the feature which is least characteristic of almost all successful staff relationships with line managers is that the staff employee

(A) is primarily a representative of the supervisor
(B) receives a salary at least equal to the average salary of the supervisor's direct line subordinates
(C) relies largely on persuasion to get his or her ideas put into effect
(D) is prepared to submerge his or her own personality and desire for recognition and see others often receive more recognition than he or she receives.

6. The one of the following systems which has, as its principle objective, the storage of items in files so that they may be readily found when needed is called

(A) information retrieval   (C) critical path
(B) simulation   (D) PERT.

7. A detailed description of the steps to be taken in order to accomplish a job is most appropriately called a

(A) policy   (C) procedure
(B) rule   (D) principle.

8. In choosing the best place in the executive hierarchy to which to assign the task of making a certain type of decision, which one of the following questions should normally be least important?

(A) Who knows the facts on which the decision will be based, or who can obtain them most readily?
(B) Who has the most adequate supply of current forms on which the decision is normally recorded?
(C) Who has the capacity to make sound decisions?
(D) How significant is the decision?

9. Of the following, the action which is least likely to be either expressed or implied every time a manager delegates work to a

subordinate is that the manager

(A) creates a need for a new class of positions
(B) indicates what work the subordinate is to do
(C) grants the subordinate some authority
(D) creates an obligation for the subordinate who accepts the work to try to complete it.

10. Of the following, the <u>least</u> appropriate use of organizational charts is to

(A) depict standard operating procedures
(B) indicate lines of responsibility
(C) indicate the relative level of key positions
(D) portray organizations graphically.

11. The one of the following considerations which is generally <u>least</u> important in deciding whether to automate a management operation by using a computer is whether the computer

(A) possesses a suitable array of programmed actions that might be taken
(B) can draw upon available data for information as to which alternative is best
(C) is already familiar to the staff of the organization
(D) can issue findings in a way that will facilitate the decision-making process.

12. In evaluating a proposal to establish a library in your agency, it is generally considered <u>least</u> necessary to determine

(A) the average time staff members spend on preparatory research when assigned to projects
(B) how often junior professional and technical staff members are sent out to "look something up" in a local library
(C) how much time and money agency executives devote to telephoning around the country seeking information before making decisions
(D) the quality of the research done by executives and scientists in the agency.

13. In determining the number and type of tasks that should be combined into a single job, the one of the following which is normally the <u>least</u> useful factor to consider is the

(A) benefit of functional specialization
(B) benefit of tall pyramid organization structure in increasing decentralization
(C) need for coordination of tasks with each other
(D) effect of the tasks assigned on the morale of the employee.

14. Of the following, the one which is <u>least</u> likely to be an objective of systems and procedures analysis is to

   (A) eliminate as many unessential forms and records as feasible
   (B) simplify forms in content and method of preparation
   (C) mechanize repetitive, routine tasks
   (D) expand as many of the forms as possible.

15. A specific managerial function encompasses all of the following: "the establishment of an intentional structure of roles through determination and enumeration of the activities required to achieve the goals of an enterprise and each part of it, the grouping of these activities, the assignment of such groups of activities to a manager, the delegation of authority to carry them out, and provision for coordination of authority and informational relationships horizontally and vertically in the organization structure." Of the following, the most appropriate term for this entire managerial function is

   (A) organizing   (C) controlling
   (B) directing   (D) staffing.

16. The optimum number of subordinates that a supervisor can supervise effectively generally tends to vary <u>inversely</u> with the

   (A) percentage of the supervisor's time devoted to supervision rather than operations
   (B) repetition of activities
   (C) degree of centralization of decision-making within the supervisor's unit
   (D) ability of subordinates.

17. Under certain circumstances, a top manager may desire to strengthen the position of staff people by granting them concurring authority, so that no action may be taken in a functional area by subordinate line officials until a designated staff employee agrees to the action. For example, office managers may have to get the approval of the agency personnel officer before hiring a new employee. This approach is likely to be most valid under which one of the following conditions?

   (A) The top manager refrains from indicating the grounds on which the staff employee may grant or withhold approval of line proposals.
   (B) The point of view represented by the staff employee is particularly important and the possible delay in action will not be serious.
   (C) It is more important to fix specific accountability for failure to take appropriate action than for wrong actions taken.
   (D) The top manager gives speed priority over prudence.

18. The inclusion of the "reason why" by a superior in written orders
to subordinates normally is most likely to

(A) encourage belief by the subordinates in the meaning and intent
of the order
(B) be a waste of valuable time for both superior and subordinates
(C) be useful principally where the superior has no power to
enforce the order
(D) discourage effective two-way communication between superior
and subordinates.

19. The one of the following which is generally the best justification
for an administrator's search for alternative methods of
attaining a given objective of the unit is that such search

(A) always turns up a better method of attaining objectives than
that currently in use
(B) helps to make certain that the best method has a chance to be
found and evaluated
(C) helps to insure that peers realize that the existing method
of attaining the objective is not the best
(D) is a good way to train the unit's staff in the organization's
operational procedures.

20. "Managing-by-objectives" tends to place principal emphasis upon
which one of the following?

(A) Use of primarily qualitative goals at all management levels.
(B) Use of trait-appraisal systems based upon personality
factors.
(C) Use of primarily qualitative goals at lower management
levels as contrasted with primarily quantitative goals at
higher management levels.
(D) Goals which are clear and verifiable.

21. Which one of the following best identifies the two most important
considerations which generally should determine the degree of
management decentralization desirable in a given situation?

(A) 1. The age of the subordinate executives to whom decisions
may be delegated and
2. The number of courses in management that they have
completed.
(B) 1. The number of skills and the competence possessed by
subordinate executives and
2. The distribution of the necessary information to the points
of decision.
(C) 1. The ratio of the salary of the superior executives to the
salary of the subordinate executives and
2. The number of titles on the executive staff.
(D) 1. The number of titles in the executive staff and
2. The distribution of information to those various titles.

22. The one of the following which is a basic advantage of a microform record system (e.g., microfilm, microfiche) over a conventional filing system is that a microform system

    (A) provides a compact method of grouping and systematizing records
    (B) provides records which are immediately available without special equipment
    (C) eliminates the need for specially trained personnel
    (D) eliminates entirely the inadvertent loss of records.

23. In the planning of office space for the various bureaus and divisions of an agency, the one of the following arrangements which is generally considered to be most desirable in a conventional layout is to

    (A) locate offices where employees do close and tedious work, such as accounting, and also offices of high-level executives away from windows, so that distractions will be minimal
    (B) locate "housekeeping" offices such as data processing and the mail room very close to the high executive offices, to increase convenience for the executives
    (C) locate departments so that the work flow proceeds in an uninterrupted manner
    (D) centralize the executive suite for maximum availability and public exposure.

24. Generally, the one of the following that is <u>least</u> likely to be an essential step in a records retention plan is

    (A) storing inactive records
    (B) checking for accuracy of all records to be retained
    (C) classification of all records
    (D) making an inventory of all agency records.

25. Which of the following is generally <u>least</u> likely to occur at mid-level management as a result of installing an electronic data processing system?

    (A) The time that managers will be required to spend on the controlling function will increase.
    (B) The number of contacts that managers will have with subordinates will increase.
    (C) Additional time will be needed to train people for managerial positions.
    (D) There will be an increase in the volume of information presented to managers for analysis.

26. The concept that the major source of managerial authority is derived from the subordinate's acceptance of the manager's power is most closely identified with

(A) Luther Gulick   (C) Frederick W. Taylor
(B) John D. Mooney   (D) Chester I. Barnard.

27. The one of the following which is generally the principal objection to a pure "functional organization," as compared with a pure "line organization," is that

(A) there is a tendency to overload intermediate and supervisory management at each succeeding level of organization with wide and varied duties
(B) authority flows in an unbroken line from top management to the worker
(C) workers must often report to two or more supervisors
(D) there is a lack of specialization at the supervisory level.

28. In the development of a sound employee relations program in a government agency, administrators have found that increased efficiency is obtained when

(A) employees are invited to consult and participate in the solution of personnel problems
(B) discussion is avoided by having the administrator make all decisions without consulting the employees
(C) decisions are made by administrators other than the immediate supervisors
(D) there are comprehensive rules and regulations to cover every situation.

29. The principal asset of an office layout diagram, as contrasted with the more abstract organization charts and flowcharts, is that an office layout diagram is

(A) more readily adaptable to strictly conceptual studies
(B) pictorial and therefore easier to understand
(C) suitable for showing both manual and machine processing operations whereas organization charts and flowcharts may only be used for manual processing operations
(D) better suited for summarizing the number of work units produced at each step.

30. One of the Office Associates whom you supervise displays apparent familiarity toward a businessman who deals with your agency. This Office Associate spends more time with this person than the nature of the business would warrant, and you have observed that they are occasionally seen leaving the office together for lunch. In several instances, when this businessman comes into the office and this Office Associate is not at his desk, the businessman will not deal with any other staff member, but will, instead, leave the office and return later when that particular employee is available. Of the following courses of action, the <u>first</u> one you should take is to

(A) audit the agency's books and records pertaining to this businessman

(B) rebuke the Office Associate for unprofessional conduct at the next staff meeting, and warn him of disciplinary action if the practice is not discontinued forthwith

(C) advise your agency head of the action by the businessman and the Office Associate described in the paragraph

(D) reassign the Office Associate to duties that will not bring him into contact with any businessmen.

31. The one of the following factors which generally is the best justification for keeping higher inventories of supplies and equipment is an expected

(A) decline in demand
(B) price increase
(C) decline in prices
(D) increase in interest charges and storage costs.

32. Statistical sampling is often used in administrative operations primarily because it enables

(A) administrators to determine the characteristics of appointed or elected officials
(B) decisions to be made based on mathematical and scientific fact
(C) courses of action to be determined by scientifically-based computer programs
(D) useful predictions to be made from relatively small samples.

33. According to United States Department of Labor figures, the principal source of disabling injuries to office workers is

(A) flying objects and falling objects
(B) striking against equipment
(C) falls and slips
(D) handling materials.

34. To expedite the processing of applications issued by your agency, you ask your assistant to design a form that will be used by your typists. After several discussions, he presents you with a draft that requires the typist to use 23 tabular-stop positions. Such a form would probably be considered

(A) undesirable; typists would now have to soft-roll the platen to make the typing fall on the lines
(B) desirable; the fill-in operation by typists would be speeded up
(C) undesirable; proper vertical alignment of data would be made difficult by the number of tabular-stop positions required
(D) desirable; it would force typists to utilize the tabular-stop device.

Following are five general instructions to file clerks which might appear in a proposed filing manual for an agency:

1. Follow instructions generally; if you have a suggestion for improvement in the filing methods, install it after notifying the file supervisor who will duly authorize a change in the manual.
2. You may discuss the contents of files with fellow employees or outsiders, but do <u>not</u> give papers from the file to any person whose duties have no relation to the material requested.
3. All special instructions must be given by the file supervisor. Any problems that arise outside the regular routine of filing must be decided by the file supervisor, not by a fellow clerk.
4. You will not be held responsible for your own errors; thus refrain from asking other workers for instructions. No one is more interested in helping you in your training than your file supervisor.
5. Speed is the first essential in filing; make it your primary consideration -- quick finding of filed material is the real test of your efficiency.

35. Which of the choices listed below best identifies those statements that should or should not be followed by agencies in the functioning of their filing sections?

(A) Instructions 1, 2, 3 should be followed;
Instructions 4, 5 should not be followed.
(B) Instruction 3 should be followed;
Instructions 1, 2, 4, 5 should not be followed.
(C) Instructions 2, 4 should be followed;
Instructions 1, 3, 5 should not be followed.
(D) Instructions 1, 3 should be followed;
Instructions 2, 4, 5 should not be followed.

Each of questions <u>36</u> through <u>40</u> consists of a quotation which contains one word that is incorrectly used because it is not in keeping with the meaning that the quotation is evidently intended to convey. Determine which word is incorrectly used. Select from the choices lettered (A), (B), (C), and (D) the word which, when substituted for the incorrectly used word, would <u>best</u> help to convey the meaning of the quotation.

36. "Whatever the method, the necessity to keep up with the dynamics of an organization is the point on which many classification plans go awry. The budgetary approach to 'positions,' for example, often leads to using for recruitment and pay purposes a position authorized many years earlier for quite a different purpose than currently contemplated -- making perhaps the title, the class,

and the qualifications required inappropriate to the current
need. This happens because executives overlook the stability
that takes place in job duties and fail to reread an initial
description of the job before saying, as they scan a list of
titles, 'We should fill this position right away.' Once a
classification plan is adopted, it is pointless to do anything
less than provide for continuous, painstaking maintenance on a
current basis, else once different positions that have actually
become similar to each other remain in different classes, and
some former cognates that have become quite different continue in
the same class. Such a program often seems expensive. But to
stint too much on this out-of-pocket cost may create still
higher hidden costs growing out of lowered morale, poor production,
delayed operating programs, excessive pay for simple work, and
low pay for responsible work (resulting in poorly qualified
executives and professionals) -- all normal concomitants of
inadequate, hasty, or out-of-date classification."

(A) evolution
(B) personnel
(C) disapproved
(D) forward.

37. "At first sight it may seem that there is little or no difference
between the usableness of a manual and the degree of its use.
But there is a difference. A manual may have all the qualities
which make up the usable manual and still not be used. Take this
instance as an example: Suppose you have a satisfactory manual
but issue instructions from day to day through the avenue of
bulletins, memorandums, and other informational releases. Which
will the employee use, the manual or the bulletin which passes
over his desk? He will, of course, use the latter, for some
obsolete material will not be contained in this manual. Here we
have a theoretically usable manual which is unused because of the
other avenues by which procedural information may be issued."

(A) countermand
(B) discard
(C) intentional
(D) worthwhile.

38. "By reconcentrating control over its operations in a central
headquarters, a firm is able to extend the influence of automation
to many, if not all, of its functions -- from inventory and
payroll to production, sales, and personnel. In so doing,
businesses freeze all the elements of the corporate function in
their relationship to one another and to the overall objectives
of the firm. From this total systems concept, companies learn
that computers can accomplish much more than clerical and
accounting jobs. Their capabilities can be tapped to perform the
traditional applications (payroll processing, inventory control,
accounts payable, and accounts receivable) as well as newer
applications such as spotting deviations from planned programs
(exception reporting), adjusting planning schedules, forecasting

business trends, simulating market conditions, and solving production problems. Since the office manager is a manager of information and each of these applications revolves around the processing of data, he must take an active role in studying and improving the system under his care."

(A) maintaining
(B) inclusion
(C) limited
(D) visualize.

39. "In addition to the formal and acceptance theories of the source of authority, although perhaps more closely related to the latter, is the belief that authority is generated by personal qualities of technical competence. Under this heading is the individual who has made, in effect, subordinates of others through sheer force of personality, and the engineer or economist who exerts influence by furnishing answers or sound advice. These may have no actual organizational authority, yet their advice may be so eagerly sought and so unerringly followed that it appears to carry the weight of an order.
But, above all, one cannot discount the importance of formal authority with its institutional foundations. Buttressed by the qualities of leadership implicit in the acceptance theory, formal authority is basic to the managerial job. Once abrogated, it may be delegated or withheld, used or misused, and be effective in capable hands or be ineffective in inept hands."

(A) selected
(B) delegation
(C) limited
(D) possessed.

40. "Since managerial operations in organizing, staffing, directing, and controlling are designed to support the accomplishment of enterprise objectives, planning logically precedes the execution of all other managerial functions. Although all the functions intermesh in practice, planning is unique in that it establishes the objectives necessary for all group effort. Besides, plans must be made to accomplish these objectives before the manager knows what kind of organization relationships and personal qualifications are needed, along which course subordinates are to be directed, and what kind of control is to be applied. And, of course, each of the other managerial functions must be planned if they are to be effective.
Planning and control are inseparable -- the Siamese twins of management. Unplanned action cannot be controlled, for control involves keeping activities on course by correcting deviations from plans. Any attempt to control without plans would be meaningless, since there is no way anyone can tell whether he is going where he wants to go -- the task of control -- unless first he knows where he wants to go -- the task of planning. Plans thus preclude the standards of control."

(A) coordinating
(B) individual
(C) furnish
(D) follow.

41. A person has been working in a city agency as a permanent employee in the title of Office Aide from January 1, 1978 to the present on the basis of the normal five-day week. He has had no other city service. Under the provisions of the Leave Regulations for Career and Salary Plan Employees, he is entitled to an Annual Leave Allowance of

(A) 14 work days   (C) 23 work days
(B) 20 work days   (D) 26 work days.

42. In a Personnel Policy and Procedure Bulletin, the City Personnel Director reminded city agencies of certain requirements relating to nomination or appointment of provisionals pursuant to Civil Service Rule 5.5.1. It was indicated in that bulletin that it is incumbent upon city agencies not to nominate or appoint a provisional under that rule if

(A) the nominee for provisional appointment has served in another title as a provisional within the preceding fiscal year
(B) the nominee for provisional appointment would receive a salary increase of more than 5% over his most recent salary prior to appointment
(C) there is an adequate eligible list in existence for the title
(D) an open-competitive examination has been ordered for the title within the past three months.

43. Listed below are five steps in the process of staffing:

1) authorization for staffing
2) manpower planning
3) development of applicant sources
4) evaluation of applicants
5) employment decisions and offers

The one of the following sequences which is generally the most logical arrangement of the above steps is

(A) 1), 2), 3), 4), 5)   (C) 3), 1), 2), 4), 5)
(B) 2), 1), 3), 4), 5)   (D) 2), 3), 1), 4), 5)

44. Job enrichment is least likely to lead to

(A) fewer employee grievances
(B) increased employee productivity
(C) people acting as adjuncts of increased automation
(D) increased employee morale.

45. Of the following, programmed instruction would usually be most effective in teaching

    (A) principles of decision-making
    (B) technical skills and knowledge
    (C) good judgment
    (D) executive management ability.

46. Of the following, the main purpose of systematic manpower planning is to

    (A) analyze the levels of skill needed by each worker
    (B) analyze causes of current vacancies, such as resignations, discharges, retirements, transfers, or promotions
    (C) save money by eliminating useless jobs
    (D) provide for the continuous and proper staffing of the workforce.

47. Many functions formerly centralized in the Department of Personnel have been decentralized, in whole or in part, to operating city agencies. The one of the following personnel functions which has been least decentralized is

    (A) position evaluation
    (B) investigation of non-competitive employees
    (C) investigation of competitive employees
    (D) jurisdictional classification.

48. The appraisal of subordinates and their performance is an integral part of the supervisor's job. There is wide agreement that several basic principles must be taken into account by supervisors involved in the appraisal process in order to perform this function correctly. The one of the statements below which least represents a basic principle of the appraisal process is:

    (A) appraisals should be based more on performance of definite tasks than on personality considerations
    (B) appraisal of long-range potential should rely most heavily on subjective judgment of that potential
    (C) appraisal involves the use of value judgments by the supervisor and does, therefore, require reference to pre-established standards
    (D) appraisal should aim at emphasizing subordinates' strengths rather than weaknesses.

49. The "grievance-arbitration" process involves systematic union-management deliberation regarding a complaint that is work- or contract-related. An outcome that does not result from this process is

    (A) a communications channel from the rank-and-file-workers to higher management is developed or improved

(B) the contract is immediately changed to provide justice for both parties

(C) both labor and management identify those parts of the contract that need to be clarified and modified in subsequent negotiations

(D) the language of the agreement is informally translated into understandable terms for the parties bound by it.

50. In city government, job evaluation is the process of determining the relative worth of the various jobs in an organization, so that differential wages can be paid. Job evaluation is based on several basic assumptions. Of the assumptions listed below, the most questionable is that

(A) the cash payments in government should be substantially higher than those in local private industry

(B) it is logical to pay the most for jobs that contribute most to the organization

(C) people feel more fairly treated if wages are based on the relative worth of their jobs

(D) the best way to achieve the goals of the enterprise is to maintain a wage structure based on job worth.

51. Of the following, the training method that normally provides the instructor with the least "feedback" from the trainees is

(A) the lecture method
(B) the conference method
(C) simulation or gaming techniques
(D) programmed instruction.

52. Insufficient and inappropriate delegation of work assignments is most often the fault of

(A) subordinates who are unwilling to accept responsibility for their own mistakes
(B) a paternal attitude on the part of management
(C) the immediate supervisor
(D) subordinates who are too willing to take on extra responsibility.

53. As contrasted with expense budgets, capital budgets are more likely to

(A) be used for construction of physical facilities
(B) be designed for a shorter time period
(C) include personal service expenditures
(D) include fringe benefits.

54. Assume that, in a New York City department, Employee X has served as a permanent Office Aide for two years and Employee Y has

served as a permanent Office Aide for four years. Neither has ever served as an Office Associate. Now, both Employee X and Employee Y are being promoted to Office Associate from the departmental promotion list. According to the Rules and Regulations of the New York City Department of Personnel, unless the appointing officer waives the requirement of satisfactory completion of the probationary term, or terminates the employment of the probationer earlier, generally, Employee X

(A) will have a probationary period of three months and Employee Y will have a probationary period of two months
(B) will have a probationary period of four months and Employee Y will have a probationary period of two months
(C) and Employee Y will both have a probationary period of three months
(D) and Employee Y will both have a probationary period of six months.

55. During the first quarter of a year, a division's production rate was 1.26 man-hours per work unit produced. For the second quarter of that year all other factors (e.g., size of staff, character of work unit, etc.) remained constant, except that the manner of reporting production rate was changed to work units per man-hour instead of man-hours per work unit. During that second quarter, the unit's production rate was .89 work units per man-hour. On the basis of the above information, it would be most nearly correct to conclude that the division's production rate during the second quarter was approximately

(A) 30% lower than during the first quarter
(B) 10% lower than during the first quarter
(C) 10% higher than during the first quarter
(D) 30% higher than during the first quarter.

56. New York City budgeting terminology would be most likely to use the abbreviation "O.T.P.S." to include

(A) salaries for permanent employees
(B) salaries for "provisional" employees
(C) salaries for permanent employees under the Managerial Pay Plan
(D) supplies and materials.

57. The largest portion of the New York City Expense Budget is allotted to

(A) capital projects   (C) salaries of city employees
(B) debt service   (D) equipment and supplies.

58. A Planning-Programming-Budget system (PPBS) is primarily intended to do which one of the following?

(A) Improve control through a budgeting-by-line-item system.
(B) Plan and program budgets by objective rather than by function.
(C) Raise money for social welfare programs.
(D) Reduce budgets by planning and programming unspent funds.

Answer questions 59 and 60 on the basis of the following information.

The five bureaus within a department sent the following budget requests to the department head:

```
Bureau  A - $10 million
   "    B - $12 million
   "    C - $18 million
   "    D - $ 6 million
   "    E - $ 4 million
```

After reviewing all of these requests, the department head decided to reduce these requests so that they would total only $40 million. He considered the following two options to accomplish this:

Option I - Reduce the requests of Bureaus A, B, and D by an equal dollar amount. Reduce the dollar amount request of Bureau C by 2½ times the dollar amount that he reduces the request of Bureau B. Reduce the dollar amount request of Bureau E by ½ of the dollar amount that he reduces the request of Bureau B.

Option II - First, reduce the dollar amount request of all five bureaus by 15%. Then the remaining reduction required by the entire department would be achieved by further reducing the resulting budget requests of Bureaus B and C by an equal dollar amount each.

59. Under Option I, the dollar amount request for Bureau E, after reduction by the department head, would be most nearly

(A) $1 2/3 million   (C) $3 1/6 million
(B) $2 1/3 million   (D) $3 1/2 million.

60. Under Option II, the dollar amount of the request of Bureau B, after both reductions were made by the department head, would be most nearly

(A) $8 million   (C) $10 million
(B) $9 million   (D) $11 million.

Answer questions 61 and 62 solely on the basis of information given in the following paragraph.

"In-basket tests are often used to assess managerial potential. The exercise consists of a set of papers that would be likely to be found in the in-basket of an administrator or manager at any given time, and requires the individuals participating in the examination to indicate how they would dispose of each item found in the in-basket. In order to handle the in-basket effectively, they must successfully manage their time, refer and assign some work to subordinates, juggle potentially conflicting appointments and meetings, and arrange for follow-up of problems generated by the items in the in-basket. In other words, the in-basket test is attempting to evaluate the participants' abilities to organize their work, set priorities, delegate, control, and make decisions."

61. According to the preceding paragraph, to succeed in an in-basket test, an administrator must

   (A) be able to read very quickly
   (B) have a great deal of technical knowledge
   (C) know when to delegate work
   (D) arrange a lot of appointments and meetings.

62. According to the preceding paragraph, all of the following abilities are indications of managerial potential, except the ability to

   (A) organize and control
   (B) manage time
   (C) write effective reports
   (D) make appropriate decisions.

Answer questions 63 and 64 solely on the basis of information given in the following paragraph.

"One of the biggest mistakes of government executives with substantial supervisory responsibility is failing to make careful appraisals of performance during employee probationary periods. Many a later headache could have been avoided by prompt and full appraisal during the early months of an employee's assignment. There is not much more to say about this except to emphasize the common prevalence of this oversight and to underscore that for its consequences, which are many and sad, the offending managers have no one to blame but themselves."

63. According to the preceding passage, probationary periods are

   (A) a mistake, and should not be used by supervisors with large responsibilities
   (B) not used properly by government executives
   (C) used only for those with supervisory responsibility
   (D) the consequence of management mistakes.

64. The one of the following conclusions which can most appropriately be drawn from the preceding passage is

(A) management's failure to appraise employees during their probationary period is a common occurrence

(B) there is not much to say about probationary periods, because they are unimportant

(C) managers should blame employees for failing to use their probationary periods properly

(D) probationary periods are a headache to most managers.

Answer questions <u>65</u> - <u>67</u> solely on the basis of information given in the following paragraph.

"The common sense character of the merit system seems so natural to most Americans that many people wonder why it should ever have been inoperative. After all, the American economic system, the most phenomenal the world has ever known, is also founded on a rugged selective process which emphasizes the personal qualities of capacity, industriousness, and productivity. The criteria may not have always been appropriate and competition has not always been fair, but competition there was, and the responsibilities and the rewards -- with exceptions, of course -- have gone to those who could measure up in terms of intelligence, knowledge or perseverance. This has been true not only in the economic area, in the money-making process, but also in achievement in the professions and other walks of life."

65. According to the preceding paragraph, economic rewards in the United States have

(A) always been based on appropriate, fair criteria
(B) only recently been based on a competitive system
(C) not gone to people who compete too ruggedly
(D) usually gone to those people with intelligence, knowledge and perseverance.

66. According to the preceding passage, a merit system is

(A) an unfair criterion on which to base rewards
(B) unnatural to anyone who is not American
(C) based only on common sense
(D) based on the same principles as the American economic system.

67. According to the preceding passage, it is most accurate to say that

(A) the United States has always had a civil service merit system
(B) civil service employees are very rugged
(C) the American economic system has always been based on a merit objective
(D) competition is unique to the American way of life.

The management study of employee absence due to sickness is an effective tool in planning. Answer questions <u>68</u> - <u>70</u> solely on the data given below.

Number of days absent per worker (sickness)	1	2	3	4	5	6	7	8 or Over
Number of workers	76	23	6	3	1	0	1	0

Total Number of Workers: 400
Period covered: January 1, 1982 - Dec. 31, 1982

68. The total number of man-days lost due to illness in 1982 was

   (A) 110   (C) 144
   (B) 137   (D) 164

69. What percent of the workers had 4 or more days absence due to sickness during 1982?

   (A) .25%   (C) 1.25%
   (B) 2.5%   (D) 12.5%

70. Of the 400 workers studied, the number who lost no days due to sickness in 1982 was

   (A) 190   (C) 290
   (B) 236   (D) 346

In the graph below, the lines labeled "A" and "B" represent the cumulative progress in the work of two file clerks, each of whom was given 500 consecutively numbered applications to file in the proper cabinets over a five-day work week. Answer questions <u>71</u> - <u>73</u> solely upon the data provided in the graph.

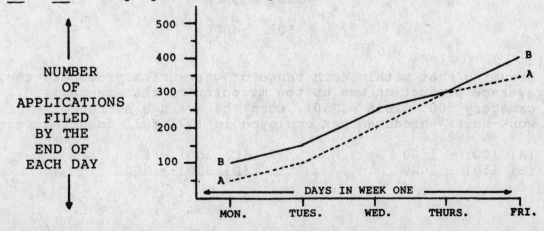

NUMBER OF APPLICATIONS FILED BY THE END OF EACH DAY

DAYS IN WEEK ONE

MON.   TUES.   WED.   THURS.   FRI.

71. The day during which the largest number of applications was filed by both clerks was

    (A) Monday
    (B) Tuesday
    (C) Wednesday
    (D) Friday.

72. At the end of the second day, the percentage of applications still to be filed was

    (A) 25%
    (B) 50%
    (C) 66%
    (D) 75%

73. Assuming that the production pattern is the same the following week as the week shown in the chart, the day on which the file clerks will finish this assignment will be

    (A) Monday
    (B) Tuesday
    (C) Wednesday
    (D) Friday.

The following chart shows the differences between the rates of production of employees in Department D in 1971 and 1981. Answer questions 74 - 76 solely on the basis of the information given in the chart.

Number of Employees Producing Work-Units Within Range in 1971	Number of Work-Units Produced	Number of Employees Producing Work-Units Within Range in 1981
7	500 - 1000	4
14	1001 - 1500	11
26	1501 - 2000	28
22	2001 - 2500	36
17	2501 - 3000	39
10	3001 - 3500	23
4	3501 - 4000	9

74. Assuming that within each range of work-units produced, the average production was at the midpoint of that range (i.e., category 500 - 1000 = 750), then the average number of work-units produced per employee in 1971 fell into the range

    (A) 1001 - 1500
    (B) 1501 - 2000
    (C) 2001 - 2500
    (D) 2501 - 3000

75. The ratio of the number of employees producing more than 2000 work-units in 1971 to the number of employees producing more than 2000 work-units in 1981 is most nearly

    (A) 1:2   (C) 3:4
    (B) 2:3   (D) 4:5

76. In Department D, which of the following were greater in 1981 than in 1971?

        1. Total number of employees
        2. Total number of work-units produced
        3. Number of employees producing 2000 or fewer work-units

    (A) 1, 2 and 3   (C) 1 and 3, but not 2
    (B) 1 and 2, but not 3   (D) 2 and 3, but not 1.

    Assume the following:

    Unit S's production fluctuated substantially from one year to another. In 1979, Unit S's production was 100% greater than in 1978. In 1980, Unit S's production was 25% <u>less</u> than in 1979. In 1981, Unit S's production was 10% greater than in 1980.

77. On the basis of this information, it is correct to conclude that Unit S's production in 1981 exceeded Unit S's production in 1978 by

    (A) 65%   (C) 95%
    (B) 85%   (D) 135%

78. Agency "X" is moving into a new building. It has 1500 employees presently on its staff and does not contemplate much variance from this level. The new building contains 100 available offices each with a maximum capacity of 30 employees. It has been decided that only 2/3 of the maximum capacity of each office will be utilized. The total number of offices that will be occupied by Agency "X" is

    (A) 30   (C) 75
    (B) 66   (D) 90

79. One typist completes a form letter every 5 minutes and another typist completes one every 6 minutes. If the two typists start together, how many minutes later will they again start typing new letters simultaneously and how many letters will they have completed by that time?

    (A) 11 minutes - 30 letters   (C) 24 minutes - 12 letters
    (B) 12 minutes - 24 letters   (D) 30 minutes - 11 letters

80. During one week a machine operator produces 10 fewer pages per hour of work than he usually does. If it ordinarily takes him six hours to produce a 300-page report, how many hours longer will that same 300-page report take him during the week when he produces more slowly?

    (A) 1 1/2 hours longer   (C) 2 hours longer
    (B) 1 2/3 hours longer   (D) 2 3/4 hours longer

81. Of the following, the biggest <u>disadvantage</u> in allowing a free flow of communications in an agency is that such a free flow

    (A) decreases creativity
    (B) increases the use of the "grapevine"
    (C) lengthens the chain of command
    (D) reduces the executive's power to direct the flow of information.

82. A downward flow of authority in an organization is one example of

    (A) horizontal communications   (C) circular communications
    (B) informal communications   (D) vertical communications.

83. Workers who belong to a cohesive group are generally thought to

    (A) have more job-related anxieties than those who do not
    (B) be less well adjusted than those who do not
    (C) derive little satisfaction from the group
    (D) conform to group norms more closely than those in noncohesive groups.

84. The one of the following which best exemplifies negative motivation is

    (A) a feeling on the part of the worker that the work is significant
    (B) monetary rewards offered the worker for high levels of output
    (C) reducing or withholding the worker's incentive rewards when performance is mediocre
    (D) nonmonetary rewards given the worker, such as publicizing a good suggestion.

85. Of the following, the initial step in the decision-making procedure normally is

    (A) evaluation of alternatives
    (B) implementing the chosen course of action
    (C) listing potential solutions
    (D) diagnosis and problem definition.

86. Management textbooks are <u>least</u> likely to define coordination as

    (A) a concern for harmonious and unified action directed toward a common objective
    (B) the essence of management, since the basic purpose of management is the achievement of harmony of individual effort toward the accomplishment of group goals
    (C) the orderly arrangement of group effort to provide unity of action in pursuit of common purpose
    (D) the transmittal of messages from senders to receivers, involving acts of persuasion or regulation, or simply the rendering of information.

87. The summary or findings of a long management report intended for the typical manager should generally appear

    (A) at the very beginning of the report
    (B) at the end of the report
    (C) throughout the report
    (D) in the middle of the report.

88. Of the following, the one that would be most likely to block effective communication is

    (A) concentration only on the issues at hand
    (B) lack of interest or commitment
    (C) use of written reports
    (D) use of charts and graphs.

89. A number of important assumptions underlie the modern human relations approach to management and administration. The one of the following which is <u>not</u> an assumption integral to the human relations school of thought is that

    (A) employee participation is essential to higher productivity
    (B) employees are motivated solely by monetary factors
    (C) teamwork is indispensable for organization growth and survival
    (D) free-flow communications must be established and maintained for organizational effectiveness.

90. Assume that a group has been working effectively with a contributing nonconformist in its midst. The best of the following reasons for the group to retain the nonconformist generally is that

    (A) nonconformists stimulate groups to think
    (B) that person may be their boss some day
    (C) nonconformists usually are fun to work with
    (D) another nonconformist will usurp the role.

91. The New York State law commonly called the "Taylor Law"

    (A) provides for housing benefits for minority groups
    (B) provides civil service test benefits for Viet Nam veterans
    (C) prohibits strikes by public employees
    (D) curtails benefits under state welfare laws.

92. After several revisions, the New York City Council is undergoing reapportionment including the drawing of new district lines. The basic purpose of this plan is to

    (A) increase representation of minority groups in the Council
    (B) establish councilmanic districts containing equal populations throughout the city
    (C) increase the number of Councilmen-at-large
    (D) draw district lines which will result in uniform, compact districts for each borough.

93. The Expense Budget for the City of New York for the Fiscal Year 1981-1982 covers the period

    (A) February 1, 1981 - January 31, 1982
    (B) April 15, 1981 - April 14, 1982
    (C) May 1, 1981 - April 30, 1982
    (D) July 1, 1981 - June 30, 1982.

94. Of the following, the best justification for a newly appointed administrator learning as much as possible about the workers under his or her supervision from their previous supervisor is that

    (A) effective handling of workers is often based upon knowledge of individual personality differences
    (B) best results in handling workers are usually obtained by treating them equally without favor
    (C) some workers often function more efficiently under one supervisor than under another supervisor
    (D) confidence of the workers in their supervisor is increased when they know he or she is interested in impartial and fair supervision.

95. In the management of a staff, an individual acting in an administrative capacity should be especially sensitive to the fatigue that results from

    (A) frustration in the handling of individuals
    (B) excessive hours on a continuous tour of duty
    (C) mental work in solving especially complex problems
    (D) widely varied duties.

96. "Too often the administrator does not realize that the organization chart is only an idealized picture of intentions, a

reflection of hopes and aims rather than a photograph of the operating facts within the organization." This statement is best supported by the fact that the organization chart

(A) cannot be a photograph of the living organization but must be either a record of past organization or proposed future organization
(B) deals in terms of positions rather than of people
(C) defines too explicitly the jurisdiction assigned to each component unit
(D) does not indicate unresolved internal ambiguities.

97. The PATH railway system, connecting New York City and New Jersey, is operated by the

(A) New York City Transit Authority
(B) New York City Department of Transportation
(C) Port Authority of New York and New Jersey
(D) State of New Jersey Transportation Department.

98. Of the following, the primary function of the New York City Office of Labor Relations is

(A) acting as a buffer between Labor and City management
(B) certifying an individual union as the collective bargaining representative for a particular group of employees
(C) representing City management in collective bargaining negotiations with unions
(D) determining which matters are bargainable.

99. If a certain public agency with a fixed number of employees has a line organizational structure, then the width of the span of supervision is

(A) inversely proportional to the length of the chain of command in the organization
(B) directly proportional to the complexity of tasks performed in the organization
(C) inversely proportional to the competence of the personnel in the organization
(D) directly proportional to the number of levels of supervision existing in the organization.

100. The role of the New York City Board of Ethics is to

(A) investigate cases of alleged police corruption and refer such cases to the Offices of the District Attorney
(B) render judgments on persons accused of violating the Hatch Act
(C) indict city officials who are suspected of having broken the law
(D) render advisory opinions at the request of city officials and employees on matters of possible conflict of interest.

Answer Key

1. D	21. B	41. B	61. C	81. D
2. C	22. A	42. C	62. C	82. D
3. D	23. C	43. B	63. B	83. D
4. D	24. B	44. C	64. A	84. C
5. B	25. A	45. B	65. D	85. D
6. A	26. D	46. D	66. D	86. D
7. C	27. C	47. D	67. C	87. A
8. B	28. A	48. B	68. D	88. B
9. A	29. B	49. B	69. C	89. B
10. A	30. C	50. A	70. C	90. A
11. C	31. B	51. A	71. C	91. C
12. D	32. D	52. C	72. D	92. A
13. B	33. C	53. A	73. B	93. D
14. D	34. C	54. D	74. C	94. A
15. A	35. B	55. C	75. A	95. A
16. C	36. A	56. D	76. B	96. B
17. B	37. D	57. C	77. A	97. C
18. A	38. D	58. B	78. C	98. C
19. B	39. D	59. C	79. D	99. A
20. D	40. C	60. B	80. A	100. D

ANSWER SHEET FOR SAMPLE PRACTICE EXAMINATION ■

1 Ⓐ Ⓑ Ⓒ Ⓓ	26 Ⓐ Ⓑ Ⓒ Ⓓ	51 Ⓐ Ⓑ Ⓒ Ⓓ	76 Ⓐ Ⓑ Ⓒ Ⓓ
2 Ⓐ Ⓑ Ⓒ Ⓓ	27 Ⓐ Ⓑ Ⓒ Ⓓ	52 Ⓐ Ⓑ Ⓒ Ⓓ	77 Ⓐ Ⓑ Ⓒ Ⓓ
3 Ⓐ Ⓑ Ⓒ Ⓓ	28 Ⓐ Ⓑ Ⓒ Ⓓ	53 Ⓐ Ⓑ Ⓒ Ⓓ	78 Ⓐ Ⓑ Ⓒ Ⓓ
4 Ⓐ Ⓑ Ⓒ Ⓓ	29 Ⓐ Ⓑ Ⓒ Ⓓ	54 Ⓐ Ⓑ Ⓒ Ⓓ	79 Ⓐ Ⓑ Ⓒ Ⓓ
5 Ⓐ Ⓑ Ⓒ Ⓓ	30 Ⓐ Ⓑ Ⓒ Ⓓ	55 Ⓐ Ⓑ Ⓒ Ⓓ	80 Ⓐ Ⓑ Ⓒ Ⓓ
6 Ⓐ Ⓑ Ⓒ Ⓓ	31 Ⓐ Ⓑ Ⓒ Ⓓ	56 Ⓐ Ⓑ Ⓒ Ⓓ	81 Ⓐ Ⓑ Ⓒ Ⓓ
7 Ⓐ Ⓑ Ⓒ Ⓓ	32 Ⓐ Ⓑ Ⓒ Ⓓ	57 Ⓐ Ⓑ Ⓒ Ⓓ	82 Ⓐ Ⓑ Ⓒ Ⓓ
8 Ⓐ Ⓑ Ⓒ Ⓓ	33 Ⓐ Ⓑ Ⓒ Ⓓ	58 Ⓐ Ⓑ Ⓒ Ⓓ	83 Ⓐ Ⓑ Ⓒ Ⓓ
9 Ⓐ Ⓑ Ⓒ Ⓓ	34 Ⓐ Ⓑ Ⓒ Ⓓ	59 Ⓐ Ⓑ Ⓒ Ⓓ	84 Ⓐ Ⓑ Ⓒ Ⓓ
10 Ⓐ Ⓑ Ⓒ Ⓓ	35 Ⓐ Ⓑ Ⓒ Ⓓ	60 Ⓐ Ⓑ Ⓒ Ⓓ	85 Ⓐ Ⓑ Ⓒ Ⓓ
11 Ⓐ Ⓑ Ⓒ Ⓓ	36 Ⓐ Ⓑ Ⓒ Ⓓ	61 Ⓐ Ⓑ Ⓒ Ⓓ	86 Ⓐ Ⓑ Ⓒ Ⓓ
12 Ⓐ Ⓑ Ⓒ Ⓓ	37 Ⓐ Ⓑ Ⓒ Ⓓ	62 Ⓐ Ⓑ Ⓒ Ⓓ	87 Ⓐ Ⓑ Ⓒ Ⓓ
13 Ⓐ Ⓑ Ⓒ Ⓓ	38 Ⓐ Ⓑ Ⓒ Ⓓ	63 Ⓐ Ⓑ Ⓒ Ⓓ	88 Ⓐ Ⓑ Ⓒ Ⓓ
14 Ⓐ Ⓑ Ⓒ Ⓓ	39 Ⓐ Ⓑ Ⓒ Ⓓ	64 Ⓐ Ⓑ Ⓒ Ⓓ	89 Ⓐ Ⓑ Ⓒ Ⓓ
15 Ⓐ Ⓑ Ⓒ Ⓓ	40 Ⓐ Ⓑ Ⓒ Ⓓ	65 Ⓐ Ⓑ Ⓒ Ⓓ	90 Ⓐ Ⓑ Ⓒ Ⓓ
16 Ⓐ Ⓑ Ⓒ Ⓓ	41 Ⓐ Ⓑ Ⓒ Ⓓ	66 Ⓐ Ⓑ Ⓒ Ⓓ	91 Ⓐ Ⓑ Ⓒ Ⓓ
17 Ⓐ Ⓑ Ⓒ Ⓓ	42 Ⓐ Ⓑ Ⓒ Ⓓ	67 Ⓐ Ⓑ Ⓒ Ⓓ	92 Ⓐ Ⓑ Ⓒ Ⓓ
18 Ⓐ Ⓑ Ⓒ Ⓓ	43 Ⓐ Ⓑ Ⓒ Ⓓ	68 Ⓐ Ⓑ Ⓒ Ⓓ	93 Ⓐ Ⓑ Ⓒ Ⓓ
19 Ⓐ Ⓑ Ⓒ Ⓓ	44 Ⓐ Ⓑ Ⓒ Ⓓ	69 Ⓐ Ⓑ Ⓒ Ⓓ	94 Ⓐ Ⓑ Ⓒ Ⓓ
20 Ⓐ Ⓑ Ⓒ Ⓓ	45 Ⓐ Ⓑ Ⓒ Ⓓ	70 Ⓐ Ⓑ Ⓒ Ⓓ	95 Ⓐ Ⓑ Ⓒ Ⓓ
21 Ⓐ Ⓑ Ⓒ Ⓓ	46 Ⓐ Ⓑ Ⓒ Ⓓ	71 Ⓐ Ⓑ Ⓒ Ⓓ	96 Ⓐ Ⓑ Ⓒ Ⓓ
22 Ⓐ Ⓑ Ⓒ Ⓓ	47 Ⓐ Ⓑ Ⓒ Ⓓ	72 Ⓐ Ⓑ Ⓒ Ⓓ	97 Ⓐ Ⓑ Ⓒ Ⓓ
23 Ⓐ Ⓑ Ⓒ Ⓓ	48 Ⓐ Ⓑ Ⓒ Ⓓ	73 Ⓐ Ⓑ Ⓒ Ⓓ	98 Ⓐ Ⓑ Ⓒ Ⓓ
24 Ⓐ Ⓑ Ⓒ Ⓓ	49 Ⓐ Ⓑ Ⓒ Ⓓ	74 Ⓐ Ⓑ Ⓒ Ⓓ	99 Ⓐ Ⓑ Ⓒ Ⓓ
25 Ⓐ Ⓑ Ⓒ Ⓓ	50 Ⓐ Ⓑ Ⓒ Ⓓ	75 Ⓐ Ⓑ Ⓒ Ⓓ	100 Ⓐ Ⓑ Ⓒ Ⓓ

SAMPLE PRACTICE EXAMINATION III

1. For sound organizational relationships, of the following, it is generally most desirable that

   (A) authority and responsibility be segregated from each other, in order to facilitate control
   (B) the authority of a manager should be commensurate with responsibility, and vice versa
   (C) authority be defined as the obligation of an individual to carry out assigned activities to the best of his or her ability
   (D) clear recognition be given to the fact that delegation of authority benefits only the manager who delegates it.

2. In utilizing a checklist of questions for general managerial planning, which one of the following generally is the first question to be asked and answered?

   (A) Where will it take place?
   (B) How will it be done?
   (C) Why must it be done?
   (D) Who will do it?

3. It is often desirable for an administrator to consult, during the planning process, the persons to be affected by those plans. Of the following, the major justification for such consultation is that it recognizes the

   (A) fact that participating in horizontal planning is almost always more effective than participating in vertical planning
   (B) principle of participation and the need for a sense of belonging as a means of

127

decreasing resistance and developing support

(C) principle that lower-level administrators normally are more likely than higher-level administrators to emphasize longer-range goals

(D) fact that final responsibility for the approval of plans should be placed in committees not individuals.

4. In evaluating performance and, if necessary, correcting what is being done to assure attainment of results according to plan, it is generally best for the administrator to do which one of the following?

(A) Make a continual effort to increase the number of written control reports prepared.

(B) Thoroughly investigate in equal detail all possible deviations indicated by comparison of performance to expectation.

(C) Decentralize, within an operating unit or division, the responsibility for correcting deviations.

(D) Concentrate on the exceptions, or outstanding variations, from the expected results or standards.

5. Generally, changes in the ways in which the supervisors and employees in an organization do things are more likely to be welcomed by them when the changes

(A) threaten the security of the supervisors than when they do not

(B) are inaugurated after prior change has been assimilated than when they are inaugurated before other major changes have been assimilated

(C) follow a series of failures in changes than when they follow a series of successful changes

(D) are dictated by personal order rather than when they result from an application of previously established impersonal principles.

6. When an additional organizational level is added within a department, that department has most directly manifested

(A) horizontal growth
(B) horizontal shrinkage
(C) vertical growth
(D) vertical shrinkage.

7. Deparmentation by function is the same as, or most similar to, departmentation by

(A) equipment
(B) clientele
(C) territory
(D) activity.

8. Such verifiable factors as turnover, absenteeism, or volume of grievances would generally best assist in measuring the effectiveness of a program to improve

(A) forms control
(B) employee morale
(C) linear programming
(D) executive creativity.

9. Of the following, the one which generally is the most intangible planning factor is

(A) budget dollars allocated to a function

(B) square feet of space for office use

(C) number of personnel in various clerical titles

(D) emotional impact of a proposed personnel policy among employees.

10. In selecting from among administrative alternatives, three general bases for decision are open to the manager -- experience, experimentation, and research and analysis. Of the following, the best argument <u>against</u> primary reliance upon experimentation as the method of evaluating administrative alternatives is that experimentation is

(A) generally the most expensive of the three techniques

(B) almost always legally prohibited in procedural matters

(C) possible only in areas where results may be easily duplicated by other experimenters at any time

(D) an approach that requires information on scientific method seldom available to administrators.

11. The administrator who utilizes the techniques of operations research, linear programming, and simulation in making an administrative decision should most appropriately be considered to be using the techniques of

(A) intuitive anlaysis

(B) quantitative analysis

(C) nonmathematical analysis

(D) qualitative analysis.

12. When the success of a plan in achieving specific program objectives is measured

against that plan's costs, the measure obtained is most directly that of the plan's

(A) pervasiveness

(B) control potential

(C) primacy

(D) efficiency.

13. Of the following, the best overall technique for choosing from among several alternative public programs proposed to try to achieve the same broad objective generally is

(A) random-sample analysis

(B) input analysis

(C) cost-effectiveness analysis

(D) output analysis.

14. "Determining what is being accomplished, that is, evaluating the performance and, if necessary, applying corrective measures so that performance takes place according to plans" is most appropriately called management

(A) actuating

(B) planning

(C) controlling

(D) motivating.

15. The term "computer hardware" is most likely to refer to

(A) machines and equipment

(C) programmed instruction texts and compiler decks

(C) training manuals

(D) documentation supporting usage of computing machines.

16. An organization increases the number of subordinates reporting to a manager up to the point where incremental savings in costs, better communication and morale, and other factors equal

incremental losses in effectiveness of control, direction, and similar factors. This action most specifically employs the technique of

(A) role playing
(B) queuing theory
(C) marginal analysis
(D) capital standards analysis.

17. As used with respect to decision-making, "the application of scientific method to the study of alternatives in a problem situation, with a view to providing a quantitative basis for arriving at an optimum solution in terms of the goals sought" is most appropriately called

(A) simple number departmentation
(B) geographic decentralization
(C) operations research
(D) trait rating.

18. Of the following, it is usually best to set administrative objectives so that they are

(A) at a level that is unattainable, so that administrators will continually be strongly motivated
(B) at a level that is attainable, but requires some stretching and reaching by administrators trying to attain them
(C) stated in qualitative rather than quantitative terms whenever a choice between the two is possible
(D) stated in a general and unstructured manner, to permit each

administrator maximum freedom in interpreting them.

19. Generally, the degree to which an organization's planning will be coordinated varies most directly with the degree to which

(A) the individuals charged with executing plans are better compensated than those charged with developing and evaluating plans
(B) the individuals charged with planning understand and agree to utilize consistent planning premises
(C) a large number of position classification titles have been established for those individuals charged with organizational planning functions
(D) subordinate unit objectives are allowed to control the overall objectives of the departments of which such subordinate units are a part.

20. The responsibility for specific types of decisions generally is best delegated to

(A) the highest organizational level at which there is an individual possessing the ability, desire, impartiality and access to relevant information needed to make these decisions
(B) the lowest organizational level at which there is an individual possessing the ability, desire, impartiality and access to relevant information needed to make these

decisions
(C) a group of executives, rather than a single executive, if these decisions deal with an emergency
(D) the organizational level midway between that which will have to carry out these decisions and that which will have to authorize the resources for their implementation.

21. The process of managing by objectives is most likely to lead to a situation in which the

(A) goal accomplishment objectives of managers tend to have a longer time span as one goes lower down the line in an organization
(B) establishment of quantitative goals for staff positions is generally easier than the establishment of quantitative goals for line positions
(C) development of objectives requires the manager to think of the way he or she will accomplish given results, and of the organization, personnel and resources that he or she will need
(D) superiors normally develop and finally approve detailed goals for subordinates without any prior consultation with either those subordinates or with the top-level executives responsible for the longer-run objectives of the organization.

22. Assume that a bureau head proposes that final responsibility and authority for all planning within the bureau is to be delegated to one employee who is to be paid at the level of an assistant division head in that bureau. Of the following, the most appropriate comment about this proposal is that it is

(A) improper; mainly because planning does not call for someone at this high a level
(B) improper; mainly because responsibility for a basic management function such as planning may not properly be delegated as proposed
(C) proper; mainly because ultimate responsibility for all bureau planning is best placed as proposed
(D) proper; mainly because every well-managed bureau should have a full-time planning officer.

23. The term "PPBS" relates most directly to one of the systems principally designed to do which one of the following?

(A) Reduce the number of mistakes resulting in spoilage and wasted effort to zero.
(B) Obtain greater cost effectiveness.
(C) Assure that all operations are performed at the highest quality level that is technically attainable at the present time.
(D) Assure that all output units are fully verified prior to being sent out.

24. Assume that you are working with a computer programmer to solve a complex problem. Together, you have defined

your problem in everyday English clearly enough to proceed. In the next step, you both start breaking down the information in the definition so that you both can decide on the operations needed for programming the problem. This next step of getting from the definition of the problem to the point where you can begin laying out the steps actually to be taken in solving the problem is most appropriately called

(A) completing the documentation
(B) implementing the solution
(C) identifying the problem statement
(D) analyzing the problem.

25. Two organizations have the same basic objectives and the same total number of employees. The span of authority of each intermediate manager is narrower in one organization than it is in the other organization. It is most likely that the organization in which each intermediate manager has a narrower span of authority will have

(A) fewer intermediate managers
(B) more organizational levels
(C) most managers reporting to a larger number of immediate supervisors
(D) more characteristics of a "flat" organizational structure.

26. The City's records retention guidelines indicate that most New York City agencies normally should retain which one of the following types

of records for the longest time period?

(A) Accident reports.
(B) Copies of Board of Estimate calendars.
(C) Motor vehicle and travel records -- daily reports, operators and mileage.
(D) Agency purchase requisitions.

27. Which one of the following is directed by the members of the Metropolitan Transportation Authority?

(A) New York City Department of Traffic.
(B) New York City Department of Highways.
(C) New York City Transit Authority.
(D) Port of New York Authority.

28. Of the following, the city official who has the principal responsibility for the overall preparation and justification of New York City's Expense Budget is the

(A) Chairman of the City Planning Commission
(B) Mayor
(C) President of the City Council
(D) Finance Administrator.

29. The fiscal year for New York City's Capital Budget begins

(A) on the same date as the fiscal year for New York City's Expense Budget
(B) two months after the fiscal year for New York City's Expense Budget
(C) two months before the fiscal year for New York City's Expense Budget
(D) six months before the fiscal year for New York City's Expense Budget.

30. For a department to plan its work schedule so as to provide a constant backlog of work would be

    (A) undesirable primarily because it is almost impossible to plan for this type of backlog
    (B) desirable primarily because the department would be in a better position to change its plans if no deadlines were involved
    (C) undesirable primarily because lists of persons eligible for appointment would not be ready when required
    (D) desirable primarily because the procedure would tend to insure continuity of work flow.

31. The <u>functional</u> type of administrative organization is a system

    (A) in which the operating units are grouped according to activities
    (B) in which the character of the activities determines the geographical jurisdiction of subordinate units
    (C) which is repudiated by highly technical departments
    (D) which lends itself most readily to the definite location of responsibility.

32. Which of the following best reflects the first step, logically and to some extent chronologically, in planning the budget for an operating unit of a large public agency?

    (A) establish a priority for each task or activity
    (B) take an inventory of present equipment and facilities
    (C) determine deficiencies in the present budget
    (D) forecast of workload.

33. The most important distinction between operating and service functions of an administrative organization is that

    (A) service activities involve public relations to a greater extent than operating activities
    (B) service activities are functional while operating activities are often termed "housekeeping"
    (C) operating activities are an end in themselves, while service activities are a means to an end
    (D) operating activities may be thought of as institutional, while service activities are of primary importance.

34. Of the following, the principal function of an "ombudsman" generally is to

    (A) review departmental requests for new data processing equipment so as to reduce duplication
    (B) receive and investigate complaints from citizens who are displeased with the actions or non-actions of administrative officials and try to effectuate warranted remedies
    (C) review proposed departmental reorganizations in order to advise the chief executive whether or not they are in accordance with the latest principles of proper management structuring

(D) preside over courts of the judiciary convened to try "sitting" judges.

35. Of the following four New York City officials, how many are removable at the pleasure of the Mayor?

    Commissioner of
        Investigation
    Deputy Mayor - City
        Administrator
    Commissioner of Health
    Commissioner of Consumer
        Affairs

    (A) Only one.
    (B) Only two.
    (C) Only three.
    (D) All four.

36. "Virtually all of us use this principle in our human communications -- perhaps without realizing it. In casual conversations, we are alert for cues to whether we are understood (e.g., attentive nod from the other person). Similarly, an instructor is always interested in reactions among those to whom he or she is giving instruction. The effective administrator is equally conscious of the need to determine subordinates' reactions to what he or she is trying to communicate."

    The principle referred to in the above selection is most appropriately called

    (A) cognitive dissonance
    (B) feedback
    (C) negative reinforcement
    (D) noise transmission.

37. Of the following, the most important reason that participation has motivating effects is generally that it gives to the individual

participating

    (A) a recognition of his or her desire to feel important and to contribute to achievement of worthwhile goals
    (B) an opportunity to participate in work that is beyond the scope of the class specification for his or her title
    (C) a secure knowledge that his or her organization's top leadership is as efficient as possible considering all major circumstances
    (D) the additional information which is likely to be crucial to his or her promotion.

38. Of the following, the most essential characteristic of an effective employee suggestion system is that

    (A) suggestions be submitted upward through the chain of command
    (B) suggestions be acted upon promptly so that employees may be promptly informed of what happens to their submitted suggestions
    (C) suggesters be required to sign their names on the material sent to the actual evaluators for evaluation
    (D) suggesters receive at least 25% of the agency's savings during the first two years after their suggestions have been accepted and put into effect by the agency.

39. Which one of the following statements is most generally supported by modern industrial and behavioral research?

(A) High productivity and high quality each show a substantial negative correlation with high morale.

(B) Where professional employees participate in defining how much and what caliber of their service should be considered acceptable, they generally will set both types of goals substantially below those which management alone would have set.

(C) Professional employees get greatest satisfaction out of work that challenges them to exert their capacities fully.

(D) The participative approach to management relieves the manager of the need to be a decision-maker.

40. A bureau has a very large number of clerical personnel engaged in very similar duties, and only a limited portion can be absent at any one time if the workload is to be handled properly. Which one of the following would generally be the bureau head's best approach toward scheduling the annual leave time (vacation, etc.) to be taken by the employees of that bureau?

(A) The bureau head personally receives from each employee a preferred schedule of annual leave time, personally decides on when the employee can most conveniently be spared from the viewpoint of the office workload, and issues decisions to all concerned in the form of a binding memorandum.

(B) The bureau head advises subordinate supervisors and employees of the parameters and constraints in time and numbers upon annual leave. The employees and subordinate supervisors prepare a proposed annual leave schedule within those limitations and submit it to the bureau head for approval or modification, and for promulgation.

(C) The bureau head initially asks subordinate supervisors to prepare a proposed annual leave schedule for employees with a minimum of consultation with the employees. The bureau head then circulates this schedule to the employees over his or her signature as a proposed schedule and invites direct reaction.

(D) The bureau head asks employee or union representatives to prepare a proposed schedule with all leave to be taken spread evenly over the entire vacation period. He or she personally reviews and accepts or modifies this proposal.

41. An agency head desires to have an estimate of the "potential" of a middle-level administrative employee for development for higher-level administrative positions. He or she also desires to try to minimize possible errors or capriciousness which might creep into that estimate. Of the following, it would generally be most desirable to have the estimate

(A) result from the pooled

judgment of three or more past or present substantial-level supervisors of the subject employee and of persons with lateral or service contacts with the subject employee

(B) made solely by substantial-level executives outside the past or present direct line of supervision above the subject employee

(C) result from the pooled judgment of substantial-level personnel staff members rather than line executives

(D) made solely by the present immediate line supervisor of the subject employee.

42. Generally, an employee receiving new information from a fellow employee is most likely to

(A) forget the new information if it is consistent with existing beliefs much more easily than he forgets the new information if it is inconsistent with existing beliefs

(B) accept the validity of the new information if it is consistent with existing beliefs more readily than he or she accepts the validity of the new information if it is inconsistent with existing beliefs

(C) have a less accurate memory of the new information if it is consistent with existing beliefs than of the new information if it is inconsistent with existing beliefs

(D) ignore the new information if it is consistent with existing beliefs more often than he or she ignores the new information if it is inconsistent with existing beliefs.

43. Of the following, the most usual reason for unsatisfactory line-staff relationships is

(A) inept use of the abilities of staff personnel by line management

(B) the higher salaries paid to line officials

(C) excessive consultation between line officials and staff officials at the same organizational level

(D) a feeling among the staff members that only lower-level line members appreciate their work.

Each of questions 44 through 48 consists of a quotation which contains one word that is incorrectly used because it is not in keeping with the meaning that the quotation is evidently intended to convey. Determine which word is incorrectly used. Select from the choices lettered (A), (B), (C), and (D) the word which, when substituted for the incorrectly used word, would best help to convey the meaning of the quotation.

44. "A complex society like our own, after all, depends on the skills of the individuals composing it. Concerns of human safety, convenience, and the quality of our collective life are of as great consequence as our

concern for equal protection of the laws. We do want a qualified surgeon when we need an operation. We assume a skilled pilot, especially when it is we who are on the plane. We want the telephone to work, and our mail to come to us, and not to someone down the street. We want competent teachers for our children. In universities, we want high standards of scholarship and research."

"Our existence places us at the mercy of persons, never invisible to us, who are certified for their qualities. While we may argue about the manner in which, in real life, skill and competence are elicited and ascertained, we can hardly argue that there are no such things as skill and competence or that there is no way of measuring them. But there are those among us who <u>do</u> make this argument and those who also accept it, and its spreading influence may well constitute the single greatest threat to the quality of our lives today."

(A) little
(B) quibble
(C) gullibility
(D) often.

45. "If strategy or policy does not further plans or make enterprise procedures more attainable, it has not done its job. No manager should ever be able to say: 'There's no good reason why we do it, it is just our policy!'"

"While many policies and some strategies are, in effect, permanent, it should never be assumed that they represent natural laws engraved on stone. If goals, premises, or major plans change, strategies and policies should be reconsidered to meet the new situation."

(A) objectives
(B) exclaim
(C) diverge
(D) reinforced.

46. "To some extent, the attitude that experience is the best teacher is justifiable. The very fact that the manager has reached his position appears to justify his decisions. Moreover, the reasoning process of thinking problems through, making decisions, and seeing programs succeed or fail, does make for a degree of good judgment (at times bordering on the intuitive). Many people, however, do not profit by their errors, and there are managers who seem never to gain the seasoned judgment required by modern enterprise."

"There is danger, however, in relying on one's past experience as a guide for future action. In the first place, it is an unusual human being who recognizes the obvious reasons for his mistakes or failures. In the second place, the lessons of experience may be entirely unsuitable to new problems. Good decisions must be evaluated against future events, while experience belongs to the past."

(A) poorest
(B) underlying
(C) principle
(D) quantified.

47. "A bit of thinking will give a clue to the variety of disciplines which are involved in the range of the personnel function. In staffing -- from initial entry to promotion and transfer -- the field of psychological measurement is brought into play. Compensation decisions require economists and statisticians. Job analysis calls for skills in research and administrative procedure. Training draws upon adult education specialists and other occupations. Health and safety measures demand the employment of medical doctors, nurses, and safety engineers. Operating a retirement system necessitates expertise in the insurance field and actuarial mathematics. Dealing with employees corporately requires knowledge in labor relations. Interpretation of rules and adjudication of claims and complaints call for the skills of lawyers. And all the elements of leadership, budgeting, incentive, evaluation, and discipline, on which the personnel program is expected to provide the principal guidance, can be fortified only by a liberal under-standing of such social sciences as social psychology and sociology, to say nothing of a healthy dose of that conventional wisdom known as common sense."

    (A) supervision
    (B) physiological
    (C) economic
    (D) purchasing.

48. "Another means of increasing participation is what has been called 'grass roots' budgeting. Instead of a budget for operations or capital expenditures being prepared at the top or departmental level, the smallest organization units prepare their budgets and submit them upward. Naturally, to be effective, these units must be aware of objectives, policies, and programs which affect their operations, must above all be given clear planning premises, and be furnished factors enabling them to convert workload into requirements for workers, material, and money. If these budget requests are reviewed and coordinated by departmental management, and if the budget makers are required to expend their budgets, this means of planning participation becomes real and purposeful. There probably exist no greater incentive to planning and no stronger sense of participation than those created in developing, defending, and selling a course of action over which the manager has control and for which he or she bears responsibility."

    (A) intermediate
    (B) productivity
    (C) defend
    (D) cut.

49. Assume that during the fiscal year 1981-1982, a bureau produced 20% more work units than it produced in the fiscal year 1980-1981. Also, assume that during the fiscal year 1981-1982 that bureau's staff was 20% _smaller_ than it was in the fiscal year 1980-1981. On the basis of this information, it would be most proper to conclude that the number of work units

produced per staff member in that bureau in the fiscal year 1981-1982 exceeded the number of work units produced per staff member in that bureau in the fiscal year 1980-1981 by which of the following percentages?

(A) 20%
(B) 25%
(C) 40%
(D) 50%

50. Assume that during the following fiscal years (FY), a bureau has received the following appropriations:

FY 1977-1978 - $200,000
FY 1978-1979 - $240,000
FY 1979-1980 - $280,000
FY 1980-1981 - $390,000
FY 1981-1982 - $505,000

The bureau's appropriation for which one of the following fiscal years showed the largest percentage of increase over the bureau's appropriation for the immediately previous fiscal year?

(A) FY 1978-1979
(B) FY 1979-1980
(C) FY 1980-1981
(D) FY 1981-1982

51. The maximum number of 2-3/4" x 4-1/4" size forms which may be obtained from one ream of 17" x 22" paper is

(A) 4,000
(B) 8,000
(C) 12,000
(D) 16,000

52. On a general organization chart, staff positions normally should be pictured

(A) directly above the line positions to which they

report
(B) to the sides of the main flow lines
(C) within the box of the highest level subordinate positions pictured
(D) directly below the line positions which report to them.

53. When an administrator is diagramming an office layout, of the following, the primary job generally should be to indicate the

(A) lighting intensities that will be required by each operation
(B) noise level that will be produced by the various equipment employed in the office
(C) direction of the work flow and the distance involved in each transfer
(D) durability of major pieces of office equipment currently in use or to be utilized.

54. Manually operated typewriters most generally tend to have which one of the following advantages, as compared with electric typewriters?

(A) lower maintenance costs
(B) higher quality copy
(C) greater output with less energy being expended
(D) greater number of legible copies per typing.

55. Generally, the actual floor space occupied by a standard letter-size office file cabinet, when closed, is most nearly

(A) 1/2 square foot
(B) 3 square feet
(C) 7 square feet
(D) 11 square feet.

56. One common guideline or

rule-of-thumb ratio for evaluating the efficiency of files is the number of records requested divided by the number of records filed. Generally, if this ratio is very low it would point most directly to the need for

(A) improving the indexing and coding system
(B) improving the charge-out procedures
(C) exploring the need for transferring records from active storage to the archives
(D) exploring the need to encourage employees to keep more records in their private files.

57. The greatest percentage of money spent on preparing and keeping the usual records in an office generally is expended for which one of the following?

(A) Renting space in which to place the record-keeping equipment.
(B) Paying salaries of record-recording and record-keeping personnel.
(C) Depreciation of purchased record-preparation and record-keeping equipment.
(D) Paper and forms upon which to place the records.

58. If we total all of the occasions in which all governmental positions are filled with new faces (persons who did not occupy those specific positions previously), we generally would find that a greater number will result from

(A) new accessions from the outside than from movement of personnel

within the organization
(B) movement of personnel within the organization than from new accessions from the outside
(C) promotion of staff personnel to higher staff jobs than from promotion of line personnel to higher line jobs
(D) filling of Exempt and Non-Competitive Class positions than from filling of Competitive Class positions.

59. Listed immediately below are four measures to be utilized to try to achieve a major personnel goal:

(1) Diversifying tasks in any one unit as much as feasible.
(2) Delegating authority to each layer in the hierarchy to the maximum extent consistent with the clarity of policy guides, training of staff, and the effectiveness of post-audit procedures.
(3) Assigning whole integrals of functions to individuals or units instead of splitting them into fine specializations with separate employees or groups concentrating on each.
(4) Permitting workers to follow through on tasks or projects from start to finish rather than carry out single segments of the process.

The major personnel goal which all of the above measures, taken together, may best be expected to serve is

(A) increasing job simplification
(B) promoting E.E.O.

affirmative action
(C) making and keeping jobs
as meaningful as they
can practically be
(D) increasing the number of
promotional levels
available so as to
maximize advancement
opportunities as much as
possible.

60. Which one of the following
is generally the best
criterion for determining
the classification title to
which a position should be
allocated?

(A) The personal
qualifications possessed
by the present or
expected appointee to
the position.
(B) The consequences of the
work of the position or
the responsibility it
carries.
(C) The number of work units
required to be produced
or completed in the
position.
(D) The consequences of
inadequate overall
governmental pay scales
upon recruitment of
outstanding personnel.

61. The ultimate controlling
factor in structuring
positions in the public
service, most generally,
should be the

(A) possibility of
providing upgrading for
highly productive
employees
(B) collective bargaining
demands initially made
by established public
employee unions
(C) positive motivational
effects upon productivity
resulting from an
inverted pyramid job
structure

(D) effectiveness of the
structuring in serving
the mission of the
organization.

62. The major decisions as to
which jobs shall be created
and who shall carry which
responsibilities should
generally be made by

(A) budgetary advisers
(B) line managers
(C) classification
specialists
(D) peer-level rating
committees.

63. Of the following, the
problems encountered by
government establishments
which are most likely to
make extensive delegation of
authority difficult to
effectuate tend to be
problems of

(A) accountability and
insuring uniform
administration
(B) line and staff
relationships within
field offices
(C) general employee
opposition to such
delegation of authority
and to the consequent
record-keeping activities
(D) use of the management-by-
objectives approach.

64. Of the following, the
promotion selection policy
generally considered most
antithetical to the merit
concept is the promotion
selection policy which

(A) is based solely on
objective tests of
competence
(B) is based solely on
seniority
(C) may require a manager to
lose the best employee
to another part of the

organization

(D) permits operating managers collectively to play a significant role in promotion decisions.

65. Which one of the following best expresses the essence of the merit idea or system in public employment?

   (A) A person's worth to the organization -- the merit of his or her attributes and capacities -- is the governing factor in his or her selection, assignment, pay, recognition, advancement and retention.
   (B) Written tests of the objective type are the only fair way to select on a merit basis from among candidates for open-competitive appointment to positions within the merit system.
   (C) Employees who have qualified for civil service positions shall have life-time tenure during good behavior in those positions regard-less of changes in public programs.
   (D) Periodic examinations with set date limits within which all persons desiring to demonstrate their merit may apply, shall be publicly advertised and held for all promotional titles.

66. Of the following, the most valid reason for recruiting an intermediate-level administrator from outside an agency, rather than from within the agency, normally is to

   (A) improve the public image of the agency as a desirable place in which

to be employed

   (B) reduce the number of potential administrators who must be evaluated prior to filling the position
   (C) minimize the morale problems arising from frequent internal staff upgradings
   (D) obtain fresh ideas and a fresh viewpoint on agency problems.

67. "A group of positions that are sufficiently similar in nature and level of duties, responsibilities, and qualifications required to warrant similar treatment for purposes of recruitment, examination, and pay" is most appropriately called

   (A) a grade
   (B) a pay range
   (C) a class
   (D) an occupational group.

68. Governmental personnel testing, most generally, has done which one of the following?

   (A) Shown greater precision in testing for creativity and courage than in testing for intelligence and achievement.
   (B) Developed more useful tests of intelligence, aptitude, and achievement than of creativity, courage, and commitment.
   (C) Failed in the attempt to develop any testing mechanisms in the areas of aptitude or achievement to the point where they are of any use in eliminating extraneous, prejudicial factors in the selection process.
   (D) Made more use of previous employment records in selecting novices from

the outside for junior
positions than it has in
selecting persons from
the outside to fill more
senior positions.

69. Of the following, the major
objective of government
managers in most job
restructuring generally
should be to

(A) reduce the percentage
that lower-level
employees in the
government service
constitute of the total
(B) reduce the percentage
range of the salaries
paid within each
classified title
(C) concentrate as much of
the higher-skill duties
in as few of the jobs as
possible
(D) package duties into job
combinations that are
the same as the job
combinations
traditionally used by
lower-paying private
employers in the
surrounding geographical
area.

Answer questions 70 through
72 on the basis of the
New York State Civil Service
Law and the Rules and
Regulations of the New York
City Civil Service Commission
as they are generally
applied.

70. Generally, the civil service
rules provide that the
duration of either an
open-competitive or a
promotion eligible list shall
be not less than

(A) six nor more than thirty
months from the date of
establishment
(B) one nor more than four
years from the date of

establishment
(C) one nor more than three
years from the date of
the first assembled test
(D) two nor more than five
years from the date of
establishment.

71. In order for a new title to
be officially included in the
Non-Competitive Class, an
appropriate resolution must
be adopted by the City
Personnel Director and also
must be officially approved
by the

(A) Mayor and the State Civil
Service Commission
(B) Comptroller and the
President of the City
Council
(C) State Civil Service
Commission and the United
States Civil Service
Commission
(D) Director of the Budget
and the Mayor.

72. No more than one appointment
can be made to or under the
title of any office or
position in the Exempt class
unless

(A) a special Personnel Order
is signed by the Mayor
allowing such appointment
(B) the classification rules
specifically state that
a different number is
prescribed
(C) the appointment is
expected to be for a
period of less than
thirty months
(D) a certificate is filed
with the Department of
Personnel showing the
appointee's educational
and experience
qualifications for the
position, and the
Department of Personnel
approves such
qualifications.

73. Which one of the following generally best characterizes the basic nature of budget making and budget administration from a managerial viewpoint?

    (A) Budget administration is control, while budget making is planning.
    (B) Budget administration is planning, while budget making is control.
    (C) Both budget making and budget administration are only control functions; neither is a planning function.
    (D) Both budget making and budget administration are only planning functions; neither is a control function.

74. A New York City department head wishes to transfer funds from one of his program appropriation units to another program appropriation unit within his own department. According to the New York City Charter, this action would require the approval of

    (A) a majority of the Board of Estimate
    (B) the Comptroller
    (C) the Mayor
    (D) the Deputy Finance Administrator.

75. In preparing his annual budget request for a large bureau with both substantial continuing and anticipated new activities, the bureau head must consider various factors (e.g., retaining credibility and obtaining required funds).

    (A) twice what is actually needed on the assumption that higher authorities will generally cut the requested amount in half
    (B) ten percent less than he actually estimates to be needed and to submit a supplementary request later for that ten percent
    (C) what is needed for the continuing activities plus twenty-five percent to allow for some slack funds
    (D) what he estimates is needed to continue existing essential programs and to fund needed new activities.

76. "Attempts should be made to permit first level supervisors to participate in the development of plans which will affect levels in the department other than their own." Following this policy, when possible, is

    (A) undesirable; conferences will tend to be overloaded with supervisors who have little to contribute
    (B) desirable; the supervisors who participate will understand the department better and will be able to make more useful suggestions in the future
    (C) undesirable; supervisors can be trained more efficiently and economically in an organized training program than by participating in plan development
    (D) desirable; supervisors can be trained more efficiently and economically by participation in plan development than by participation in an organized training program.

77. "Data relating to the detailed operations of the different units in a department should be accumulated and periodically summarized and analyzed." The primary reason for this from the viewpoint of the administrator is to

    (A) point out which are the most efficient workers
    (B) show the importance of maintaining operating records and quotas
    (C) compare the amount of work done by different kinds of units
    (D) locate those operations which are unusually efficient or inefficient.

78. The more complex the organization, the more highly specialized the division of work, the greater the need for

    (A) strict line discipline
    (B) inter (or intra) departmental council for cooperation
    (C) finer division of supervision
    (D) coordinating authority.

79. Of the following, the chief detriment to a department which is overstaffed is that of

    (A) too many workers competing for too few supervisory jobs
    (B) facilities are usually inadequate causing crowded conditions and personality conflicts among workers
    (C) workers become dissatisfied because they are not kept busy
    (D) danger of laxness in efficiency, because inefficiency can be

covered up by workers.

80. Of the following, the least important factor for sound organization is the

    (A) individual and his or her position
    (B) hierarchical form of organization
    (C) location and delegation of authority
    (D) standardization of salary schedules.

81. Although authorities in public administration generally recommend that activities of a department should be as closely integrated as possible, they recommend granting a status of considerable independence to those activities which

    (A) are purely of an emergency or temporary character
    (B) are in the period of decline and liquidation
    (C) are in the period of initiation and development
    (D) render service of a routine nature.

82. Organizational problems are concerned chiefly with the

    (A) ways in which work is to be done, and the establishment and maintenance of routines and procedures to perform the work
    (B) types of employees needed, the obtaining, training, and developing of these employees, and their supervision and direction
    (C) disposition of forces, the logical grouping of activities, the assigning of duties and responsibilities, and the

coordination of efforts
(D) actions to be taken
under any given
circumstances, and the
setting of major
objectives and the
formulation of plans of
action to attain them.

83. In a municipal budget
context, the distinguishing
characteristic of "general
funds" is that they

(A) are derived from the
general population
rather than any special
segment thereof
(B) are not earmarked and
may be expended for any
municipal activity
(C) must be expended for
governmental rather than
proprietary functions
(D) must be expended on
matters of legal
necessity rather than
administrative
convenience.

84. Basically, the determination
of the adequacy of
governmental services is a
function of which of the
following elements

(A) administrative
(B) legislative
(C) operating
(D) technical or professional
groups outside the
government.

85. Which type of writ could a
court be likely to issue in
order to compel a public
official to perform some
duty required by law?

(A) injunction
(B) habeas corpus
(C) certiorari
(D) mandamus.

86. What private business calls
"profit and loss" government
calls

(A) revenue and expenditure
(B) premature and deferred
charges
(C) taxation and assessment
(D) surplus and deficit.

87. "Definite mechanisms and
routines must be provided
to the end of causing all
groups within an organization
to function harmoniously
toward the attainment of the
common objective." According
to this statement, a definite
system must be established
for the purpose of

(A) specialization
(B) discipline
(C) coordination
(D) line and staff control.

88. In regard to reorganizational
procedure in a bureau, the
chief administrators should
constantly guard against

(A) rotating personnel
(B) considering established
organizational structure
as being infallible just
because of custom and
long use
(C) any marked change from
long-established
practice that has been
successful in the past
(D) making any substantial
changes in organizational
structure lest they be
branded radicals.

89. The one of the following
problems that represents the
greatest difficulty in the
supervision of workers in an
agency is

(A) insufficient opportunity
to gain a knowledge of
the capabilities and
deficiencies of
subordinate staff members
(B) the absence of concrete

and measurable indexes
of work performance
(C) the difficulty of
identifying and
maintaining satisfactory
lines of authority in
the agency
(D) the channelling of
loyalties into the most
desirable goals.

90. To be effective, the
supervisory methods of an
administrator should be
flexible primarily because

(A) new procedures may render
established methods
obsolete
(B) such methods should
conform to the
preferences of the
superior
(C) workers under supervision
differ in their needs and
responses
(D) the greater the number of
tasks performed by
workers, the greater
must be the variety of
supervising methods
used.

91. The span of control, the
number of persons who can
be effectively supervised by
an administrator depends
least on the

(A) number of levels in the
chain of command
(B) routine nature of the
work
(C) amount of planning and
control required
(D) ability of subordinates
to work independently
(E) amount of time available
for supervising each
subordinate.

92. Suppose that you have the
task of formulating a plan
for the purpose of making
more efficient the operation
of a particular activity. In
general, you should pay least
regard to

(A) the length of time which
is consumed in the
activity
(B) the degree of prestige
which will accrue to you
(C) the value of the end
product resulting from
the activity
(D) the desirability of
providing work
schedules for the
participants in the
activity.

93. The principal cause for a
good administrator's failure
to do well in a department
of the next higher level is
most likely due to

(A) unwillingness to assume
the administrative and
supervisory
responsibilities of the
new position
(B) a sense of inferiority or
frustration
(C) reluctance to give up
routine company
responsibilities with
which he or she is
familiar
(D) a lack of appreciation
for the new
responsibilities involved.

94. A supervisor in a department
is responsible for the
efficient operation of the
department, yet the employee
can go to the agency head and
receive permission for
special privileges. The
thing essential in good
organization which is lacking
in this organization is

(A) that there is no limit on
the number of
subordinates who can be
supervised by one
supervisor
(B) that there is not "unity of

command" as far as the supervisor is concerned

(C) that the supervisor has not had his or her authority and responsibility fully defined

(D) that the supervisor does not have authority commensurate with responsibility.

95. A full investigation of the facts should precede the solution of a supervisory problem primarily because

(A) subordinates are usually critical of an administrator's decision

(B) an incomplete or unwise solution is likely to create new problems

(C) the evidence should be recorded for future reference

(D) the facts discovered can be used to solve other problems.

96. A department consists of several independent bureaus each responsible to the commissioner for its own planning, operation and reporting, a central personnel unit and the commissioner's office consisting of a secretary and several clerks to handle public relations. The one of the following undersirable characteristics which is most likely to arise in this organization is

(A) absence of planning

(B) duplication of work

(C) failure to have employees properly trained

(D) a lack of an easily understandable goal.

97. The one of the following which is a fundamental obstacle to effective

planning in most governmental agencies is

(A) inadequate staff or resources

(B) the absence of the properly centralized administration

(C) the absence of functional boundaries for units and individuals

(D) the neglect of analysis of ways and means.

98. Of the following, the major function of an administrative planning and research staff unit is to

(A) investigate trouble points in the organization

(B) reorganize inefficient units

(C) assist the executive to plan future operations

(D) conduct continuous investigations and planning.

99. "It is desirable and advantageous to leave a maximum measure of planning responsibility to operating agencies or units, rather than to remove the responsibility to a central planning staff agency." Adoption of the former policy (decentralized planning) would lead to

(A) less effective planning; operating personnel do not have the time to make long-term plans

(B) more effective planning; operating units are usually better equipped technically than any staff agency and consequently are in a better position to set up valid plans

(C) less effective planning;

a central planning
agency has a more
objective point of view
than any operating agency
can achieve
  (D) more effective planning;
      plans are conceived in
      terms of the existing
      situation and their
      execution is carried out
      with the will to succeed.

100. "The central staff planning
     unit within any organization
     includes in its functions

helping to plan policy at one
extreme and planning detailed
execution at the other
extreme." With respect to
the actual execution, the
planning activity should

(A) keep track of how the
    plans are working out but
    make no attempt to
    supervise their execution
(B) simply forward and
    explain new ideas
(C) supervise the execution
    of new plans
(D) have no concern with it.

Answer Key

1. B	21. C	41. A	61. D	81. C
2. C	22. B	42. B	62. B	82. C
3. B	23. B	43. A	63. A	83. B
4. D	24. D	44. D	64. B	84. B
5. B	25. B	45. A	65. A	85. D
6. C	26. A	46. B	66. D	86. D
7. D	27. C	47. A	67. C	87. C
8. B	28. B	48. C	68. B	88. B
9. D	29. A	49. D	69. C	89. B
10. A	30. D	50. C	70. B	90. C
11. B	31. D	51. D	71. A	91. A
12. D	32. D	52. B	72. B	92. B
13. C	33. C	53. C	73. A	93. A
14. C	34. B	54. A	74. C	94. B
15. A	35. D	55. B	75. D	95. B
16. C	36. B	56. C	76. B	96. B
17. C	37. A	57. B	77. D	97. C
18. B	38. B	58. B	78. D	98. D
19. B	39. C	59. C	79. D	99. D
20. B	40. B	60. B	80. D	100. A

ANSWER SHEET FOR SAMPLE PRACTICE EXAMINATION IV

1 Ⓐ Ⓑ Ⓒ Ⓓ   26 Ⓐ Ⓑ Ⓒ Ⓓ   51 Ⓐ Ⓑ Ⓒ Ⓓ   76 Ⓐ Ⓑ Ⓒ Ⓓ

2 Ⓐ Ⓑ Ⓒ Ⓓ   27 Ⓐ Ⓑ Ⓒ Ⓓ   52 Ⓐ Ⓑ Ⓒ Ⓓ   77 Ⓐ Ⓑ Ⓒ Ⓓ

3 Ⓐ Ⓑ Ⓒ Ⓓ   28 Ⓐ Ⓑ Ⓒ Ⓓ   53 Ⓐ Ⓑ Ⓒ Ⓓ   78 Ⓐ Ⓑ Ⓒ Ⓓ

4 Ⓐ Ⓑ Ⓒ Ⓓ   29 Ⓐ Ⓑ Ⓒ Ⓓ   54 Ⓐ Ⓑ Ⓒ Ⓓ   79 Ⓐ Ⓑ Ⓒ Ⓓ

5 Ⓐ Ⓑ Ⓒ Ⓓ   30 Ⓐ Ⓑ Ⓒ Ⓓ   55 Ⓐ Ⓑ Ⓒ Ⓓ   80 Ⓐ Ⓑ Ⓒ Ⓓ

6 Ⓐ Ⓑ Ⓒ Ⓓ   31 Ⓐ Ⓑ Ⓒ Ⓓ   56 Ⓐ Ⓑ Ⓒ Ⓓ   81 Ⓐ Ⓑ Ⓒ Ⓓ

7 Ⓐ Ⓑ Ⓒ Ⓓ   32 Ⓐ Ⓑ Ⓒ Ⓓ   57 Ⓐ Ⓑ Ⓒ Ⓓ   82 Ⓐ Ⓑ Ⓒ Ⓓ

8 Ⓐ Ⓑ Ⓒ Ⓓ   33 Ⓐ Ⓑ Ⓒ Ⓓ   58 Ⓐ Ⓑ Ⓒ Ⓓ   83 Ⓐ Ⓑ Ⓒ Ⓓ

9 Ⓐ Ⓑ Ⓒ Ⓓ   34 Ⓐ Ⓑ Ⓒ Ⓓ   59 Ⓐ Ⓑ Ⓒ Ⓓ   84 Ⓐ Ⓑ Ⓒ Ⓓ

10 Ⓐ Ⓑ Ⓒ Ⓓ   35 Ⓐ Ⓑ Ⓒ Ⓓ   60 Ⓐ Ⓑ Ⓒ Ⓓ   85 Ⓐ Ⓑ Ⓒ Ⓓ

11 Ⓐ Ⓑ Ⓒ Ⓓ   36 Ⓐ Ⓑ Ⓒ Ⓓ   61 Ⓐ Ⓑ Ⓒ Ⓓ   86 Ⓐ Ⓑ Ⓒ Ⓓ

12 Ⓐ Ⓑ Ⓒ Ⓓ   37 Ⓐ Ⓑ Ⓒ Ⓓ   62 Ⓐ Ⓑ Ⓒ Ⓓ   87 Ⓐ Ⓑ Ⓒ Ⓓ

13 Ⓐ Ⓑ Ⓒ Ⓓ   38 Ⓐ Ⓑ Ⓒ Ⓓ   63 Ⓐ Ⓑ Ⓒ Ⓓ   88 Ⓐ Ⓑ Ⓒ Ⓓ

14 Ⓐ Ⓑ Ⓒ Ⓓ   39 Ⓐ Ⓑ Ⓒ Ⓓ   64 Ⓐ Ⓑ Ⓒ Ⓓ   89 Ⓐ Ⓑ Ⓒ Ⓓ

15 Ⓐ Ⓑ Ⓒ Ⓓ   40 Ⓐ Ⓑ Ⓒ Ⓓ   65 Ⓐ Ⓑ Ⓒ Ⓓ   90 Ⓐ Ⓑ Ⓒ Ⓓ

16 Ⓐ Ⓑ Ⓒ Ⓓ   41 Ⓐ Ⓑ Ⓒ Ⓓ   66 Ⓐ Ⓑ Ⓒ Ⓓ   91 Ⓐ Ⓑ Ⓒ Ⓓ

17 Ⓐ Ⓑ Ⓒ Ⓓ   42 Ⓐ Ⓑ Ⓒ Ⓓ   67 Ⓐ Ⓑ Ⓒ Ⓓ   92 Ⓐ Ⓑ Ⓒ Ⓓ

18 Ⓐ Ⓑ Ⓒ Ⓓ   43 Ⓐ Ⓑ Ⓒ Ⓓ   68 Ⓐ Ⓑ Ⓒ Ⓓ   93 Ⓐ Ⓑ Ⓒ Ⓓ

19 Ⓐ Ⓑ Ⓒ Ⓓ   44 Ⓐ Ⓑ Ⓒ Ⓓ   69 Ⓐ Ⓑ Ⓒ Ⓓ   94 Ⓐ Ⓑ Ⓒ Ⓓ

20 Ⓐ Ⓑ Ⓒ Ⓓ   45 Ⓐ Ⓑ Ⓒ Ⓓ   70 Ⓐ Ⓑ Ⓒ Ⓓ   95 Ⓐ Ⓑ Ⓒ Ⓓ

21 Ⓐ Ⓑ Ⓒ Ⓓ   46 Ⓐ Ⓑ Ⓒ Ⓓ   71 Ⓐ Ⓑ Ⓒ Ⓓ   96 Ⓐ Ⓑ Ⓒ Ⓓ

22 Ⓐ Ⓑ Ⓒ Ⓓ   47 Ⓐ Ⓑ Ⓒ Ⓓ   72 Ⓐ Ⓑ Ⓒ Ⓓ   97 Ⓐ Ⓑ Ⓒ Ⓓ

23 Ⓐ Ⓑ Ⓒ Ⓓ   48 Ⓐ Ⓑ Ⓒ Ⓓ   73 Ⓐ Ⓑ Ⓒ Ⓓ   98 Ⓐ Ⓑ Ⓒ Ⓓ

24 Ⓐ Ⓑ Ⓒ Ⓓ   49 Ⓐ Ⓑ Ⓒ Ⓓ   74 Ⓐ Ⓑ Ⓒ Ⓓ   99 Ⓐ Ⓑ Ⓒ Ⓓ

25 Ⓐ Ⓑ Ⓒ Ⓓ   50 Ⓐ Ⓑ Ⓒ Ⓓ   75 Ⓐ Ⓑ Ⓒ Ⓓ   100 Ⓐ Ⓑ Ⓒ Ⓓ

SAMPLE PRACTICE EXAMINATION IV

DIRECTIONS FOR ANSWERING QUESTIONS

Each question has four suggested answers, lettered A, B, C, and D. Decide which one is the best answer and on the sample answer sheet find the question number and darken the area with a soft pencil which corresponds to the answer that you have selected.

The time allowed for the entire examination is 4 hours.

1. A supervisor notices that one of his more competent subordinates has recently been showing less interest in his work. The work performed by this employee has also fallen off and he seems to want to do no more than the minimum acceptable amount of work. When his supervisor questions the subordinate about his decreased interest and his mediocre work performance, the subordinate replies: "Sure, I've lost interest in my work. I don't see any reason why I should do more than I have to. When I do a good job, nobody notices it. But, let me fall down on one minor job and the whole place knows about it! So why should I put myself out on this job?" If the subordinate's contentions are true, it would be correct to assume that the

(A) subordinate has not received adequate training
(B) subordinate's workload should be decreased
(C) supervisor must share responsibility for this employee's reaction
(D) supervisor has not been properly enforcing work standards.

2. "How many subordinates should report directly to each supervisor? While there is agreement that there are limits to the number of subordinates that a manager can supervise well, this limit is determined by a number of important factors." Which of the following factors is most likely to increase the number of subordinates that can be effectively supervised by one supervisor in a particular unit?

(A) The unit has a great variety of activities.

153

(B) A staff assistant handles the supervisor's routine duties.
(C) The unit has a relatively inexperienced staff.
(D) The office layout is being rearranged to make room for more employees.

3. Mary Smith, a Principal Administrative Associate, heads the Inspection Records Unit of Department Y. She is a dedicated supervisor who not only strives to maintain an efficient operation, but she also tries to improve the competence of each individual member of her staff. She keeps these considerations in mind when assigning work to her staff. Her bureau chief asks her to compile some data based on information contained in her records. She feels that any member of her staff should be able to do this job. The one of the following members of her staff who would probably be given least consideration for this assignment is

(A) Jane Abel, a capable Office Associate with considerable experience in the unit
(B) Kenneth Brown, an Office Aide recently transferred to the unit who has not had an opportunity to demonstrate his capabilities
(C) Laura Chance, an Office Aide who spends full time on a single routine assignment
(D) Michael Dunn, an Office Aide who works on several minor jobs but still has the lightest work load.

4. "There are very few aspects of a supervisor's job that do not involve communication, either in writing or orally." Which of the following statements regarding oral and written orders is not correct?

(A) Oral orders usually permit more immediate feedback than do written orders.
(B) Written orders, rather than oral orders, should generally be given when the subordinate will be held strictly accountable.
(C) Oral orders are usually preferable when the order contains lengthy detailed instructions.
(D) Written orders, rather than oral orders, should usually be given to a subordinate who is slow to understand or is forgetful.

5. Assume that you are the head of a large clerical unit in Department R. Your department's personnel office has appointed an Office Aide, Roberta Rowe, to fill a vacancy in your unit. Before bringing this appointee to your office, the personnel officer has given Roberta the standard orientation on salary, fringe benefits, working conditions, attendance, and the department's personnel rules. In addition, she has been supplied with literature covering these areas. Of the following, the action that you should take first after Roberta has been brought to your office is to

(A) give her an opportunity to read the literature furnished by the personnel office so that she can ask you questions about it

(B) escort her to the desk she will use and assign her to work with an experienced employee who will act as her trainer

(C) explain the duties and responsibilities of her job and its relationship with the jobs being performed by the other employees of the unit.

(D) summon the employee who is currently doing the work that will be performed by Roberta and have that employee explain and demonstrate how to perform the required tasks.

6. Your superior informs you that the employee turnover rate in your office is well above the norm and must be reduced. Which one of the following initial steps would be least appropriate in attempting to overcome this problem?

(A) Decide to be more lenient about performance standards and about employee requests for time off, so that your office will gain a reputation as an easy place to work.

(B) Discuss the problem with a few of your key people whose judgment you trust to see if they can shed some light on the underlying causes of the problem.

(C) Review the records of employees who have left during the past year to see if there is a pattern that will help you understand the problem.

(D) Carefully review your training procedures to see whether they can be improved.

7. In issuing instructions to a subordinate on a job assignment, the supervisor should ordinarily explain why the assignment is being made. Omission of such an explanation is best justified when the

(A) subordinate is restricted in the amount of discretion to be exercised in carrying out the assignment

(B) assignment is one that will be unpopular with the subordinate

(C) subordinate understands the reason as a result of previous similar assignments

(D) assignment is given to an employee who is in need of further training.

8. When a supervisor allows sufficient time for training and makes an appropriate effort in the training of subordinates, his or her chief goal is to

(A) increase the dependence of one subordinate upon another in their everyday work activities

(B) spend more time with subordinates in order to become more involved in their work

(C) increase the capability and independence of subordinates in carrying out their work

(D) increase frequency of contact with subordinates in order to better evaluate their performance.

9. In preparing an evaluation of a subordinate's performance, which one of the following items is usually irrelevant?

(A) Remarks about tardiness or absenteeism.
(B) Mention of any unusual contributions or accomplishments.
(C) A summary of the employee's previous job experience.
(D) An assessment of the employee's attitude toward the job.

10. The ability to delegate responsibility while maintaining adequate controls is one key to a supervisor's success. Which one of the following methods of control would minimize the amount of responsibility assumed by the subordinate?

(A) Asking for a monthly status report in writing.
(B) Asking to receive copies of important correspondence so that you can be aware of potential problems.
(C) Scheduling periodic project status conferences with your subordinate.
(D) Requiring that your subordinate confer with you before making decisions on a project.

11. You wish to assign an important project to a subordinate who you think has good potential. Which one of the following approaches would be most effective in successfully completing the project while developing the subordinate's abilities?

(A) Describe the project to the subordinate in general terms and emphasize that it must be completed as quickly as possible.
(B) Outline the project in detail to the subordinate and emphasize that its successful completion could lead to career advancement.
(C) Develop a detailed project outline and timetable, discuss the details and timing with the subordinate and assign the subordinate to carry out the plan on his or her own.
(D) Discuss the project objectives and suggested approaches with the subordinate, and ask the subordinate to develop a detailed project outline and timetable for your approval.

12. Research studies reveal that an important difference between high-production and low-production supervisors lies not in their interest in eliminating mistakes, but in their manner of handling mistakes. High-production supervisors are most likely to look upon mistakes as primarily

(A) an opportunity to provide training
(B) a by-product of subordinate negligence
(C) an opportunity to fix blame in a situation
(D) a result of their own incompetence.

13. Supervisors should try to establish what has been called "positive discipline," an atmosphere in which subordinates willingly abide by rules which they consider fair. When a supervisor

notices a subordinate violating an important rule, the <u>first</u> course of action should be to

(A) stop the subordinate and tell him what he is doing wrong
(B) wait a day or two before approaching the employee involved
(C) call a meeting of all subordinates to discuss the rule
(D) forget the matter in the hope that it will not happen again.

14. The working climate is the feeling, degree of freedom, the tone and the mood of the working environment. Which of the following contributes most to determining the working climate in a unit or group?

(A) The rules set for rest periods.
(B) The example set by the supervisor.
(C) The rules set for morning check in.
(D) The wages paid to the employees.

15. John Polk is a bright, ingenious Office Aide with a lot of initiative. He has made many good suggestions to his supervisor in the Training Division of Department T, where he is employed. However, last week one of his bright ideas literally "blew up." In setting up some electronic equipment in the training classroom, he crossed some wires resulting in a damaged tape recorder and a classroom so filled with smoke that the training class had to be held in another room. When Mr. Brown, his supervisor, learned of this occurrence, he immediately summoned John to his private office. There Mr. Brown spent five minutes bawling John out, calling him an overzealous, overgrown kid, and sent him back to his job without letting John speak once. Of the following the action of Mr. Brown that most deserves approval is that he

(A) took disciplinary action immediately without regard for past performance
(B) kept the disciplinary interview to a brief period
(C) concentrated his criticism on the root cause of the occurrence
(D) held the disciplinary interview in his private office.

16. Typically, when the technique of "supervision by results" is practiced, higher management sets down, either implicitly or explicitly, certain performance standards or goals that the subordinate is expected to meet. As long as these standards are met, management interferes very little. The most likely result of the use of this technique is that it will

(A) lead to ambiguity in terms of goals
(B) be successful only to the extent that close direct supervision is practiced
(C) make it possible to evaluate both employee and supervisory effectiveness
(D) allow for complete autonomy on the subordinate's part.

17. Assume that you, a Principal Administrative Associate, are the supervisor of a large

clerical unit performing routine clerical operations. One of your clerks consistently produces much less work than other members of your staff performing similar tasks. Of the following, the action you should take <u>first</u> is to

(A) ask the clerk if he or she wants to be transferred to another unit

(B) reprimand the clerk for poor performance and issue a warning stating that further disciplinary action will be taken if work does not improve

(C) quietly ask the clerk's co-workers whether they know the reason for the poor performance

(D) discuss the matter with the clerk to work out plans for improving performance.

18. When making written evaluations and reviews of the performance of subordinates, it is usually advisable to

(A) avoid informing the employee of the evaluation if it is critical because it may create hard feelings

(B) avoid informing the employee of the evaluation whether critical or favorable because it is tension-producing

(C) permit the employee to see the evaluation but not to discuss it because the supervisor cannot be certain where the discussion might lead

(D) discuss the evaluation openly with the employee because it helps the employee understand what is expected.

19. There are a number of well-known and respected human relations principles that successful supervisors have been using for years in building good relationships with their employees. Which of the following does <u>not</u> illustrate such a principle?

(A) Give clear and complete instructions.

(B) Let each person know how he or she is getting along.

(C) Keep an open-door policy.

(D) Make all relationships personal ones.

20. Assume that it is your responsibility as a Principal Administrative Associate to maintain certain personnel records that are continually being updated. You have three office aides assigned specifically to this task. Recently you have noticed that the volume of work has increased substantially, and the processing of personnel records by the office aides is backlogged. Your supervisor is now receiving complaints due to the processing delay. Of the following, the best course of action for you to take <u>first</u> is to

(A) have a meeting with the office aides, advise them of the problem and ask that they do their work faster; then confirm your meeting in writing for the record

(B) request that an additional position be authorized for your unit

(C) review the procedures being used for processing the work, and try to determine if you can improve the flow of work

(D) get the system moving faster by spending some of your own time processing the backlog.

21. Assume that you are in charge of a payroll unit consisting of four office aides. It is Friday, November 14. You have just arrived in the office after a conference. Your staff is preparing a payroll that must be forwarded the following Monday. Which of the following new items on your desk should you attend to <u>first</u>?

(A) A telephone message regarding very important information needed for the statistical summary of salaries paid for the month of November.

(B) A memorandum regarding a new procedure that should be followed in preparing the payroll.

(C) A telephone message from an employee who is threatening to endorse his pay check "Under Protest" because he is dissatisfied with the amount.

(D) A memorandum from your supervisor reminding you to submit the probationary period report on a new employee.

22. You are Principal Administrative Associate in charge of a unit that orders and issues supplies. On a particular day you are faced with the following four situations. Which one should you take care of <u>first</u>?

(A) One of your employees who is in the process of taking the quarterly inventory of supplies has telephoned and asked that you return the call as soon as possible.

(B) A representative of a company that is noted for producing excellent office supplies will soon arrive with samples for you to distribute to the various offices in your agency.

(C) A large order of supplies which was delivered this morning has been checked and counted and a deliveryman is waiting for you to sign the receipt.

(D) A clerk from the purchase division asks you to search for a bill you failed to send to them which is urgently needed in order for them to complete a report due this morning.

23. As Principal Administrative Associate, assume that it is necessary for you to give an unpleasant assignment to one of your subordinates. You expect this employee to raise some objections to this assignment. The most appropriate of the following actions for you to take <u>first</u> is to issue the assignment

(A) orally, with the further statement that you will not listen to any complaints

(B) in writing, to forestall any complaints by the employee

(C) orally, permitting the employee to express his feelings

(D) in writing, with a note that any comments should be submitted in writing.

24. Your office has recently acquired its own electrostatic copier. During the first two months of use, copying costs

have greatly exceeded the budgeted amount, and you have been asked to take steps to reduce this cost. Which one of the following steps would be least effective in solving this problem?

(A) Making sure that employees use carbons, rather than the copier, for file copies of ordinary correspondence.
(B) Turning off the copier for two hours each day.
(C) Analyzing the need for copies of routine reports, and eliminating useless copies.
(D) Requiring that a different copying process, such as mimeograph, be used when large numbers of copies are needed.

25. A Centrex telephone system allows both incoming and outgoing calls to be completed directly without going through a switchboard operator. An outside caller can reach a particular employee by direct dialing. For which one of the following types of offices would this system be most desirable?

(A) An office dealing chiefly with complaints from tenants.
(B) An office whose primary function is to maintain accounting records.
(C) An office that receives and processes applications for certain kinds of city permits.
(D) A purchasing office where each employee maintains contact with a number of regular suppliers.

26. "Cycling is an arrangement where papers are processed throughout a period according to an orderly plan rather than as a group all at one time. This technique has been used for a long time by public utilities in their cycle billing." Of the following practices, the one that best illustrates this technique is that in which

(A) paychecks for per annum employees are issued bi-weekly and those for per diem employees are issued weekly
(B) field inspectors report in person to their offices one day a week, on Fridays, when they do all their paperwork and also pick up their paychecks
(C) the dates for issuing relief checks to clients vary depending on the last digit of the clients' social security numbers
(D) the last day for filing and paying income taxes is the same for Federal, State, and City income taxes.

27. The employees in your division have recently been given an excellent up-to-date office manual, but you find that a good number of employees are not following the procedures outlined in it. Which one of the following would be most likely to ensure that employees begin using the manual effectively?

(A) Require each employee to keep a copy of the manual in plain sight on the desk.

(B) Issue warnings periodically to those employees who deviate most from procedures prescribed in the manual.

(C) Tell an employee to check the manual when he or she does not follow the proper procedures.

(D) Suggest to the employees that the manual be studied thoroughly.

28. The one of the following factors which should be considered <u>first</u> in the design of <u>office</u> forms is the

(A) information to be included in the form
(B) sequence of the information
(C) purpose of the form
(D) persons who will be using the form.

29. "Window envelopes are being used to an increasing extent by government and private industry." The one of the following that is <u>not</u> an advantage of window envelopes is that they

(A) cut down on addressing costs
(B) eliminate the need to attach envelopes to letters being sent forward for signature by a superior
(C) are less costly to buy that regular envelopes
(D) reduce the risk of having letters placed in wrong envelopes.

30. Your bureau's typing unit is getting bogged down with work. Your bureau head wants you to look into this problem. You find that much time is spent by the typists in inserting and then removing carbons used in preparing form notices in

quadruplicate. The carbon copies are kept by the units to which they are routed for a maximum of two years. You suggest, as a time-saver, that these notices be printed as 4-part carbon interleaved sets. In selecting the paper to be used for these 4-part carbon interleaved forms, you would find it most desirable to use

(A) 16-lb., 100% rag content paper
(B) 16-lb., 100% sulphite paper
(C) 20-lb., 25% rag content paper
(D) 20-lb., ledger paper.

31. Your bureau head asks you to prepare the office layouts for several of his units being moved to a higher floor in your office building. Of the following possibilities, the one that you should <u>avoid</u> in preparing the layouts is to

(A) place the desks of the first-line supervisors near those of the staffs they supervise
(B) place the desks of employees whose work is most closely related near one another
(C) arrange the desks so that employees do not face one another
(D) locate desks with many outside visitors farthest from the office entrance.

32. Which one of the following conditions would be <u>least</u> important in considering a change of the layout in a particular office?

(A) Installation of a new office machine.
(B) Assignment of five additional employees to your office.

(C) Poor flow of work.
(D) Employees' personal preferences of desk location.

33. Your bureau head asks you to design an application form that will be filled out either in handwriting or by typewriter. The information supplied on this form will be keypunched for subsequent processing on a computer. In designing this form, you intend to make it as easy as possible for the keypunch operator to transcribe the information that is to be keypunched. The one of the following considerations that will contribute <u>least</u> to carrying out this intention is the

(A) color of the ink to be used in printing the form
(B) similarity in sequence of items on the form and the key punch card
(C) size of the type to be used in printing the form
(D) substance and weight of the paper used for the form.

34. Which of the following duplicating processes should be used to make 10,000 copies of a letter-sized form?

(A) Photo-offset process.
(B) Xerox process.
(C) Mimeograph process.
(D) Spirit duplicating process.

35. Suppose Mr. Bloom, Principal Administrative Associate, is dictating a letter to a stenographer. His dictation begins with the name of the addressee and continues to the body of the letter.

However, Mr. Bloom does not dictate the address of the recipient of the letter. He expects the stenographer to locate it. The use of this practice by Mr. Bloom is

(A) acceptable, especially if he gives the stenographer the letter to which he is responding
(B) acceptable, especially if the letter is lengthy and detailed
(C) unacceptable, because it is not part of a stenographer's duties to search for information
(D) unacceptable, because he should not rely on the accuracy of the stenographer.

36. Assume that there are no rules, directives, or instructions concerning the filing of materials in your office or the retention of such files. A system is now being followed of placing in "inactive" files any materials that are more than one year old. Of the following, the most appropriate thing to do with material that has been in an "inactive" file in your office for over one year is to

(A) inspect the contents of the file and then use the material for scrap paper
(B) transfer the material to a remote location, where it can be obtained if necessary
(C) keep the material intact for a minimum of another three years
(D) destroy the material which has not been needed for at least a year.

37. Suppose you, a Principal Administrative Associate, have just returned to your desk after engaging in an

all-morning conference. Joe Burns, an Office Aide, informs you that Clara McClough, an administrator in another agency, telephoned during the morning and that, although she requested to speak with you, he was able to give her the desired information. Of the following, the most appropriate action for you to take in regard to Mr. Burns' action is to

(A) thank him for assisting Ms. McClough in your absence
(B) explain to him the proper telephone practice to use in the future
(C) reprimand him for not properly channeling Ms. McClough's call
(D) issue a memo to all clerical employees regarding proper telephone practices.

38. "When interviewing subordinates with problems, supervisors frequently find that asking direct questions of the employee results only in evasive responses. The supervisor may therefore resort to the 'non-directive' interview technique. In this technique the supervisor avoids pointed questions; he leads the employee to continue talking freely uninfluenced by the supervisor's preconceived notions. This technique often enables the employee to bring the problem into sharp focus and to reach a solution to the problem."

Suppose that you are a supervisor interviewing a subordinate about his recent poor attendance record. On calling his attention to his excessive lateness

record, he replies: "I just don't seem to be able to get up in the morning. Frankly, I've lost interest in this job. I don't care about it. When I get up in the morning, I have to skip breakfast and I'm still late. I don't care about this job." If you are using the "non-directive" technique in this interview, the most appropriate of the following responses for you to make is

(A) "You don't care about this job?"
(B) "Don't you think you are letting the department down?"
(C) "Are you having trouble at home?"
(D) "Don't you realize your actions are childish?"

Questions 39 through 43 are to be answered solely on the basis of the following passage.

General supervision, in contrast to close supervision, involves a high degree of delegation of authority and requires some indirect means to insure that employee behavior conforms to management needs. Not everyone works well under general supervision, however. General supervision works best where subordinates desire responsibility. General supervision also works well where individuals in work groups have strong feelings about the quality of the finished work products. Strong identification with management goals is another trait of persons who work well under general supervision. There are substantial differences in the amount of responsibility people are willing to accept on the job. One person may flourish under supervision that another might find extremely restrictive.

Psychological research provides evidence that the nature of a person's personality affects his or her attitude toward supervision. There are some employees with a low need for achievement and high fear of failure who shy away from challenges and responsibilities. Many seek self-expression off the job and ask only to be allowed to daydream on it. There are others who have become so accustomed to the authoritarian approach in their culture, family, and previous work experience that they regard general supervision as no supervision at all. They abuse the priveleges it bestows on them and refuse to accept the responsibilities it demands.

Different groups develop different attitudes toward work. Most college graduates, for example, expect a great deal of responsibility and freedom. People with limited education, on the other hand, often have trouble accepting the concept that people should make decisions for themselves, particularly decisions concerning work. Therefore, the extent to which general supervision will be effective varies greatly with the subordinates involved.

39. According to the preceding passage, which one of the following is a necessary part of management policy regarding general supervision?

(A) Most employees should formulate their own work goals.
(B) Deserving employees should be rewarded periodically.
(C) Some controls on employee work patterns should be established.
(D) Responsibility among employees should generally be equalized.

40. It can be inferred from the preceding passage that an employee who avoids responsibilities and challenges is most likely to

(A) gain independence under general supervision
(B) work better under close supervision than under general supervision
(C) abuse the liberal guidelines of general supervision
(D) become more restricted and cautious under general supervision.

41. Based on the preceding passage, employees who succeed under general supervision are most likely to

(A) have a strong identification with people and their problems
(B) accept work obligations without fear
(C) seek self-expression off the job
(D) value the intellectual aspects of life.

42. Of the following, the best title for the passage is

(A) Benefits and Disadvantages of General Supervision
(B) Production Levels of

Employees under General Supervision
(C) Employee Attitudes Toward Work and the Work Environment
(D) Employee Background and Personality as a Factor in Utilizing General Supervision.

43. It can be inferred from the preceding passage that the one of the following employees who is most likely to work best under general supervision is one who

(A) is a part-time graduate student
(B) was raised by very strict parents
(C) has little self-confidence
(D) has been closely supervised in past jobs.

44. At the request of your bureau head you have designed a simple visitor's referral form. The form will be cut from 8 1/2" x 11" stock. Which of the following should be the dimensions of the form if you want to be sure that there is no waste of paper?

(A) 2 3/4" x 4 1/4"
(B) 3 1/4" x 4 3/4"
(C) 3 3/4" x 4 3/4"
(D) 4 1/2" x 5 1/2"

45. An office contains six file cabinets, each containing three drawers. One of your responsibilities as a new Principal Administrative Associate is to see that there is sufficient filing space. At the present time, 1/4 of the file space contains forms, 2/9 contains personnel records, 1/3 contains reports, and 1/7 of the remaining space

contains budget records. If each drawer may contain more than one type of record, how much drawer space is now empty?

(A) 0 drawers
(B) 13/14 of a drawer
(C) 3 drawers
(D) 3 1/2 drawers

46. Assume that there were 21 working days in March. The five clerks in your unit had the following number of absences in March:

Clerk H - 2 absences
Clerk J - 1 absence
Clerk K - 6 absences
Clerk L - 0 absences
Clerk M - 10 absences

To the nearest day, what was the average attendance in March for the five clerks in your unit?

(A) 4
(B) 17
(C) 18
(D) 21

Answer questions 47 through 51 solely on the basis of the information in the following passage.

The concept of "program management" was first developed in order to handle some of the complex projects undertaken by the U.S. Department of Defense in the 1950's. Program management is an administrative system combining planning and control techniques to guide and coordinate all of the activities which contribute to one overall program or project. It has been used by the federal government to manage space exploration and other programs involving many contributing organizations. It is also used by state and local governments and by some large firms to provide administrative integration of work from a number of sources, be they individuals, departments, or outside companies.

One of the specific administrative techniques for program management is Program Evaluation Review Technique (PERT). PERT begins with the assembling of a list of all the activities needed to accomplish an overall task. The next step consists of arranging these activities in a sequential network showing both how much time each activity will take and which activities must be completed before others can begin. The time required for each activity is estimated by simple statistical techniques by the persons who will be responsible for the work, and the time required to complete the entire string of activities along each sequential path through the network is then calculated. There may be dozens or hundreds of these paths, so the calculation is usually done by computer. The longest path is then labelled the "critical path" because no matter how quickly events not on this path are completed, the events along the longest path must be finished before the project can be terminated. The overall starting and completion dates are then pinpointed, and target dates are established for each task. Actual progress can later be checked by comparison to the network plan.

47. Judging from the information in the preceding passage, which one of the following projects is most suitable for handling by a program management technique?

(A) Review and improvement of the filing system used by a city office.
(B) Computerization of accounting data already on file in an office.
(C) Planning and construction of an urban renewal project.
(D) Announcing a change in city tax regulations to thousands of business firms.

48. The passage indicates that program management methods are now in wide use by various kinds of organizations. Which one of the following organizations would you least expect to make use of such methods today?

(A) An automobile manufacturer.
(B) A company in the aerospace business.
(C) The government of a large city.
(D) A library reference department.

49. In making use of the PERT technique, the first step is to determine

(A) every activity that must take place in order to complete the project
(B) a target date for completion of the project
(C) the estimated time required to complete each activity which is related

to the whole
(D) which activities will
make up the longest
path on the chart.

50. Who estimates the time
required to complete a
particular activity in a
PERT program?

(A) The people responsible
for the particular
activity.
(B) The statistician assigned
to the program.
(C) The organization that
has commissioned the
project.
(D) The operator who
programs the computer.

51. Which one of the following
titles best describes the
contents of the passage?

(A) "The Need for Computers
in Today's Projects."
(B) "One Technique for
Program Management."
(C) "Local Governments Can
Now Use Space-Age
Techniques."
(D) "Why Planning Is
Necessary for Complex
Projects."

Questions 52 through 60 each
consist of a sentence which
may or may not be an example
of good English usage.
Consider grammar,
punctuation, spelling,
capitalization, verbosity,
awkwardness, etc. Examine
each sentence, and then
choose the correct statement
about it from the four
choices below it. If the
English usage in the
sentence is better as given
than with any of the changes
suggested in options B, C,
or D, choose option A. Do
not choose an option that
will change the meaning of

the sentence.

52. "The stenographers who are
secretaries to commissioners
have more varied duties than
the stenographic pool."

(A) This is an example of
effective writing.
(B) In this sentence there
should be a comma after
"commissioners" in order
to break up the sentence
into clauses.
(C) In this sentence the
words "stenographers in"
should be inserted after
the word "than."
(D) In this sentence the word
"commissioners" is
misspelled.

53. "A person who becomes an
Administrative Assistant will
be called upon to provide
leadership, to insure proper
quantity and quality of
production, and many
administrative chores must
be performed."

(A) This sentence is an
example of effective
writing.
(B) The sentence should be
divided into three
separate sentences, each
describing a duty.
(C) The words "many
administrative chores
must be performed" should
be changed to "to perform
many administrative
chores."
(D) The words "to provide
leadership" should be
changed to "to be a
leader."

54. "A complete report has been
submitted by our branch
office, giving details about
this transaction."

(A) This sentence is an
example of effective

writing.

(B) The phrase "giving details about this transaction" should be placed between the words "report" and "has."

(C) A semi-colon should replace the comma after the word "office" to indicate independent clauses.

(D) A colon should replace the comma after the word "office" since the second clause provides further explanation.

55. "The report was delayed because of the fact that the writer lost his rough draft two days before the deadline."

(A) This sentence is an example of effective writing.

(B) In this sentence the words "of the fact that" are unnecessary and should be deleted.

(C) In this sentence the words "because of the fact that" should be shortened to "due to."

(D) In this sentence the word "before" should be replaced by "prior to."

56. "Included in this offer are a six months' guarantee, a complete set of instructions, and one free inspection of the equipment."

(A) This sentence is an example of effective writing.

(B) The word "is" should be substituted for the word "are."

(C) The word "months'" should have been spelled "month's."

(D) The word "months'" should have been spelled "months."

57. "Certain employees come to the attention of their employers. Especially those with poor work records and excessive absences."

(A) This is an example of effective writing.

(B) The period after the word "employers" should be changed to a comma, and the first letter of the word "Especially" should be changed to a small "e."

(C) The period after the word "employers" should be changed to a semicolon, and the first letter of the word "Especially" should be changed to a small "e."

(D) The period after the word "employers" should be changed to a colon.

58. "The applicant had decided to decline the appointment by the time he was called for the interview."

(A) This sentence is an example of effective writing.

(B) In this sentence the word "had" should be deleted.

(C) In this sentence the phrase "was called" should be replaced by "had been called."

(D) In this sentence the phrase "had decided to decline" should be replaced by "declined."

59. "There are two elevaters, each accommodating ten people."

(A) This sentence is correct.

(B) In this sentence the word "elevaters" should be spelled "elevators."

(C) In this sentence the word "each" should be replaced

by the word "both."

(D) In this sentence the word "accommodating" should be spelled "accomodating."

60. "With the aid of a special device, it was possible to alter the letterhead on the department's stationary."

(A) This sentence is correct.
(B) The word "aid" should be spelled "aide."
(C) The word "device" should be spelled "devise."
(D) The word "stationary" should be spelled "stationery."

61. Examine the following sentence and then choose from the options below the correct word to be inserted in the blank space.

"Everybody in both offices _____ involved in the project."

(A) are
(B) feel
(C) is
(D) were.

Answer questions 62 through 66 solely on the basis of the information in the following passage.

A new way of looking at job performance promises to be a major advance in measuring and increasing a person's true effectiveness in business. The fact that individuals differ enormously in their judgment of when a piece of work is actually finished is significant. It is believed that more than half of all people in the business world are defective in the "sense of closure," that is they do not know the

proper time to throw the switch that turns off their effort in one direction and diverts it to a new job. Only a minority of workers at any level have the required judgment and the feeling of responsibility to work on a job to the point of maximum effectiveness. The vast majority let go of each task far short of the completion point.

Very often, a defective sense of closure exists in the entire staff. When that occurs, it usually stems from a long-standing laxness on the part of higher management. A low degree of responsibility has been accepted and it has come to be standard. Combating this requires implementation of a few basic policies. Firstly, it is important to make each responsibility completely clear and to set certain guideposts as to what constitutes complete performance. Secondly, excuses for delays and failures should not be dealt with too sympathetically, but interest should be shown in the encountered obstacles. Lastly, a checklist should be used periodically to determine whether new levels of expectancy and new closure values have been set.

62. According to the preceding passage, a majority of people in the business world

(A) do not complete their work on time
(B) cannot properly determine when a particular job is completed
(C) make lame excuses for not completing a job on time
(D) can adequately judge

their own effectiveness at work.

63. It can be inferred from the preceding passage that when a poor sense of closure is observed among all the employees in a unit, the responsibility for raising the performance level belongs to

(A) non-supervisory employees
(B) the staff as a whole
(C) management
(D) first-line supervisors.

64. It is implied by the preceding passage that, by the establishment of work guideposts, employees may develop a

(A) better understanding of expected performances
(B) greater interest in their work relationships
(C) defective sense of closure
(D) lower level of performance.

65. It can be inferred from the preceding passage that an individual's idea of whether a job is finished is most closely associated with his

(A) loyalty to management
(B) desire to overcome obstacles
(C) ability to recognize his own defects
(D) sense of responsibility.

66. Of the following, the best heading for the preceding passage is

(A) Management's Role In a Large Bureaucracy
(B) Knowing When a Job Is Finished
(C) The Checklist, a Supervisor's Tool for Effectiveness
(D) Supervisory Techniques

In answering questions 67 through 73, assume that you are in charge of public information for an office which issues reports and answers questions from other offices and from the public on changes in land use. The charts below represent comparative land use in four neighborhoods. The area of each neighborhood is expressed in city blocks. Assume that all city blocks are the same size.

NEIGHBORHOOD A - 10 CITY BLOCKS

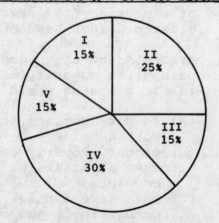

NEIGHBORHOOD B - 20 CITY BLOCKS

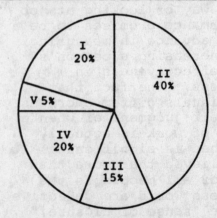

NEIGHBORHOOD C - 8 CITY BLOCKS

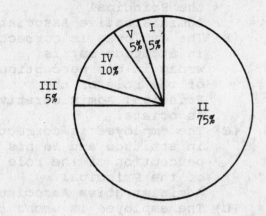

NEIGHBORHOOD D - 16 CITY BLOCKS

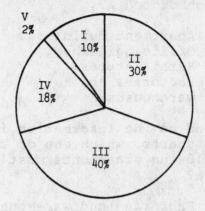

KEY:

        I - One- and two-family houses
       II - Apartment buildings
      III - Office buildings
       IV - Retail stores
        V - Factories and warehouses

67. In how many of these neighborhoods does residential use (categories I and II together) account for more than 50% of the land use?

   (A) One
   (B) Two
   (C) Three
   (D) Four

68. How many of the neighborhoods have an area of land occupied by apartment buildings which is greater than the area of land occupied by apartment buildings in Neighborhood C?

   (A) None
   (B) One
   (C) Two
   (D) Three

69. Which neighborhood has the largest land area occupied by factories and warehouses?

   (A) Neighborhood A.

   (B) Neighborhood B.
   (C) Neighborhood C.
   (D) Neighborhood D.

70. In which neighborhood is the largest percentage of the land devoted to both office buildings and retail stores?

   (A) Neighborhood A.
   (B) Neighborhood B.
   (C) Neighborhood C.
   (D) Neighborhood D.

71. What is the difference, to the nearest city block, between the amount of land devoted to one- and two-family houses in Neighborhood A and the amount devoted to similar use in Neighborhood C?

   (A) 1 block.
   (B) 2 blocks.
   (C) 5 blocks.
   (D) 10 blocks.

72. Which one of the following types of buildings occupies the same amount of land area

in Neighborhood B as the amount of land area occupied by retail stores in Neighborhood A?

(A) Apartment buildings.
(B) Office buildings.
(C) Retail stores.
(D) Factories and warehouses.

73. Based on the information in the charts, which one of the following statements must be true?

(A) Factories and warehouses are gradually disappearing from all the neighborhoods except Neighborhood A.
(B) Neighborhood B has more land area occupied by retail stores than any of the other neighborhoods.
(C) There are more apartment dwellers living in Neighborhood C than in any of the other neighborhoods.
(D) All four of these neighborhoods are predominantly residential.

74. An employee in a work group made the following comment to a co-worker: "It's great to be a lowly employee instead of a Principal Administrative Associate because you can work without thinking. The Principal Administrative Associate is getting paid to plan, schedule, and think. Let him see to it that you have a productive day." Which of the following statements about this quotation best reflects an understanding of good personnel management techniques and the role of the supervising Principal Administrative Associate?

(A) The employee is wrong in attitude and in his perception of the role of the Principal Administrative Associate.
(B) The employee is correct in attitude but is wrong in his perception of the role of the Principal Administrative Associate.
(C) The employee is correct in attitude and in his perception of the role of the Principal Administrative Associate.
(D) The employee is wrong in attitude but is right in his perception of the role of the Principal Administrative Associate.

75. A Principal Administrative Associate has been criticized for the low productivity in the group which he supervises. Which of the following best reflects an understanding of supervisory responsibilities in the area of productivity? Principal Administrative Associates should be held responsible for

(A) their own individual productivity and the productivity of the group they supervise, because they are in positions where they maintain or increase production through others
(B) their own personal productivity only, because supervisors are not likely to have any effect on the productivity of subordinates
(C) their own individual productivity but only for a drop in the productivity of the group they supervise,

since subordinates will
receive credit for
increased productivity
individually

(D) their own personal
productivity only,
because this is how
they would be evaluated
if they were not
supervisors.

76. A supervisor has held a
meeting in his office with
an employee about the
employee's grievance. The
grievance concerned the
sharp way in which the
supervisor reprimanded the
employee for an error the
employee made in the
performance of an assigned
task. The problem was not
resolved. Which one of the
following statements about
this meeting best reflects
an understanding of good
supervisory techniques?

(A) It is awkward for a
supervisor to handle a
grievance involving
himself. The supervisor
should not have held the
meeting.
(B) It would have been
better if the supervisor
had held the meeting at
the employee's workplace,
even though there would
have been frequent
distractions, because
the employee would have
been more relaxed.
(C) The resolution of a
problem is not the only
sign of a successful
meeting. The
achievement of
communication is
worthwhile.
(D) The supervisor should
have been forceful.
There is nothing wrong
with raising your voice
to an employee every
once in a while.

77. John Hayden, the owner of a
single family house in the
Bronx, complains that he
submitted an application for
reduction of assessment that
obviously was not acted upon
before his final assessment
notice was sent to him. The
timely receipt of the
application has been verified
in a departmental log book.
As the supervisor of the
clerical unit through which
this application was
processed and where this
delay occurred, you should
be least concerned with

(A) what happened
(B) who is responsible
(C) why it happened
(D) what can be learned from
it.

78. The one of the following that
applies most appropriately to
the role of the first-line
supervisor is that usually he
or she is

(A) called upon to help
determine agency policy
(B) involved in long-range
agency planning
(C) responsible for
determining some aspects
of basic organization
(D) a participant in
developing procedures
and methods.

79. Sally Jones, a Principal
Administrative Associate,
gives clear and precise
instructions to Robert
Warren, an Office Aide. In
these instructions, Ms.
Jones clearly delegates
authority to Mr. Warren to
undertake a well-defined
task. In this situation
Ms. Jones should expect
Mr. Warren to

(A) come to her to check out
details as he progresses

with the task
(B) come to her only with exceptional problems
(C) ask her permission if he wishes to use his delegated authority
(D) use his authority to redefine the task and its related activities.

80. Planning involves establishing departmental goals and programs and determining ways of reaching them. The main advantage of such planning is that

(A) there will be no need for adjustments once a plan is put into operation
(B) it insures that everyone is working on schedule
(C) it provides the framework for an effective operation
(D) unexpected work problems are easily overcome.

81. As a result of reorganization, the jobs in a large clerical unit were broken down into highly specialized tasks. Each specialized task was then assigned to a particular employee to perform. This action will probably lead to an increase in

(A) flexibility
(B) job satisfaction
(C) need for coordination
(D) employee initiative.

82. Your office carries on a large volume of correspondence concerned with the purchase of supplies and equipment for city offices. You use form letters to deal with many common situations. In which one of the following situations would use of a

form letter be <u>least</u> appropriate?

(A) Informing suppliers of a change in city regulations concerning purchase contracts.
(B) Telling a new supplier the standard procedures to be followed in billing.
(C) Acknowledging receipt of a complaint and saying that the complaint will be investigated.
(D) Answering a City Councilman's request for additional information on a particular regulation affecting suppliers.

83. Assume that you are Principal Administrative Associate heading a large clerical unit. Because of the great demands being made on your time, you have designated Tom Smith, an Office Associate, to be your assistant and to assume some of your duties. Of the following duties performed by you, the most appropriate one to assign to Tom Smith is to

(A) conduct the on-the-job training of new employees
(B) prepare the performance appraisal reports on your staff members
(C) represent your unit in dealings with the heads of other units
(D) handle matters that require exception to general policy.

84. In establishing rules for subordinates, a superior should be primarily concerned with

(A) creating sufficient flexibility to allow for

exceptions
(B) making employees aware
of the reasons for the
rules and the penalties
for infractions
(C) establishing the
strength of his or her
own position in relation
to subordinates
(D) having subordinates know
that such rules will be
imposed in a personal
manner.

85. The practice of conducting
staff training sessions on
a periodic basis is generally
considered

(A) poor; it takes employees
away from their work
assignments
(B) poor; all staff training
should be done on an
individual basis
(C) good; it permits the
regular introduction of
new methods and
techniques
(D) good; it insures a high
employee productivity
rate.

86. Suppose, as a Principal
Administrative Associate,
you have just announced at a
staff meeting with your
subordinates that a radical
reorganization of work will
take place next week. Your
subordinates at the meeting
appear to be excited, tense,
and worried. Of the
following, the best action
for you to take at that time
is to

(A) schedule private
conferences with each
subordinate to obtain
individual reactions to
the meeting
(B) close the meeting and
tell your subordinates to
return immediately to
their work assignments

(C) give your subordinates
some time to ask
questions and discuss
your announcement
(D) insist that your
subordinates do not
discuss your announcement
among themselves or with
other members of the
agency.

87. Assume that you are a Principal
Administrative Associate
supervising the Duplicating
and Reproduction Unit of
Department B. One of your
responsibilities is to
prepare a daily schedule
showing when and on which of
your unit's four duplicating
machines jobs are to be run
off. Of the following, the
factor that should be given
least consideration in
preparing the schedule is the

(A) priority of each of the
jobs to be run off
(B) production speed of the
different machines that
will be used
(C) staff available to
operate the machines
(D) date on which the job
order was received.

88. Suppose that as a Principal
Administrative Associate you
were recently placed in
charge of the Duplicating
and Stock Unit of Department
Y. From your observation of
the operations of your unit
during your first week as its
head, you get the impression
that there are inefficiencies
in its operations causing low
productivity. To obtain an
increase in its productivity,
the first of the following
actions you should take is to

(A) seek the advice of your
immediate superior on how
he or she would tackle
this problem

(B) develop plans to correct any unsatisfactory conditions arising from other than manpower deficiencies

(C) identify the problems causing low productivity

(D) discuss your productivity problem with other unit heads to find out how they handled similar problems.

89. Assume that you are a Principal Administrative Associate recently placed in charge of a large clerical unit. At a meeting, the head of another unit tells you, "My practice is to give a worker more than he can finish. In that way you can be sure that you are getting the most out of him." For you to adopt this practice would be

(A) advisable, since your actions would be consistent with those practiced in your agency

(B) inadvisable, since such a practice is apt to create frustration and lower staff morale

(C) advisable, since a high goal stimulates people to strive to attain it

(D) inadvisable, since management may, in turn, set too high a productivity goal for the unit.

90. Suppose that you are the supervisor of a unit in which there is an increasing amount of friction among several of your staff members. One of the reasons for this friction is the the work of some of these staff members cannot be completed by them until other staff members complete related work. Of the following, the most

appropriate action for you to take is to

(A) summon these employees to a meeting to discuss the responsibilities each has and to devise better methods of coordination

(B) have a private talk with each employee involved and make each understand that there must be more cooperation among the employees

(C) arrange for interviews with each of the employees involved to determine what the problems are

(D) shift the assignments of these employees so that each will be doing a job different from the current one.

91. An office supervisor has a number of responsibilities with regard to subordinates. Which one of the following functions should not be regarded as a basic responsibility of the office supervisor?

(A) Telling employees how to solve personal problems that may be interfering with their work.

(B) Training new employees to do the work assigned to them.

(C) Evaluating employees' performance periodically and discussing the evaluation with each employee.

(D) Bringing employee grievances to the attention of higher-level administrators and seeking satisfactory resolutions.

92. One of your most productive subordinates frequently demonstrates a poor attitude

towards her job. She seems unsure of herself, and she annoys her co-workers because she is continually belittling herself and the work that she is doing. In trying to help her overcome this problem, which of the following approaches is least likely to be effective?

(A) Compliment her on her work and assign her some additional responsibilities, telling her that she is being given these responsibilities because of her demonstrated ability.
(B) Discuss with her the problem of her attitude, and warn her that you will have to report it on her next performance evaluation.
(C) Assign her a particularly important and difficult project, stressing your confidence in her ability to complete it successfully.
(D) Discuss with her the problem of her attitude, and ask her for suggestions as to how you can help her overcome it.

93. You come to realize that a personality conflict between you and one of your subordinates is adversely affecting job performance. Which one of the following would be the most appropriate first step to take?

(A) Report the problem to your superior and request assistance. Your superior's experience may be helpful in resolving this problem.
(B) Discuss the situation

with several of the subordinate's co-workers to see if they can suggest any remedy.
(C) Suggest to the subordinate that professional counseling or therapy be obtained.
(D) Discuss the situation candidly with the subordinate, with the objective of resolving the problem between yourselves.

94. Assume that you are a Principal Administrative Associate supervising the Payroll Records Section in Department G. Your section has been requested to prepare and submit to the department's budget officer a detailed report giving a breakdown of labor costs under various departmental programs and sub-programs. You have assigned this task to an Office Aide, giving him full authority for seeing that this job is performed satisfactorily. You have given him a written statement of the job to be done and explained the purpose and use of this report. The next step that you should take in connection with this delegated task is to

(A) assist the Office Aide in the step-by-step performance of the job
(B) assure the Office Aide that you will be understanding of mistakes if made at the beginning
(C) require him to receive your approval for interim reports submitted at key points before he can proceed further with his task

(D) give him a target date for the completion of this report.

95. Assume that you are a Principal Administrative Associate heading a unit staffed with six clerical employees. One Office Aide, John Snell, is a probationary employee appointed four months ago. During the first three months, John learned his job quickly, performed his work accurately and diligently, and was cooperative and enthusiastic in his attitude. However, during the past few weeks his enthusiasm seems dampened, he is beginning to make mistakes, and at times appears bored. Of the following, the most appropriate action for you to take is to

(A) check with John's co-workers to find out whether they can explain John's change in attitude and work habits
(B) wait a few more weeks before taking any action, so that John will have an opportunity to make the needed changes on his own initiative
(C) talk to John about the change in his work performance and his decreased enthusiasm
(D) change John's assignment since this may be the basic cause of John's change in attitude and performance.

96. The supervisor of a clerical unit, on returning from a meeting, finds that one of his subordinates is performing work that has not been assigned. The subordinate explains that the group supervisor had come into the office while the unit supervisor was out and directed the employee to work on an urgent assignment. This is the first time the group supervisor had bypassed the unit supervisor. Of the following, the most appropriate action for the unit supervisor to take is to

(A) explain to the group supervisor that bypassing the unit supervisor is an undesirable practice
(B) have the subordinate stop work on the assignment until the entire matter can be clarified with the group supervisor
(C) raise the matter of bypassing a supervisor at the next staff conference held by the group supervisor
(D) forget about the incident.

97. Assume that you are a Principal Administrative Associate in charge of the Mail and Records Unit of Department K. On returning from a meeting, you notice that Jane Smith is not at her regular work location. You learn that another employee, Ruth Reed, had become faint, and that Jane took Ruth outdoors for some fresh air. It is a long-standing rule in your unit that no employee is to leave the building during office hours except on official business or with the unit head's approval. Only a few weeks ago, John Duncan was reprimanded by you for going out at 10:00 a.m. for a cup of coffee. With respect to Jane Smith's violation of this rule, the most appropriate of the following actions for you to take is to

(A) issue a reprimand to Jane Smith, with an

explanation that all employees must be treated in exactly the same way
(B) tell Jane that you should reprimand her, but you will not do so in this instance
(C) overlook this rule violation in view of the extenuating circumstances
(D) issue the reprimand with no further explanation, treating her in the same manner that you treated John Duncan.

98. Assume that you are a Principal Administrative Associate recently assigned as supervisor of Department X's Mail and Special Services Unit. In addition to processing your department's mail, your clerical employees are often sent on errands in lower Manhattan. You have learned that, while on such official errands, these employees sometimes take care of their own personal matters or those of their co-workers. The previous supervisor had tolerated this practice even though it violated a departmental personnel rule. The most appropriate of the following actions for you to take is to

(A) continue to tolerate this practice so long as it does not interfere with the work of your unit
(B) take no action until you have proof that an employee has violated this rule; then give the employee a mind reprimand
(C) wait until an employee has committed a gross violation of this rule; then bring the employee up on charges

(D) discuss this rule with your staff and caution them that its violation might necessitate disciplinary action.

99. "Supervisors who exercise 'close supervision' over their subordinates usually check up on their employees frequently, give them frequent instructions, and in general limit their freedom to do their work in their own way. Those who exercise 'general supervision' usually set forth the objectives of a job, tell their subordinates what they want accomplished, fix the limits within which the subordinates can work, and let the employees (if they are capable) decide how the job is to be done." Which one of the following conditions would contribute least to the success of the "general supervision" approach in an organizational unit?

(A) Employees in the unit welcome increased responsibilities.
(B) Work assignments in the unit are often challenging.
(C) Work procedures must conform with those of other units.
(D) Staff members support the objectives of the unit.

100. Assume that you are Principal Administrative Associate assigned as supervisor of the Clerical Services Unit of a large agency's Labor Relations Division. A member of your staff comes to you with a criticism of a policy followed by the Labor Relations Division. You also have similar views regarding this policy. Of the

following, the most appropriate action for you to take in response to her criticism is to

(A) agree with her, but tell her that nothing can be done about it at your level
(B) suggest to her that it is not wise for her to express criticism of policy
(C) tell the employee that she should direct her criticism to the head of the agency if she wants quick action
(D) ask the employee if she has suggestions for revising the policy.

Answer Key

1. C	21. B	41. B	61. C	81. C
2. B	22. C	42. D	62. B	82. D
3. A	23. C	43. A	63. C	83. A
4. C	24. B	44. A	64. A	84. B
5. C	25. D	45. C	65. D	85. C
6. A	26. C	46. B	66. B	86. C
7. C	27. C	47. C	67. B	87. D
8. C	28. C	48. D	68. B	88. C
9. C	29. C	49. A	69. A	89. B
10. D	30. D	50. A	70. D	90. A
11. D	31. D	51. B	71. A	91. A
12. A	32. D	52. C	72. B	92. B
13. A	33. D	53. C	73. B	93. D
14. B	34. A	54. B	74. D	94. D
15. D	35. A	55. B	75. A	95. C
16. C	36. B	56. A	76. C	96. D
17. D	37. A	57. B	77. B	97. C
18. D	38. A	58. A	78. D	98. D
19. D	39. C	59. B	79. B	99. C
20. C	40. B	60. D	80. C	100. D

ANSWER SHEET FOR SAMPLE PRACTICE EXAMINATION V

1 Ⓐ Ⓑ Ⓒ Ⓓ	26 Ⓐ Ⓑ Ⓒ Ⓓ	51 Ⓐ Ⓑ Ⓒ Ⓓ	76 Ⓐ Ⓑ Ⓒ Ⓓ
2 Ⓐ Ⓑ Ⓒ Ⓓ	27 Ⓐ Ⓑ Ⓒ Ⓓ	52 Ⓐ Ⓑ Ⓒ Ⓓ	77 Ⓐ Ⓑ Ⓒ Ⓓ
3 Ⓐ Ⓑ Ⓒ Ⓓ	28 Ⓐ Ⓑ Ⓒ Ⓓ	53 Ⓐ Ⓑ Ⓒ Ⓓ	78 Ⓐ Ⓑ Ⓒ Ⓓ
4 Ⓐ Ⓑ Ⓒ Ⓓ	29 Ⓐ Ⓑ Ⓒ Ⓓ	54 Ⓐ Ⓑ Ⓒ Ⓓ	79 Ⓐ Ⓑ Ⓒ Ⓓ
5 Ⓐ Ⓑ Ⓒ Ⓓ	30 Ⓐ Ⓑ Ⓒ Ⓓ	55 Ⓐ Ⓑ Ⓒ Ⓓ	80 Ⓐ Ⓑ Ⓒ Ⓓ
6 Ⓐ Ⓑ Ⓒ Ⓓ	31 Ⓐ Ⓑ Ⓒ Ⓓ	56 Ⓐ Ⓑ Ⓒ Ⓓ	81 Ⓐ Ⓑ Ⓒ Ⓓ
7 Ⓐ Ⓑ Ⓒ Ⓓ	32 Ⓐ Ⓑ Ⓒ Ⓓ	57 Ⓐ Ⓑ Ⓒ Ⓓ	82 Ⓐ Ⓑ Ⓒ Ⓓ
8 Ⓐ Ⓑ Ⓒ Ⓓ	33 Ⓐ Ⓑ Ⓒ Ⓓ	58 Ⓐ Ⓑ Ⓒ Ⓓ	83 Ⓐ Ⓑ Ⓒ Ⓓ
9 Ⓐ Ⓑ Ⓒ Ⓓ	34 Ⓐ Ⓑ Ⓒ Ⓓ	59 Ⓐ Ⓑ Ⓒ Ⓓ	84 Ⓐ Ⓑ Ⓒ Ⓓ
10 Ⓐ Ⓑ Ⓒ Ⓓ	35 Ⓐ Ⓑ Ⓒ Ⓓ	60 Ⓐ Ⓑ Ⓒ Ⓓ	85 Ⓐ Ⓑ Ⓒ Ⓓ
11 Ⓐ Ⓑ Ⓒ Ⓓ	36 Ⓐ Ⓑ Ⓒ Ⓓ	61 Ⓐ Ⓑ Ⓒ Ⓓ	86 Ⓐ Ⓑ Ⓒ Ⓓ
12 Ⓐ Ⓑ Ⓒ Ⓓ	37 Ⓐ Ⓑ Ⓒ Ⓓ	62 Ⓐ Ⓑ Ⓒ Ⓓ	87 Ⓐ Ⓑ Ⓒ Ⓓ
13 Ⓐ Ⓑ Ⓒ Ⓓ	38 Ⓐ Ⓑ Ⓒ Ⓓ	63 Ⓐ Ⓑ Ⓒ Ⓓ	88 Ⓐ Ⓑ Ⓒ Ⓓ
14 Ⓐ Ⓑ Ⓒ Ⓓ	39 Ⓐ Ⓑ Ⓒ Ⓓ	64 Ⓐ Ⓑ Ⓒ Ⓓ	89 Ⓐ Ⓑ Ⓒ Ⓓ
15 Ⓐ Ⓑ Ⓒ Ⓓ	40 Ⓐ Ⓑ Ⓒ Ⓓ	65 Ⓐ Ⓑ Ⓒ Ⓓ	90 Ⓐ Ⓑ Ⓒ Ⓓ
16 Ⓐ Ⓑ Ⓒ Ⓓ	41 Ⓐ Ⓑ Ⓒ Ⓓ	66 Ⓐ Ⓑ Ⓒ Ⓓ	91 Ⓐ Ⓑ Ⓒ Ⓓ
17 Ⓐ Ⓑ Ⓒ Ⓓ	42 Ⓐ Ⓑ Ⓒ Ⓓ	67 Ⓐ Ⓑ Ⓒ Ⓓ	92 Ⓐ Ⓑ Ⓒ Ⓓ
18 Ⓐ Ⓑ Ⓒ Ⓓ	43 Ⓐ Ⓑ Ⓒ Ⓓ	68 Ⓐ Ⓑ Ⓒ Ⓓ	93 Ⓐ Ⓑ Ⓒ Ⓓ
19 Ⓐ Ⓑ Ⓒ Ⓓ	44 Ⓐ Ⓑ Ⓒ Ⓓ	69 Ⓐ Ⓑ Ⓒ Ⓓ	94 Ⓐ Ⓑ Ⓒ Ⓓ
20 Ⓐ Ⓑ Ⓒ Ⓓ	45 Ⓐ Ⓑ Ⓒ Ⓓ	70 Ⓐ Ⓑ Ⓒ Ⓓ	95 Ⓐ Ⓑ Ⓒ Ⓓ
21 Ⓐ Ⓑ Ⓒ Ⓓ	46 Ⓐ Ⓑ Ⓒ Ⓓ	71 Ⓐ Ⓑ Ⓒ Ⓓ	96 Ⓐ Ⓑ Ⓒ Ⓓ
22 Ⓐ Ⓑ Ⓒ Ⓓ	47 Ⓐ Ⓑ Ⓒ Ⓓ	72 Ⓐ Ⓑ Ⓒ Ⓓ	97 Ⓐ Ⓑ Ⓒ Ⓓ
23 Ⓐ Ⓑ Ⓒ Ⓓ	48 Ⓐ Ⓑ Ⓒ Ⓓ	73 Ⓐ Ⓑ Ⓒ Ⓓ	98 Ⓐ Ⓑ Ⓒ Ⓓ
24 Ⓐ Ⓑ Ⓒ Ⓓ	49 Ⓐ Ⓑ Ⓒ Ⓓ	74 Ⓐ Ⓑ Ⓒ Ⓓ	99 Ⓐ Ⓑ Ⓒ Ⓓ
25 Ⓐ Ⓑ Ⓒ Ⓓ	50 Ⓐ Ⓑ Ⓒ Ⓓ	75 Ⓐ Ⓑ Ⓒ Ⓓ	100 Ⓐ Ⓑ Ⓒ Ⓓ

SAMPLE PRACTICE EXAMINATION V

DIRECTIONS FOR ANSWERING QUESTIONS

Each question has four suggested answers, lettered A, B, C, and D. Decide which one is the best answer and on the sample answer sheet find the question number and darken the area with a soft pencil which corresponds to the answer that you have selected.

The time allowed for the entire examination is 4 hours.

1. A management approach widely used today is based on the belief that decisions should be made and actions should be taken by managers closest to the organization's problems. This style of management is most appropriately called

   (A) scientific management
   (B) means-end management
   (C) decentralized management
   (D) internal process management.

2. As contrasted with tall organization structures with narrow spans of control, flat organization structures with wide spans of control most usually provide

   (A) fast communication and information flows
   (B) more levels in the organizational hierarchy

   (C) fewer workers reporting to supervisors
   (D) lower motivation because of tighter control standards.

3. Use of the systems approach is most likely to lead to

   (A) consideration of the impact on the whole organization of actions taken in any part of that organization
   (B) the placing of restrictions on departmental authority
   (C) use of mathematical models to suboptimize production
   (D) consideration of the activities of each unit of an organization as a totality without regard to the remainder of the organization.

183

4. An administrator, with overall responsibility for all administrative operations in a large operating agency, is considering organizing the agency's personnel office around either of the following two alternative concepts:

Alternative I - a corps of specialists for each branch of personnel subject matter, whose skills, counsel, or work products are coordinated only by the agency personnel officer.

Alternative II - a crew of so-called "personnel generalists," who individually work with particular segments of the organization but deal with all subspecialties of the personnel function.

The one of the following which most tends to be a drawback of Alternative I, as compared with Alternative II, is that

(A) training and employee relations work call for education, interests, and talents that differ from those required for classification and compensation work
(B) personnel office staff may develop only superficial familiarity with the specialized areas to which they have been assigned
(C) supervisors may fail to get continuing, overall personnel advice on an integrated basis
(D) the personnel specialists are likely to become so interested in and identified with the operating view as to particular cases that they lose their professional objectivity and become merely advocates of what some supervisor wants.

5. The matrix summary or decision matrix is a useful tool for making choices. Its effectiveness is most dependent upon the user's ability to

(A) write a computer program (Fortran or Cobol)
(B) assign weights representing the relative importance of the objectives
(C) solve a set of two equations with two unknowns
(D) work with matrix algebra.

6. An organizational form which is set up only on an ad hoc basis to meet specific goals is said primarily to use

(A) clean break departmentation
(B) matrix or task force organization
(C) scaler specialization
(D) geographic or area-wide decentralization.

7. The concept of job enlargement would least properly be implemented by

(A) permitting workers to follow through on tasks or projects from start to finish
(B) delegating the maximum authority possible for decision-making to lower levels in the hierarchy
(C) maximizing the number of professional classes in the classification plan
(D) training employees to grow beyond whatever

tasks they have been performing.

8. As used in the area of administration, the principle of "unity of command" most specifically means that

(A) an individual should report to only one superior for any single activity
(B) individuals make better decisions than do committees
(C) in large organizations, chains of command are normally too long
(D) an individual should not supervise over five subordinates.

9. The methods of operations research, statistical decision-making and linear programming have been referred to as "the tool kit of the manager" by Peter Drucker. Utilization of these tools is least useful in the performance of which of the following functions?

(A) Elimination of the need for using judgment when making decisions.
(B) Facilitation of decision-making without the need for sub-optimization.
(C) Reduction of time and cost in various management areas.
(D) Accounting for risks and assumptions in the decision-making process.

10. "When acting in their respective managerial capacities, the chief executive officer and the office supervisor both perform the fundamental functions of management." Of the following differences between

the two, the one which is generally considered to be the least significant is the

(A) breadth of the objectives
(B) complexity of measuring actual efficiency of performance
(C) number of decisions made
(D) organizational relationships affected by actions taken.

11. The ability of operations researchers to solve complicated problems rests on their use of models. These models can best be described as

(A) mathematical statements of the problem
(B) physical constructs that simulate a work layout
(C) toy-like representations of employees in work environments
(D) role-playing simulations.

12. Of the following, it is most likely to be proper for the agency head to allow the agency personnel officer to make final selection of appointees from certified eligible lists where there are

(A) small numbers of employees to be hired in newly-developed professional fields
(B) large numbers of persons to be hired for key managerial positions
(C) large numbers of persons to be hired in very routine occupations and the individual discretion of operating officials is not vital
(D) small numbers of persons to be hired in highly specialized professional occupations

which are vital to the agency's operations.

13. Of the following, an operating agency personnel office is <u>least</u> likely to be able to exert strong influence or control within the operating agency by

   (A) intepreting to the operating agency head what is intended by the directives and rules emanating from the central personnel agency
   (B) establishing the key objectives of those line divisions of the operating agency employing large numbers of staff and operating under the management-by-objectives approach
   (C) formulating and proposing to the agency head the internal policies and procedures on personnel matters required within the operating agency
   (D) exercising certain discretionary authority in the application of the agency head's general personnel policies to actual specific situations.

14. PERT is a system used primarily to

   (A) evaluate the quality of applicants' backgrounds
   (B) analyze and control the timing aspects of a major project
   (C) control the total expenditure of agency funds within a monthly or quarterly time period
   (D) analyze and control the differential effect on costs of purchasing in different quantities.

15. Assume that an operating agency has among its vacant positions two positions each of which encompasses mixed duties. Both require appointees to have considerable education and experience but these requirements are essential only for the more difficult duties of these positions. In the place of these positions, an administrator creates two new positions, one in which the higher duties are concentrated and the other with the lesser functions requiring only minimum preparation. Of the following, it is generally most appropriate to characterize the administrator's action as

   (A) an undesirable example of deliberate downgrading of standards and requirements
   (B) an undesirable manipulation of the classification system for non-merit purposes
   (C) a desirable broadening of the definition of a class of positions
   (D) a desirable example of job redesign.

16. Of the following, the <u>least</u> important stumbling block to the development of personnel mobility among governmental jurisdictions is the

   (A) limitations on lateral entry above junior levels, in many jurisdictions
   (B) continued collection of filing fees for civil service tests by many governmental jurisdictions
   (C) absence of reciprocal exchange of retirement benefit eligibility

between governments
(D) disparities in salary
scales between
governments.

17. Of the following, the major
<u>disadvantage</u> of a personnel
system that features the
"selection out" (forced
retirement) of those who have
been passed over a number of
times for promotion is that
such a system

(A) wastes manpower which is
perfectly competent at
one level but unable to
rise above that level
(B) wastes funds by
requiring review boards
(C) leads to excessive
recruiting of newcomers
from outside the system
(D) may not be utilized in
"closed" career systems
with low maximum age
limits for entrance.

18. Of the following, the fields
in which operating agency
personnel offices generally
exercise the most
stringent controls over
first-line supervisors in
the agency are

(A) methods analysis and
work simplification
(B) selection and position
classification
(C) vestibule training and
Gantt charting
(D) suggestion systems and
staff development.

19. Of the following, computers
are normally most effective
in handling

(A) large masses of data
requiring simple
processing
(B) small amounts of data
requiring constantly
changing complex
processing

(C) data for which reported
values are often subject
to inaccuracies
(D) large amounts of data
requiring continual
programming and
reprocessing.

20. Contingency planning, which
has long been used by the
military and is assuming
increasing importance in
other organizations, may
best be described as a
process which utilizes

(A) alternative plans based
on varying assumptions
(B) "crash programs" by
organizations
departmentalized along
process lines
(C) plans which mandate
substitution of
equipment for manpower at
predetermined operational
levels
(D) plans that individually
and accurately predict
future events.

21. In the management of
inventory, two kinds of
costs normally determine when
to order and in what amounts.
The one of the following
choices which includes both
of these kinds of costs is

(A) carrying costs and
storage costs
(B) personnel costs and
order costs
(C) carrying costs and order
costs
(D) personnel costs and
computer costs.

22. At top management levels,
the one of the following
which is generally the most
important executive skill is
skill in

(A) budgeting procedures
(B) a technical discipline

(C) controlling actions in accordance with previously approved plans

(D) seeing the organization as a whole.

23. Of the following, the best way to facilitate the successful operation of a committee is to set guidelines establishing its

(A) budget exclusive of personnel costs
(B) location
(C) schedule of meetings or conferences
(D) scope or purpose.

Answer questions 24 through 28 on the basis of the New York State Civil Service Law and the Rules and Regulations of the New York City Civil Service Commission as they apply generally to clerical, administrative, and similar titles.

24. A person who has never before worked for the City is appointed to the Competitive Class title of Office Aide. Unless otherwise set forth in the terms and conditions of the certification for appointment, such appointment shall be for a probationary period of

(A) one month
(B) three months
(C) six months
(D) twelve months.

25. An eligible list consisting of ten (10) eligibles in list order (#1 through #10) has been certified only to one agency. This agency has two persons serving provisionally in permanent vacancies in the list title. There are no other vacancies

in the agency. All persons on the list are qualified and willing to accept appointment to the agency. On the basis of this information, which one of the following is most likely to be a legally proper disposition of that certification?

(A) Appointed - #1, #8
Considered but passed over - #2, #3, #4, #5, #6, #7
Not reached for consideration - #9, #10

(B) Appointed - #3, #4
Considered but passed over - #1, #2
Not reached for consideration - #5, #6, #7, #8, #9, #10

(C) Appointed - #2, #6
Considered but passed over - #1, #3, #4, #5
Not reached for consideration - #7, #8, #9, #10

(D) Appointed - #1, #6
Considered but passed over - #2, #3, #4, #5
Not reached for consideration - #7, #8, #9, #10.

26. Every transfer, other than a functional transfer, shall require the consent, in writing, of the proposed transferee and of the

(A) appointing officer of the department or agency to which the transfer is being made and the approval of the Comptroller
(B) respective appointing officers concerned therewith and the approval of the City Civil Service Commission
(C) respective appointing officers concerned therewith and the

approval of the State
Civil Service Commission
(D) City Personnel Director
and the Mayor.

27. Except as otherwise provided
in the announcement of
examination, eligibility for
certification from a
departmental or unit
promotion list generally
shall be limited to permanent
employees of such department
whose names appear on such
list and who have served
permanently in the eligible
title or titles for a total
period of not less than

(A) six months prior to the
date of the written
promotion test
(B) six months prior to the
date of promotion
(C) one year prior to the
date of promotion
(D) eighteen months prior
to the date of
promotion.

28. "Rule 5.5.3. -- A
provisional appointment to
any position shall be
terminated within (X)
months following the
establishment of an
appropriate eligible list
for filling vacancies in
such positions; provided,
however, that when there is
a large number of
provisional appointees in
any department or agency to
be replaced by permanent
appointees from a newly
established eligible list
and the appointing officer
deems that the termination
of the employment of all
such provisional appointees
within (X) months following
the establishment of such
list would disrupt or
impair essential public
services, evidence thereof
may be presented to the

director, who, after due
inquiry, and upon finding
that it is in the best
interest of the public
service, may waive the
provision of this paragraph
requiring the termination
of the employment of
provisional employees
within (X) months following
the establishment of an
appropriate eligible list
and authorize the
termination of the employment
of various numbers of such
provisional appointees at
stated intervals prescribed
by him; provided, however,
that in no case shall the
employment of such
provisional appointee be
continued longer than (Y)
months following the
establishment of such
eligible list."

The numbers that should be
substituted for (X) and (Y)
to correctly complete
Rule 5.5.3 are

(A) (X) two   (Y) four
(B) (X) three   (Y) six
(C) (X) three   (Y) nine
(D) (X) four   (Y) eight.

29. Executive training programs
that single out particular
administrators and groom them
for promotion create the
so-called organizational
"crown princes." Of the
following, the most serious
problem that arises in
connection with this practice
is that

(A) the administrators chosen
for promotion seldom turn
out to be the best
administrators since the
future potential of
persons cannot be
predicted
(B) not enough effort is made
to remove organizational

obstacles in the way of
their development and
achievement

(C) the resentment of the
administrators not
selected for the program
has an adverse effect on
the motivation of those
administrators not
selected

(D) performance appraisal
and review are not
carried out
systematically enough.

30. Of the following, the <u>least</u>
likely result of the use of
the concept of job
enlargement is that

(A) coordination will be
simplified
(B) the individual's job
will become less
challenging
(C) worker satisfaction will
increase
(D) fewer people will have
to give attention to
each piece of work.

31. The one of the following
which is most likely to be
emphasized in the use of the
brainstorming technique is
the

(A) early consideration of
cost factors of all
ideas which may be
suggested
(B) avoidance of impractical
suggestions
(C) separation of the
generation of ideas from
their evaluation
(D) appraisal of
suggestions concurrently
with their initial
presentation.

32. Of the following, the best
method for assessing
administrative performance
is generally to

(A) compare the
administrator's
accomplishments against
clear, specific,
agreed-upon goals
(B) compare the
administrator's traits
with those of his or her
peers on a predetermined
objective scale
(C) measure the
administrator's behavior
against a listing of
itemized personal traits
(D) measure the
administrator's success
according to the
enumeration of the
"satisfaction" principle.

33. As compared with recruitment
from outside, selection from
within the service must
generally show greater
concern for the

(A) prestige in which the
public service as a whole
is held by the public
(B) morale of the candidate
group comprising the
recruitment field
(C) cost of examining per
candidate
(D) benefits of the use of
standardized and
validated tests.

34. Class specifications issued
by the New York City
Department of Personnel
for such Rule XI Competitive
Class titles as Clerk,
Administrative Associate, and
Stockman are <u>least</u> likely to
contain a section entitled

(A) General Statement of
Duties and
Responsibilities
(B) Examples of Typical Tasks
(C) Qualification Requirements
(D) Types of Examination
Required.

35. Performance budgeting focuses primary attention upon which one of the following?

    (A) The things to be acquired, such as supplies and equipment.
    (B) The general character and relative importance of the work to be done or the service to be rendered.
    (C) The list of personnel to be employed, by specific title.
    (D) The separation of employee performance evaluations from employee compensation.

36. Of the following, the <u>first</u> step in the installation and operation of a performance budgeting system generally should be the

    (A) identification of program costs in relationship to the accounting system and operating structure
    (B) identification of the specific end results of past programs in other jurisdictions
    (C) identification of work programs that are meaningful for management purposes
    (D) establishment of organizational structures each containing only one work program.

37. Of the following, the most important purpose of a system of quarterly allotments of appropriated funds generally is to enable the

    (A) head of the judicial branch to determine the legality of agency requests for budget increases
    (B) operating agencies of government to upgrade the quality of their services without increasing costs
    (C) head of the executive branch to control the rate at which the operating agencies obligate and expend funds
    (D) operating agencies of government to avoid payment for services which have not been properly rendered by employees.

38. In the preparation of the agency's budget, the agency's central budget office has two responsibilities: program review and management improvement. Which one of the following questions concerning an operating agency's program is most closely related to the agency budget officer's program review responsibility?

    (A) Can expenditures for supplies, materials or equipment be reduced?
    (B) Will improved work methods contribute to a more effective program?
    (C) What is the relative importance of this program as compared with other programs?
    (D) Will a realignment of responsibilities contribute to a higher level of program performance?

39. Of the following, the method of evaluating relative rates of return normally and generally thought to be most useful in evaluating government operations is

    (A) cost-benefit analysis
    (B) budget variance analysis
    (C) investment capital

analysis

(D) budget planning program analysis.

40. The one of the following assumptions that is <u>least</u> likely to be made by a democratic or permissive type of leader is that

(A) commitment to goals is seldom a result of monetary rewards alone

(B) people can learn not only to accept, but also to seek, responsibility

(C) the average person prefers security over advancement

(D) creativity may be found in most segments of the population.

41. City Charter provisions on budget administration state, in part, "Except as otherwise provided by law, no unit of appropriation shall be available for expenditure by any agency until a schedule fixing positions and salaries or setting forth other expenses within such unit of appropriation, established subject to the provisions of this charter, of the civil service law and of other applicable statutes shall have been approved by the

(A) finance administrator."

(B) chairman of the City Council Finance Committee."

(C) Mayor."

(D) Deputy Comptroller."

42. City Charter provisions require that the Mayor's expense budget message, which shall not be deemed a part of the expense budget, shall include

(A) a statement of the cost per work unit for each work unit to be produced during the coming year and a comparison with such costs during each of the past five years

(B) a listing of the names and proposed salaries of each employee for whom a salary of $25,000 or more is proposed in the budget

(C) an itemized statement of the proposed duties of all additional Exempt Class positions proposed in the budget

(D) an explanation, in general summary terms, of the major emphasis and objectives of the budget.

43. The date by which City agency heads must submit to the Bureau of the Budget estimates of their expense requirements is not later than

(A) October 1

(B) January 1

(C) March 1

(D) July 1.

44. In attempting to motivate subordinates, an administrator should principally be aware of the fact that

(A) the psychological qualities of people, in general, are easily predictable

(B) fear, as a traditional form of motivation, has lost much of its former power to motivate people in our modern industrial society

(C) fear is still the most potent force in motivating the behavior of subordinates in the public service

(D) the worker has very
little control over the
quality and quantity of
output.

45. Which of the following best
describes a way in which the
appointment or tenure of
heads of city agencies
generally differs from the
appointment or tenure of
heads of major Federal
agencies (departments)?

(A) Appointments of heads of
city agencies usually
must be confirmed by the
City Council, whereas
appointments of Federal
Department heads usually
do not require Senate
confirmation.
(B) Appointments of Federal
Department heads usually
require Senate
confirmation, whereas
appointments of heads
of city agencies usually
do not require City
Council confirmation.
(C) Heads of city agencies
usually are appointed
for a fixed number of
years, whereas Federal
Department heads
usually serve at the
pleasure of the chief
executive.
(D) Heads of city agencies
usually serve at the
pleasure of the chief
executive, whereas
Federal Department heads
are usually appointed
for a fixed number of
years.

46. The New York City Department
of Investigation is
principally charged with the
responsibility for
investigating

(A) the legality of proposed
amendments to the City
Charter

(B) the character and fitness
of all applicants for
City jobs
(C) charges made by the
Department of Consumer
Affairs of possible
advertising and marketing
fraud
(D) City personnel or
agencies as directed by
the Mayor or the City
Council.

47. A primary function of the
Board of Certification of the
New York City Office of
Collective Bargaining is to
certify that

(A) union wage demands do not
exceed the President's
wage guidelines
(B) a group of employees has
been designated as a
bargaining unit and a
specific union or
association has been
designated their
exclusive representative
(C) a municipal union has
been granted membership
in the Municipal Labor
Committee
(D) offers made by the City's
bargaining
representatives are in
accordance with the
Mayor's wage and fringe
benefit policies.

48. When an administrator
receives an inquiry from a
union regarding
interpretation of its
collective bargaining
agreement with the city, the
standard procedure for the
administrator to take is to

(A) interpret the agreement
personally
(B) consult with the
Chairman of the Office
of Collective Bargaining
and then carry out the
Chairman's instructions

(C) notify the city's Director of Labor Relations

(D) notify the City Personnel Director.

49. The City Charter under which New York City is currently governed was adopted in the early

(A) 1920's
(B) 1930's
(C) 1950's
(D) 1960's.

50. In accordance with Local Law 73 of 1959, the New York City agency that is primarily charged by rendering advisory opinions on potential conflicts of interest by city employees and officers is the

(A) Department of Investigation
(B) Department of Personnel
(C) Board of Ethics
(D) Law Department.

51. Of the following, the primary method for selecting members of community school boards in New York City is

(A) election by the members of the City Board of Education
(B) appointment by the Chancellor
(C) election by proportional representation within the community school district
(D) appointment by the Mayor and confirmation by the City Council.

Each of questions 52 through 57 consists of a quotation which contains one word that is incorrectly used because it is not in keeping with the meaning that the quotation is evidently intended to convey. Determine which word is incorrectly used. Select from the choices lettered (A), (B), (C), and (D) the word which, when substituted for the incorrectly used word, would best help to convey the meaning of the quotation.

52. "One of the considerations likely to affect the currency of classification, particularly in professional and managerial occupations, is the impact of the incumbent's capacities on the job. Some work is highly susceptible to change as the result of the special talents or interests of the classifier. Organization should never be so rigid as not to capitalize on the innovative or unusual proclivities of its key employees. While a machine operator may not be able, even subtly, to change the character or level of his or her job, the design engineer, the attorney, or the organization and methods analyst might readily do so. Reliance on his or her judgment and the scope of his or her assignments may both grow as the result of skill, insight, and capacity."

(A) unlikely
(B) incumbent
(C) directly
(D) scope.

53. "The supply of services by the state is not governed by market price. The aim is to supply such services to all who need them and to treat all consumers equally. This objective especially compels the civil servant to maintain a role of strict impartiality, based on the

principle of equality of individual citizens vis-a-vis their government. However, there is a clear difference between being neutral and being impartial. If the requirement is construed to mean that all civil servants should be political eunuchs, devoid of the drive and motivation essential to dynamic administration, then the concept of impartiality is being seriously utilized. Modern governments should not be stopped from demanding that their hirelings have not only the technical but the emotional qualifications necessary for wholehearted effort."

(A) determined
(B) rule
(C) stable
(D) misapplied.

54. "The manager was barely listening. Recently, at the divisional level, several new fronts of troubles had erupted, including a requirement to increase production yet hold down operating costs and somehow raise quality standards. Though the three objectives were basically obsolete, top departmental management was insisting on the simultaneous attainment of them, an insistence not helping the manager's ulcer, an old enemy within. Thus, the manager could not find time for interest in individuals only in statistics which regiments of individuals, like unconsidered Army privates, added up to."

(A) quantity
(B) battalion
(C) incompatible
(D) quiet.

55. "When a large volume of data flows directly between operators and first-line supervisors, senior executives tend to be out of the mainstream of work. Summary reports can increase their remoteness. An executive needs to know the volume, quality and cost of completed work, and exceptional problems. In addition, the executive may desire information on key operating conditions. Summary reports on these matters are, therefore, essential features of a communications network and make delegation without loss of control possible."

(A) unimportant
(B) quantity
(C) offset
(D) incomplete.

56. "Of major significance in management is harmony between the overall objectives of the organization and the managerial objectives within that organization. In addition, harmony among goals of managers is impossible; they should not be at cross-purposes. Each manager's goal should supplement and assist the goals of his or her colleagues. Likewise, the objectives of individuals or nonmanagement members should be harmonized with those of the manager. When this is accomplished, genuine teamwork is the result, and human relations are aided materially. The integration of managers' and individuals' goals aids in achieving greater work satisfaction at all levels."

(A) competition
(B) dominate

(C) incremental
(D) vital.

57. "Change constantly challenges the manager. Some of this change is evolutionary, some revolutionary, some recognizable, some nonrecognizable. Both forces within an enterprise and forces outside the enterprise cause managers to act and react in initiating changes in their immediate working environment. Change invalidates existing operations. Goals are not being accomplished in the best manner, problems develop, and frequently because of the lack of time, only patched-up solutions are followed. The result is that the mode of management is profound in nature and temporary in effectivenss. A complete overhaul of managerial operations should take place. It appears quite likely that we are just beginning to see the real effects of change in our society; the pace probably will accelerate in ways that few really understand or know how to handle."

(A) confirms
(B) decline
(C) instituting
(D) superficial.

Answer questions 58 and 59 on the basis of the passage below.

"Management by objectives (MBO) may be defined as the process by which the superior and subordinate managers of an organization jointly define its common goals, define each individual's major areas of responsibility in terms of the results expected of him or her and use these measures as guides for operating the unit and assessing the contribution of each of its members.

The MBO approach requires that after organizational goals are established and communicated, targets must be set for each individual position which are congruent with organizational goals. Periodic performance reviews and a final review using the objectives set as criteria are also basic to this approach.

Recent studies have shown that MBO programs are influenced by attitudes and perceptions of the boss, the company, the reward-punishment system and the program itself. In addition, the manner in which the MBO program is carried out can influence the success of the program. A study done in the late sixties indicates that the best results are obtained when the manager sets goals which deal with significant problem areas in the organizational unit, or with the subordinate's personal deficiencies. These goals must be clear with regard to what is expected of the subordinate. The frequency of feedback is also important in the success of a management by objectives program. Generally, the greater the amount of feedback, the more successful the MBO program."

58. According to the preceding passage, the expected output for individual employees should be determined

(A) after a number of reviews of work performance
(B) after common organizational goals are defined
(C) before common organizational goals are defined
(D) on the basis of an employee's personal qualities.

59. According to the preceding passage, the management-by-objective approach requires

(A) less feedback than other types of management programs
(B) little review of on-the-job performance after the initial setting of goals
(C) general conformance between individual goals and organizational goals
(D) the setting of goals which deal with minor problem areas in the organization.

Answer questions 60 through 62 on the basis of the passage below.

"During the last decade, a great deal of interest has been generated around the phenomenon of 'organizational development, or the process of developing human resources through conscious organization effort. Organizational development (OD) stresses improving interpersonal relationships and organizational skills, such as communication, to a much greater degree than individual training ever did.

The kind of training that an organization should emphasize depends upon the present and future structure of the organization. If future organizations are to be unstable, shifting coalitions, then individual skills and abilities, particularly those emphasizing innovativeness, creativity, flexibility and the latest technological knowledge, are crucial and individual training is most appropriate.

But if there is to be little change in organizational structure, then the main thrust of training should be group-oriented or organizational development. This approach seems better designed for overcoming hierarchical barriers, for developing a degree of interpersonal relationships which make communication along the chain of command possible, and for retaining a modicum of innovation and/or flexibility."

60. According to the preceding passage, group-oriented training is most useful in

(A) developing a communications system that will facilitate understanding through the chain of command
(B) highly flexible and mobile organizations
(C) preventing the crossing of hierarchical barriers within an organization
(D) saving energy otherwise wasted on developing methods of dealing with rigid hierarchies.

61. The one of the following conclusions which can be drawn most appropriately from the preceding passage is that

(A) behavioral research

supports the use of organizational development training methods rather than individualized training
(B) it is easier to provide individualized training in specific skills than to set up sensitivity training programs
(C) organizational development eliminates innovative or flexible activity
(D) the nature of an organization greatly influences which training methods will be most effective.

62. According to the preceding passage, the one of the following which is <u>least</u> important for large-scale organizations geared to rapid and abrupt change is

(A) current technological information
(B) development of a high degree of interpersonal relationships
(C) development of individual skills and abilities
(D) emphasis on creativity.

63. Assume that the following figures represent the number of work-units that were produced during a week by each of sixteen employees in a division:

12	16	13	18
21	12	16	13
16	13	17	21
13	15	18	20

If all of the employees of the division who produced thirteen work-units during the week had instead produced fifteen work-units during

that same week, then for that week the

(A) mean, median, and mode would all change
(B) mean and mode would change, but the median would remain the same
(C) mode and median would change, but the mean would remain the same
(D) mode, mean, and median would all still remain unchanged in value.

64. An important law in motivation theory is called the "law of effect." This law says that behavior which satisfies a person's needs tends to be repeated; behavior which does not satisfy a person's needs tends to be eliminated. The one of the following which is the best interpretation of this law is that

(A) productivity depends on personality traits
(B) diversity of goals leads to instability of motivation
(C) the greater the satisfaction, the more likely it is that the behavior will be reinforced
(D) extrinsic satisfaction is more important than intrinsic reward.

65. Of the following, the most acceptable reason an administrator can give for taking advice from other employees in the organization only when he or she asks for it, is that the administrator wants to

(A) encourage creativity and high morale
(B) keep dysfunctional pressures and inconsistent recommendations to a

minimum
(C) show superiors and peers who is in charge
(D) show subordinates who is in charge.

66. A complete picture of the communication channels in an organization can best be revealed by

(A) observing the planned paperwork system
(B) recording the highly intermittent patterns of communication
(C) plotting the entire flow of information over a period of time
(D) monitoring the "grapevine."

Column I includes characteristics associated with different types of organizations. By selecting the proper option in Column II, indicate whether each item in Column I is most closely associated with (A) functional organizations, (B) line and staff organizations, (C) line organizations, or whether it is associated with (D) none of these types of organizations.

Column I

67. Complete accuracy in communication

68. Expert knowledge and authority combined

69. Expert knowledge distinct from authority

70. Simplicity

71. Speed in communication

72. More than one supervisor for each organizational element.

Column II

(A) functional organizations
(B) line and staff organizations
(C) line organizations
(D) none of the above.

73. Which of the following is the most important characteristic of a good operational plan?

(A) Responsibility for execution is vested in one administrator
(B) Presents only objectives of the plan and allocation of authority; does not specify methods
(C) Need for on-the-scene modification or amplification is minimized
(D) Effectively serves as a training device.

74. There is a continuous need for reorganization in any department; however, the administrator should realize that even though certain improvements should be made, reorganization generally should be accomplished

(A) more or less gradually in an unfolding sort of way
(B) only after a plan is submitted to a vote of department employees
(C) before the beginning of the next fiscal year
(D) after plan is unanimously approved by department personnel.

75. In measuring the cost of a certain operation or function, the first step is to

(A) calculate the average cost of supplies and equipment per person and add it to the average current salary

(B) determine the work or units
(C) calculate the cost of labor, supplies, equipment, etc., per unit of working time
(D) determine the rate of production.

76. When it is said that the functions of management may be divided between planning and control, the term "control" means

(A) restricting the powers of those who plan the policies of an organization by independent review of all policies
(B) making sure that the policies of the organization are carried out
(C) determining the specific objectives of the organization
(D) the enforcement of uniform standards of discipline.

77. In the field of public administration, there currently appears to be the most pressing need for planning and research aimed at

(A) standardization of the basis of personnel morale and loyalty
(B) formulation of exact standards for selection and promotion
(C) development of work units and performance standards
(D) long range prediction of community trends.

78. One method of organizing a complex operation is to subdivide the work into small units, with each employee specializing in one phase of the operation. Which of the

following is a likely disadvantage of this subdivision of work? The

(A) work will be harder to coordinate
(B) quality of work will be lower
(C) employees will require more training
(D) work will be more costly in terms of salaries.

79. One of the principal disadvantages of a strictly line organization is that it

(A) is ineffective in emergencies
(B) makes for lax discipline
(C) does not fix responsibility
(D) tends to overload executives.

80. Fundamentally, the purpose of governmental accounting is to

(A) insure efficiency
(B) prevent defalcation
(C) provide information
(D) control expenditures.

81. "His attitude is as provincial as an isolationist country's unwillingness to engage in any international trade whatever, on the ground that it will be required to buy something from outsiders which could possible be produced by local talent, although not as well and not as cheaply." This statement is most descriptive of the attitude of the division chief in a government agency who

(A) wishes to restrict promotions to supervisory positions in his division exclusively to employees in his division
(B) refuses to delegate

responsible tasks to
subordinates qualified
to perform these tasks
(C) believes that informal
on-the-job training of
new staff members is
superior to formal
training methods
(D) frequently makes personal
issues out of matters
that should be handled
on an impersonal basis.

82. "No matter how elaborate a
formal system of
communication is in an
organization, the system
will always be supplemented
by informal channels of
communication, such as the
'grapevine.' Although
such informal channels of
communication are usually
not highly regarded, they
sometimes are of value to
an organization." Of the
following, the chief value
of informal channels of
communication is that they
serve to

(A) transmit information
that management has
neglected to send through
the formal system of
communication
(B) confirm information that
has already been received
through the formal system
of communication
(C) hinder the formation of
employee cliques in the
organization
(D) revise information sent
through the formal system
of communication.

83. If a certain public agency
with a fixed number of
employees has a line
organizational structure,
then the width of the span of
supervision is

(A) inversely proportional to
the length of the chain

of command in the
organization
(B) directly proportional to
the complexity of tasks
performed in the
organization
(C) inversely proportional
to the competence of the
personnel in the
organization
(D) directly proportional to
the number of levels of
supervision existing in
the organization.

84. Some policy-making commissions
are composed of members who
are appointed to overlapping
terms. Of the following,
the chief advantage of
appointing members to
overlapping terms in such
commissions is that

(A) continuity of policy is
promoted
(B) the likelihood of
compromise policy
decisions is reduced
(C) responsibility for
policy decisions can be
fixed upon individual
members
(D) the likelihood of
unanimity of opinion is
increased.

85. In organization terminology,
the function of the
management section is
considered primarily to be

(A) auxiliary
(B) line
(C) planning
(D) staff.

86. Of the following, the most
common characteristic of
hierarchical organizations
is that they

(A) are based upon work
specialization
(B) are structured according
to ability

(C) fix authority
(D) promote on the basis of merit.

87. An organization which emphasizes uniformity is most likely to suffer from a lack of

(A) centralization
(B) economy
(C) flexibility
(D) standardization.

88. "A danger which exists in any organization as complex as that required for administration of a large city is that each department comes to believe that it exists for its own sake." The one of the following which has been attempted in some organizations as a cure for this condition is to

(A) build up the departmental esprit de corps
(B) expand the functions and jurisdictions of the various departments so that better integration is possible
(C) systematically transfer administrative personnel from one department to another
(D) delegate authority to the lowest possible echelon.

89. "Work measurement is an essential control tool to an office administrator." Of the following, the least important reason for using work measurement as a control tool is that work measurement

(A) may indicate training needs of subordinates
(B) simplifies the procedures used by the administrator's

subordinates in carrying out their assignments
(C) can indicate whether the administrator is employing more subordinates than is really needed
(D) is a basis for determining which of the subordinates are the most efficient workers.

90. "It is possible to have accurate work measurement without having satisfactory work standards but it is not possible to have satisfactory work standards unless they are based upon accurate work measurement." The one of the following statements which is the most direct implication of this quotation is that

(A) the number of lines that a typist types must be compared with a satisfactory work standard
(B) satisfactory work standards for the number of lines that a typist is required to type depend upon accurate work measurement
(C) the establishment of satisfactory work standards is necessary before work can be accurately measured
(D) accurate work measurement is of most value when it is used for the development of satisfactory work standards.

91. "Scheduling work within a unit requires a knowledge of the length of time it takes to perform the component parts of a task and of the precedence which certain tasks should take over others." The one of the following which is the most valid implication of this

quotation is that

(A) the priority which is given some tasks over others is determined by the length of time it takes to perform the component parts of each task
(B) only those tasks can be scheduled which have been performed in the unit in the past
(C) some tasks in a unit do not have component parts
(D) in order to estimate the time required to complete an assignment, a knowledge of the rate of performance of each part of the assignment is necessary.

92. Assume that you devised a new procedure which you expected would result in a substantial reduction in the amount of paper used in performing the work of the unit you supervise. After trying out this new procedure in your unit for several weeks, you find that the quantity of paper saved is considerably less than you anticipated. Of the following, the best action for you to take first is to

(A) inform your staff that they are probably using paper unnecessarily, and that in view of the current paper shortage, you expect them to conserve paper as much as possible
(B) suspend the use of this new procedure until you can discover why it has not worked out as you anticipated
(C) invite your subordinates to submit suggestions as to how the procedure may be improved

(D) analyze the various processes involved in the new procedure to determine whether there are any factors which you may have overlooked.

93. "The use of standard practices and procedures in large organizations is often essential in order to insure a smooth, efficient, and controlled flow of work. A strict adherence to standard practices and procedures to the extent that unnecessary delay is created is known, in general, as 'red tape.'" On the basis of this quotation, the most accurate of the following statements is that

(A) although the use of standard practices and procedures promotes efficiency, it also creates unnecessary delays and "red tape"
(B) in order to insure a smooth, efficient and controlled plan of work, "red tape" should be eliminated by a strict adherence to standard practices and procedures
(C) "red tape" is a necessary evil which invariably creeps into any large organization which uses standard practices and procedures
(D) "red tape" exists when delay takes place as a result of too rigid conformity with standard practices and procedures.

94. While setting up a reporting system to help the department planning section, an administrator proposed the policy that no overlap or duplication be permitted even if it meant that some minor areas were left uncovered.

This policy is

(A) undesirable; duplication is preferable to leaving any area uncovered
(B) desirable; the presence of overlap and duplication indicates defective planning
(C) undesirable; setting up general policy in advance of the specific reporting system may lead to inflexibility
(D) desirable; it is not necessary to get complete coverage in order to be able to plan operations.

95. The work reports of employees of a unit reveal that a few employees are producing much less work than the other members of the unit. These few employees appear to be working as conscientiously as the others. Of the following, the first action for the unit supervisor to take in connection with these few employees is to

(A) recognize the fact that individuals differ in native ability and that some individuals are naturally slower workers than others
(B) organize a training program to assist these employees in improving their skill and speed of work
(C) find out the reasons for their relatively poor performance and help them increase their production rate
(D) assign these employees to work which is more suitable to their temperament and ability.

96. The criteria used by an administrator to evaluate the performance by an employee of a routine task might differ from those used to evaluate a subordinate's performance of a complicated task. Of the following, the criterion best suited to evaluate the performance of a routine task is the

(A) ingenuity employed in solving unexpected problems
(B) rapidity of performance and quality of the finished product
(C) initiative displayed in developing new methods of work
(D) orderly arrangement and clarity of presentation of conclusions and recommendations.

97. The flow of work in a public agency may be impeded by a number of factors. Some of the factors impeding the flow of work may be controlled or corrected more easily than others. Of the following, the factor impeding flow of work which is most difficult for a public agency to control is

(A) a lack of adequate standards of performance
(B) unexpected changes in the volume of work
(C) unforeseen vacation requests by employees
(D) assignment of employees without considering their abilities.

98. The degree of decentralization that is effective and economical in an organization tends to vary inversely with the

(A) size of the organization

(B) availability of adequate numbers of competent personnel

(C) physical dispersion of the organization's activities

(D) adequacy of the organization's communications system.

99. "In order to promote efficiency and economy in an agency, it is advisable for the management to systematize and standardize procedures and relationships in so far as this can be done; however, excessive routinizing which does not permit individual contributions or achievements should be avoided." On the basis of this quotation, it is most accurate to state that

(A) systematized procedures should be designed mainly to encourage individual achievements

(B) standardized procedures should allow for individual accomplishments

(C) systematization of procedures may not be possible in organizations which have a large variety of functions

(D) individual employees of an organization must fully accept standardized procedures if the procedures are to be effective.

100. "A governmental agency may establish and maintain certain types of communications for use primarily within its own organization. These communications are intended to be directed primarily to persons who are members of that organization, or subject to that organization's authority and control, and represent what is sometimes called 'administrative communication.'" On the basis of this quotation, the one of the following which may not properly be called an example of administrative communication is that of

(A) a Principal Administrative Associate issuing a press release to a newspaper reporter

(B) a unit supervisor issuing written instructions to subordinates for carrying out of long range assignment

(C) the personnel officer of an agency issuing a memorandum to the employees of the agency listing changes in annual and sick leave regulations

(D) the head of an agency issuing an announcement to the staff concerning a new suggestion system.

Answer Key

1.	C	26.	B	51.	C	76.	B
2.	A	27.	C	52.	B	77.	C
3.	A	28.	A	53.	D	78.	A
4.	C	29.	C	54.	C	79.	D
5.	B	30.	B	55.	C	80.	C
6.	B	31.	C	56.	D	81.	A
7.	C	32.	A	57.	D	82.	A
8.	A	33.	B	58.	B	83.	A
9.	A	34.	D	59.	C	84.	A
10.	C	35.	B	60.	A	85.	D
11.	A	36.	C	61.	D	86.	C
12.	C	37.	C	62.	B	87.	C
13.	B	38.	C	63.	B	88.	C
14.	B	39.	A	64.	C	89.	C
15.	D	40.	C	65.	B	90.	D
16.	B	41.	C	66.	C	91.	D
17.	A	42.	D	67.	D	92.	D
18.	B	43.	B	68.	A	93.	D
19.	A	44.	B	69.	B	94.	A
20.	A	45.	B	70.	C	95.	C
21.	A and C	46.	D	71.	C	96.	B
22.	D	47.	B	72.	A	97.	B
23.	D	48.	C	73.	C	98.	D
24.	D	49.	D	74.	A	99.	B
25.	B	50.	C	75.	B	100.	A

BOOKS FOR JOB HUNTERS

CAREERS / STUDY GUIDES

Airline Pilot
Allied Health Professions
Automobile Technician Certification Tests
Federal Jobs for College Graduates
Federal Jobs in Law Enforcement
Getting Started in Film
How to Pass Clerical Employment Tests
How You Really Get Hired
Law Enforcement Exams Handbook
Make Your Job Interview a Success
Mechanical Aptitude and Spatial Relations Tests
Mid-Career Job Hunting
100 Best Careers for the Year 2000
Passport to Overseas Employment
Postal Exams Handbook
Real Estate License Examinations
Refrigeration License Examinations
Travel Agent

RESUME GUIDES

The Complete Resume Guide
Resumes for Better Jobs
Resumes That Get Jobs
Your Resume: Key to a Better Job

AVAILABLE AT BOOKSTORES EVERYWHERE

PRENTICE HALL